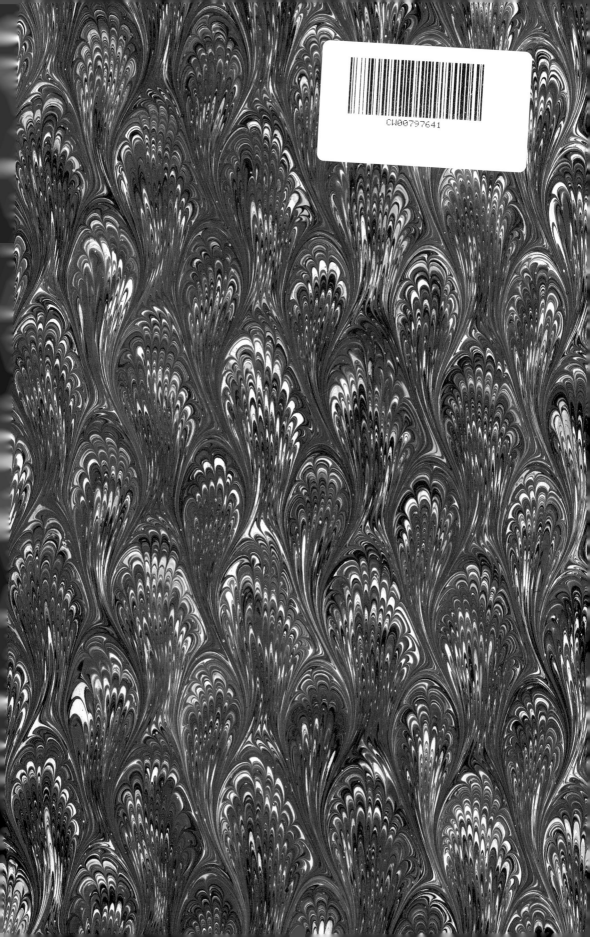

The House of Lords
a thousand years of British tradition

The House of Lords
a thousand years of British tradition

The House of Lords
a thousand years of British tradition

Published by Smith's Peerage Limited, Heron Place, 3 George Street, London W1H 6AD

ISBN 0 9524229 0 5

British Library Cataloguing in Publication Data. A catalogue record for this book is available from the British Library; Great Britain - History - early medieval to present (R Smith and J S Moore, joint Eds).

This book originated at a Conference held by the Manorial Society of Great Britain at University College, Oxford, in September 1992. *The House of Lords, a thousand years of British tradition*, is the first in a series of three books about the British Constitution. *The Monarchy, a thousand years of British tradition,* will be published in spring 1995; and *The House of Commons, seven hundred years of British tradition,* will be published in autumn 1995.

The Manorial Society of Great Britain
(founded 1906)

104 Kennington Road, London SE11 6RE

Governing Council:
The Lord Sudeley MA(Oxon) FSA,
Sir Colin Cole KCB KCVO TD FSA (sometime Garter Principal King of Arms),
Desmond de Silva QC KStJ, Norman J Fisher LLB,
Cecil R Humphery-Smith BSc FSA, Bruce King-Siem JP (Australia),
Gerald F Rand, Denis B Woodfield DPhil (Oxon) (United States),
Robert Smith BA Chairman of the Governing Council

Typeset by RPMS Ltd, 23 Harrison Avenue, Bournemouth, Dorset BH1 4NT
Printed by Staples Printers Rochester Limited, Neptune Close,
Medway City Estate, Frindsbury, Rochester, Kent ME2 4LT England

London 1994

LIST OF SUBSCRIBERS

THE PEERAGE

The Duke of Abercorn
The Lord Aberdare
The Lord Alexander of Weedon
The Earl of Annandale and Hartfell
The Earl of Aylesford
The Lord Bellwin
The Earl of Bessborough
The Lord Biddulph
The Baroness Blatch
The Viscount Brookeborough
The Duke of Buccleuch KT
The Earl of Carlisle
The Lord Carnock
The Lord Carter
The Lord Chalfont
The Earl of Clarendon
The Lord Clark of Kempston
The Lord Clifford
The Lord Clinton
The Viscount Cobham
The Lord Colyton
The Lord Cooke of Islandreagh
Lord Courtenay
The Lord Croft
The Viscount Cross
The Lord Cudlipp
The Lord Dainton
The Lord De Ramsey
The Viscount Devonport
The Duke of Devonshire
The Marquess of Donegall
The Baroness Dunn
The Lord Eden of Winton
The Lord Fanshawe
The Earl Ferrers
The Lord Feversham
The Lord Fisher
The Baroness Flather
The Lord Flowers
The Countess of Galloway
The Lord Goold
The Viscount Gormanston

The Baroness Gould
The Lord Grantchester
The Lord Gray of Contin
The Lord Grey of Codnor
The Lord Gridley
The Lord Griffiths
The Lord Hanson
The Earl of Harrington
The Lord Hastings
The Lord Hill-Norton
The Lord Hirshfield
The Lady Hirshfield
The Lord Howell
The Earl of Iddesleigh
Ther Earl of Ilchester
The Lord Kagan
The Lord Kensington
The Lord Kings Norton
The Lord Kissen
The Lord Laing of Dunphail
The Viscount Leathers
The Lord Lilford
The Viscount Long
The Lord Macfarlane of Bearsdon
The Viscount Mackintosh of Halifax
The Duke of Manchester
The Lord Marshall of Goring
The Lord Martonmere
The Lord Matthews
The Lord MacAlpine of West Green
The Lord McColl
The Lord Menuhin OM
The Lord Middleton
The Baroness Miller of Hendon
The Lord Milner of Leeds
The Lord Mostyn
The Lord Mottistone
The Lord Mowbray Segrave and Stourton
The Earl of Munster
The Lord Nelson of Stafford
The Duke of Northumberland
The Lord O'Neill
The Lord Oranmore and Brown
The Lord Palmer
The Lord Palumbo
The Lord Parkinson
The Lord Penrhyn

The Lord Perry of Walton
The Lord Peyton of Yeovil
The Lord Plummer of St Marylebone
The Lord Prentice
The Lord Prys-Davies
The Lord Rankeillour
The Lord Rawlinson of Ewell
The Lord Rayner
The Lord Renton
The Viscount Ridley KG
The Lord Rippon of Hexham
The Lady Saltoun
The Baroness Seccombe
The Earl of Shaftesbury
The Earl of Shannon
The Lord Sieff
The Lord Skelmersdale
The Viscount Slim
The Lord Slynn of Hadley
The Lord Somers
The Earl St Aldwyn
The Lord St Oswald
The Viscount St Vincent
The Lord Strathclyde
The Viscount Stuart of Findhorn
The Lord Taylor of Gosforth
The Viscount Thurso
The Viscount Tonypandy
The Lord Vivian
The Lord Waddington
The Lord Wakeham
The Lord Walker of Worcester
The Lord Wallace of Campsie
The Earl of Wemyss KT
The Lord Westbury
The Lord White of Hull
The Viscount Whitelaw KT
The Lord Wigram
The Lady Willoughby de Eresby
The Lord Wolfson of Marylebone
The Earl of Yarborough

THE FEUDAL BARONS

David Ainger Turner, Baron of Tirreragh
Leon Carter, Baron of Connello
John de Ayton, Baron of Corran
Raymond and Wendy de Vere Austin, Baron and Baroness of Delvin
Alan Duckett, Baron of Kendal
Charles Eugster, Baron of Callan
George Mitchell, Baron of Kilnalea
Jean Pierre Piffre, Baron of Courcy
Michel Pilette of Kinnear
Heather Previn, Baroness of Tirrerill
Daniel Sharpe of Twynehame
Paul Sleigh, Baron of Carbury
Maurice Taylor of Portlethen
Melody Urquhart, Baroness of Eye and Leyny
Douglas Wagland of Pitcruivie
Robert Williamson of Ballumbie
Anne Wood, Baroness of Lune
Fritz A Ziegler, Baron of Ibane

THE MANORIAL LORDS

Gerald T Andrews, Lord of Grayrigg
Anthony Appleton, Lord of Great Baddow
J Armitage, Lady of Knockaline
Bupendra Arora, Lord of Grittenham
Richard Ayearst, Lord of Bothamshall
Anthony Aylmer, Lord of Antingham
Arnold Baker, Lord of Barton
Sir Robert Balchin, Lord of Lingfield
Misao Batts, Lady of Birch and Lyth
Daniel and Shirley Beirne, Lord & Lady of Downholme
Jacques Bichsel, Lord of Hackford
William Bowmore, Lord of Heywood Hall in Diss
L L Brandt-Bull, Lord of Itton
Syed Bukhari, Lord of Bendysh Hall
Leonard Bull, Lord of Thoby
Brian Bullas, Lord of Scalthwaiterigg
Martin Burton, Lord of Tandridge
Malcolm Buxton, Lord of Larges
Cliifford Buxton, Lord of Tibenham Hastings
Brian Callan, Lord of Athlone
Kenneth Cater, Lord of Geltsdale
Ralph Cavenagh-Mainwaring, Lord of Whitmore
Peter Chancellor, Lord of West Hartford
D F Chapman, Lord of Casterton
Murray Chapman
P Chapman, Lord of Dodford
Achille Chiorando, Lord of Brampton
Timothy Clark, Lord of Soham with Netherhall Wygorne & Fordham
L A Coleman, Lord of Ugborough
Jack Connolly, Lord of Cheam and Cuddington
Robert Coombes, Lord of St Winnow
Arnold J Davis, Lord of Barnham Broom
Thomas Dawson, Lord of Hazelwood
Desmond de Silva
Douglas Densmore, Lord of Stratford St Andrew
Elsie Downer, Lady of Crouch
Ruth Drury
Barry Drury, Lord of Wiveton
Carl and Vindis Dunning Gribble, Lord & Lady of Marnhull
John Dyehouse, Lord of Woodford Halse
Nabil El Nagy, Lord of Wicklewood
Peter Falcon-Uff, Lord of Eynesford
Malcolm Falconer, Lord of Bere & Faconshall
Anthony Farnath, Lord of Woodcote
William Ferris, Lord of Stainburn

Norman Fisher
SG Flavell Matts, Lord of Mountsorrel
Ronald Fletcher, Lord of Dagnall
Andrew Forster, Lord of Mynchens
Raymond Franks, Lord Barwick-in-Elmet and Thorner
Mellvine Fuchs, Lord of Dunton Waylett
Theodore Gamble, Lord of Kettleburgh
James Gardiner Garrison
Robert Adam Garrison
Susan Alexandra Garrison
David Garrison, Lord of Byng
Ole Georg, Lord of Sheldowne
Ramesh Ghatge, Lord of Harthill
K K Gibson-Wynes, Lord of Bottitors in Kimberley
Deborah Gilbert, Lady of Gratwich
Christopher Golding, Lord of Kempshott
John Grant, Lord of Walton Wood
Richard Grayson, Lord of Mursley
Gillian Green, Lady of Alveston
Ronald Green, Lord of Welshampton
Leonard Grimwood, Lord of Horsey
Harold Hall, Lord of Hudnall
Bernard Hammond, Lord of Colchester Hall
Jeffrey Hardwick, Lord of Laneham
Joseph A Hardy III, Lord of Henly in Arden
Jacqueline Harris, Lady of Caldwell
Wilhelm Henriques, Lord of Perrywood
Peter Herring, Lord of Berewyk Hall
James Hilton, Lord of Lytham
Kenneth Hobday, Lord of Ruislip
John Holland, Lord of Boyland
Charles Holloway, Lord of Seavington Dennis
Niall Horan
John Hornchurch, Lord of Hornchurch Hall
Geoffrey Horne, Lord of Wakes Colne
Cecil Humphery-Smith
John Hunt, Lord of Worksop
Sandro Iaria, Lord of Tillingdon
Roy Jennings, Lord of Minterne
F A Jones, Lord of Haxey
Countess Joussineau de Tourdonnet, Lady of Kenninghall
Simon Kearey, Lord of Kersall
Matthew Keiser, Lord of Tuxford
Steven Kellner, Lord of Blencogo
Nicholas Kittrie, Lord of Croughton
J V Knight, Lady of Cooling
Frederick Lambert, Lord of Tockington

Cyril Lane, Lord of Shrewsburys Fee
Elvin Lashbrooke Jr, Lord of Duston
Abdul Latif, Lord of Harpole
James Laurie, Lord of Boylands, Beauchamp and Facons
David Legg-Willis
Alan Littlewood, Lord of Wharton
Harry Lockett, Lord of Willoughby
John Longford-Lewis, Lord of More Malherbe and Cotley
Peter Magauran, Lord of Santon
Sadie Marks, Lady of Shovelstrode
Antonio Mas-Perez, Lord of Egmanton and Elkesley
Malcolm McConaghy, Lord of Mickle Trafford
Royston McCracken, Lord of Crofton & Winnow
Patrick McKenna, Lord of Ashridge
Bruce Merivale-Austin, Lord of Horton
John Montgomery, Lord of Thirlwall
Frederick Morgan, Lord of Kenfig
Maurice Mottram, Lord of Chatteris Nunns
John Mulvihill, Lord of Abbas Hall
William and Nancy Neville, Lord & Lady of Pounceneys
Norman Newlands, Lord of Postling
Arthur Newton, Lord of Brauncewell
Peter Norton, Lord of Stratford upon Avon
David Nugent, Lord of Castletown Delvin
Donald Olliff
Colin Palmer, Lord of Manton
Michael Pendred, Lord of Frithsden
David Person, Lord of the Hundred of Forehoe
Harold Piggott, Lord of Netherhall
Victor T Podd, Lord of Newcastle
Stephen D Podd, Lord of Winston
Victor I Podd, Lord of Wightfield
Britanny Victoria Podd, Lady of Little Holland on the Sea
Natasha Renee Podd, Lady of Halton
P F Poeliejoe-Zewald, Lord of St Aylotts
C W Poole. Lord of Upton Warren
Edward Race, Lord of Felixstowe
Raymond Rayner, Lord of Chepstow
Roger Reed, Lord of Coffinswell
Leslie Retford, Lord of Pleshey
Mark Tudor Roberts, Lord of Merrion
Leslie Rosan, Lord of Haverhill
David Rosow, Lord of Godington
Hans Rösner-Mautby, Lord of Mautby
V Rubinstein, Lord of Garford
Terence Rutter, Lord of Linghall
Leslie Ryder, Lord of Tixall

L H Sanders, Lord of Broomholm
Valerie Sayer, Lady of Bures at the Mount
Gordon Scott-Morris, Lord of Madfreys
Louis-Marc Servien, Lord of Quendon
Brian Sewell, Lord of Hardingham and Flockthorpe
John Sherringham, Lord of Talkin
Timothy Shorland, Lord of Hempton & Northwick
Jacob Sigamoney, Lord of Earls Hall
John Skelton
P C K Sladden, Lord of South Repps
Patricia Slocombe, Lady of Hinton
Allan Smart, Lord of Edingale
John Stedman, Lord of Irthington
Mark Steele, Lord of Hassenbrook
Howard Steers, Lord of High Hoyland
Robert Steventon, Lord of Thistleton
Gunter Streib, Lord of Westhall
Michael Sullivan, Lord of Newenham
R S Suri, Lord of Great Bealings
Roger Taylor, Lord of Stony Stratford
Barry Theobald-Hicks, Lord of Danbury
Peter Trapp, Lord of Ulpha
Peter Tray
H B Trevor-Cox, Lord of East Winterslow
Robert Turrall-Clarke, Lord of Overhall in Hildersham
Thomas van Schoonbeek, Lord of Lambrigg
Richard Varmer, Lord of Burstall
A W Vidler, Lord of Lanhadron
Ernst Ludwig von Kuthy, Lord of Worminghall
John Waller, Lord of Cumrew
Graig and Marjorie Walsh, Lord & Lady of Lucies
Sheila Watson-Challis
Edgar Wayman
George Webb, Lord of Distington
A Weems Mcfadden, Lord of Deopham
Simon Wheaton-Smith, Lord of Romburgh
Gordon Whitehead, Lord of Cockshutt
Robert Williams, Lord of Allerby
Raymond Woodberry, Lord of Prittlewell
Denis B Woodfield, Lord of Hamptonet
Clifford Worthing

Contents

Notes on Contributors

The Hon Adam Bruce (chapter 6) read History at Balliol College, Oxford, where he was President of the Oxford Union. He then returned to study Law at Edinburgh University and now works for a firm of solicitors in Edinburgh.

Professor David Cannadine (chapter 8) is Moore Collegiate Professor of History at Columbia University and Fellow of King's College, Cambridge. His most recent books are *The Decline and Fall of the British Aristocracy* (New Haven (USA), 1990), *G M Trevelyan: A Life in History* (London, 1992), and *Aspects of Aristocracy: Grandeur and Decline in Modern Britain* (London, 1994).

Professor John Cannon CBE FRHistS FRSA (chapter 7) was Professor of Modern History at the University of Newcastle-upon-Tyne from 1976 until his retirement in 1992. He was educated at Cambridge University and was successively Lecturer, Senior Lecturer and Reader in History at Bristol University (1961-76). He was a member of the University Grants Committee (1983-89) and its Vice-Chairman (1986-89). His books include *The Fox-North Coalition: crisis of the constitution* (Cambridge, 1969), *Parliamentary Reform, 1640-1832* (Cambridge 1972) and *Aristocratic Century: the peerage of eighteenth-century England* (Cambridge 1984), and he has edited numerous other historical works including (with R A Griffiths) *The Blackwell Dictionary of Historians* (Oxford, 1988).

Dr David Carpenter FRHistS (chapter 2) is a leading authority on English medieval history. His publications include *The Battles of Lewes and Evesham* (Keele, 1987), *The Minority of Henry III* (London, 1990) and numerous articles in books and learned journals. He was educated at Westminster School and Christ Church College, Oxford. He has held lectureships at Christ Church and St Hilda's Colleges, Oxford, at the University of Aberdeen, and at Queen Mary College, London. He is now a lecturer in History at King's College, London.

Sir Colin Cole KCB KCVO TD BCL FSA (chapter 9) was Garter Principal King of Arms from 1978 to 1992 and is a member of the Governing Council of the Manorial Society of Great Britain.

Dr John Fines PhD (chapter 3) studied at Cambridge University and took his PhD at Sheffield University on the theme of Lollardy. Much of his academic work has concentrated on the development of the Reformation in England. He has been a teacher in schools and in Higher Education and, now retired, directs the Nuffield History Project. He has published widely in historical journals and in educational publications.

Dr Steven Gunn FRHistS (chapter 4) is Fellow and Tutor in Modern History at Merton College, Oxford. He is author of *Charles Brandon, Duke* *of Suffolk, c1484-1545* (Oxford, 1988), and editor with P G Lindley of *Cardinal Wolsey: Church, State and Art* (Cambridge, 1991), and is currently writing a book on early Tudor government.

Professor Henry R Loyn DLitt FBA FSA FRHistS (chapter 1) is Professor Emeritus of the University of London, where he was Professor of Medieval History at Westfield College (1977-87); previously he was Professor of Medieval History at University College, Cardiff (1967-77). He is the author of many books, including *The Governance of Anglo-Saxon England* (London, 1984), and *Anglo-Saxon England and the Norman Conquest* (London, 2nd edn, 1991), and has contributed many articles on early medieval topics to historical journals. He was President of the Historical Association (1976-79).

Professor John Miller FRHistS (chapter 5) is Head of the History Department, Queen Mary and Westfield College, University of London, and was educated at Jesus College, Cambridge. He was a Research Fellow at Gonville and Caius College, Cambridge (1971-5); since 1975 he has been at Queen Mary College as Lecturer in History, subsequently Reader and Professor. His books include *Popery and Politics in England, 1660-88* (Cambridge 1973), *James II: a study in Kingship* (Hove, 1978, repr London, 1989), *Charles II* (London, 1991), and *An English Absolutism? The later Stuart Monarchy, 1660-88* (London, 1992), and he has edited *Absolutism in Seventeenth-Century Europe* (London, 1990).

John S Moore FRHistS (General Editor; Introduction) was educated at Brighton Technical College and the Institute of Historical Research, London. He was awarded the Alexander Prize of the Royal Historical Society and the John Nichols Local History Prize of Leicester University. Since 1968 he has been Lecturer in Economic History at Bristol University. His main research interests are in the economic and social history of medieval and early modern England; his books include *The Goods and Chattels of Our Forefathers* (Chichester, 1976), and *Domesday Book: Gloucestershire* (Chichester, 1981), and he has also written articles in *Anglo-Norman Studies*, *Economic History Review* and other historical journals. He is now writing a book on the population of Tudor England.

The Rt Hon J Enoch Powell MBE (chapter 11) was a member of the House of Commons from 1950 until 1987, exept for a few months in 1974. He served in the Cabinet of the late Harold Macmillan (Earl of Stockton). With many other books to his credit, he co-authored with Keith Wallis *The House of Lords in the Middle Ages* (London, 1968).

Robert Smith BA (chapter 13) read history at Nottingham University and graduated as BA in 1969. He is the Chairman of the Manorial Society of Great Britain and Publisher of Smith's Peerage Ltd. *The Peerage, Baronetage and Feudal Title Holders* in four volumes is in the process of research for publication in 1998. He edited and published *Domesday, 900 Years of England's Norman Heritage* (joint editor with H R Loyn) for the Public Record Office (1986); *Royal Armada, 400 Years* for the National Maritime Museum (1988); and *Against the Odds, the 50th Anniversary of the Battle of Britain* for the Royal Air Force Museum (1990).

Lord Sudeley MA FSA (chapter 10) is President of the Monday Club, Patron of the Prayer Book Society and of the Bankruptcy Association, and Vice-Chancellor of the Monarchist League. He cleared the *Prayer Book (Protection) Bill* in the House of Lords in 1981, and introduced debates in the House of Lords on the export of historical manuscripts (1973), on Cathedral finance (1980) and the use of the Prayer Book in theological colleges (1987). He edited *The Sudeleys: Lords of Toddington* (London, 1987) jointly with Robert Smith, in which he wrote a chapter, and has contributed to numerous journals. He is a member of the Governing Council of the Manorial Society of Great Britain.

Keith Wallis (chapter 12) was educated privately and was awarded a BA from William College, Williamstown, Mass, in 1952. He collaborated with J Enoch Powell on *The House of Lords in the Middle Ages* (1968), and now lives in London.

Picture Captions

A: Conspicuous consumption and display have been the hallmark of all European nobilities until the 20th century when taxation, or democracy, or revolution, or all three brought radical changes in lifestyles. This picture is of John of Gaunt (Plantagenet), Duke of Lancaster, at dinner with King John of Portugal, *circa* 1389. Gaunt was the fourth son of Edward III, victor over the French at Crécy and Poitiers. The King of Portugal is seated under a canopy with his coat of arms above. Gaunt sits on the King's right beneath the Royal Arms of England. The youths who are serving at the table are probably the sons of other noblemen sent to be trained in manners, as well as the martial arts, at the Royal Household. Good manners, literacy, and an appreciation of music, and heroic and religious literature became increasingly important among the aristocracy as the Middle Ages drew to a close. This picture was painted almost 100 years later, circa 1475, by an unknown artist of Bruges, for Edward IV who at the time had grand ideas of his role as arbiter of European politics. *Courtesy British Library, Royal MS, 14 EIV fol 244v.* See John Fines, p44.

B: John, fifth Lord Lovel of Tichmersh KG, receiving a book of hours (daily devotions). Lord Lovel commissioned this *circa* 1400 for Salisbury Cathedral. The artist was John Siferwas, a Dominican friar. Lord Lovel, like many English noblemen in the 15th century, was a valiant soldier. John Tiptoft, Earl of Worcester, known as the Butcher of England, was one of the greatest collectors of illuminated manuscripts, but this was not ironic in the late medieval mind. *Courtesy British Library, Harl MS 7026 fol 4v.* See John Fines, p44.

C: John Plantagenet, Duke of Bedford, kneels in supplication before St George, Patron Saint of England, who is wearing the badge of the Order of the Garter. The Duke was the third son of Henry IV and younger brother of the brilliant Henry V, who made himself *de facto* King of France. On his brother's untimely death, in 1422, Duke John ruled France as Regent for the English. *Courtesy British Library, Add MS 18850 fol 256v.* See John Fines, p44.

D: Thomas Cromwell, first and last Earl of Essex, the son of a blacksmith who rose to become Henry VIII's Lord Chancellor and presided over the Dissolution of the monasteries. The Tudors plucked many of their chief ministers out of obscurity, sometimes to the chagrin of the old nobility, and elevated them to the peerage. Some, like Lord Essex, fell foul of their royal masters and mistresses, and died on the block. Others, such as Robert Cecil, of minor gentry, rose to found the great aristocratic Earldom and later Marquessate of Salisbury. Ironically, Lord Essex's kinsman, Sir Richard Williams, who changed his name to Cromwell, was grandfather of Oliver Cromwell, who was to overthrow the Monarchy in the following century. Painted "after

Hans Holbein". *Courtesy National Portrait Gallery, London.* See Steven Gunn, p52.

E: George Villiers, first Duke of Buckingham, being, says William Dugdale, the antiquarian, "of stature tall and comely, his comportment graceful and of a most sweet disposition". His rise from plain George Villiers, of insignificant gentle stock, was perhaps the most rapid outside the Royal Family and not a little to do with James I's predeliction for handsome young men. At 24 he became a Knight of the Garter, and in the same year Baron Whaddon. In the following year (1616), he became Viscount Villers, Earl of Buckingham in 1617, and in 1618, Marquess of Buckingham. He was created Duke in 1623. After the parsimony of Elizabeth, James lavished titles on his favourite and on his favourite's friends, family, and clients. Buckingham even sold titles for cash so that, by his assassination in 1628, the peerage had been seriously devalued. Painting attributed to William Larkin. *Courtesy National Portrait Gallery, London.* See John Miller, p66.

F: William Russell, first Duke of Bedford KG, a Whig grandee who supported the invitation to the Prince William of Orange in 1688 to come to England to save the realm from the Catholic James II. James fled and Parliament accordingly offered William and his wife, Mary, King James' daughter, the Throne as William III and Mary II in 1689 in what is called the Glorious Revolution. It must have been sweet revenge for the Duke to drive James from the land, for in 1681 James, as Duke of York and brother and heir to Charles II, had been the object of a move to exclude him from the succession, led by Bedford's son, William, Lord Russell, for which Lord Russell was beheaded. The Glorious Revolution was pivotal to the constitutional development of Britain and heralded the golden age of the aristocracy, the 18th century. Painting by Sir Godfrey Kneller. *Courtesy National Portrait Gallery, London.* See John Miller, p66 and John Cannon, p98.

G: The reigns of William III followed by that of his sister-in-law, Anne, consolidated the revolution of 1689 and laid the foundation of aristocratic power in the 18th century. Astronomic rises for the minor gentry were not uncommon as John Churchill, first Duke of Marlborough KG (attributed to J Closterman after J Riley), in this picture demonstrates. The grandson of a Devon knight, John Churchill rose in the army under the patronage of the Duke of York (later King James II). Seeing how the political wind was blowing in autumn 1688, Churchill (by then Baron Churchill of Sandridge and commander of James II's army) joined William of Orange and helped to install that Prince on the Throne (for which, William made him Earl of Marlborough). His wife Sarah's friendship with the future Queen Anne obtained for John the Marquessate of Blandford and the Dukedom of Marlborough when she ascended the Throne in 1702. Marlborough's renown on the battlefield came in Anne's reign when he trounced the French at Blenheim (1704), Ramilles (1706), Oudenard (1708) and Malplaquet (1709). A grateful nation bestowed on him the valuable Manor of Woodstock,

Oxfordshire, together with enough cash to build Blenheim Palace, and an annual subsidy of £5,000, which was paid to the family until 1947 when such pensions were abolished by the postwar Labour Government of Clement Attlee. By 1706, the Duke's only son had died and the Duke obtained an Act of Parliament allowing all his titles to pass first to his eldest daughter, Henrietta, who died childless, and then to his grandson by his second daughter, Anne, who was married to Charles Spencer, third Earl of Sunderland KG. Such was the influence of the nobility over the Crown - which might even be said to have been in tutelage - that arrangements of this sort (special remainders) were possible. *Courtesy National Portrait Gallery, London.* See John Miller, p66 and John Cannon, p98.

H: Sir Robert Walpole, first Earl of Orford KG, accounted the first of the line of British prime ministers, becoming First Lord of the Treasury briefly in 1716, and continuously from 1721 until 1742. Walpole is another example of the possibilities that were open to men of talent in the Aristocratic Century. He was little more than the son of a Norfolk squire, but Kings George I and II came to rely on him, as did the "Whig Party" and many Tories. His fall from power was against the wishes of George II and sheds an interesting light on the power of the Monarchy and that of the landed aristocracy. No prime minister could remain in power without the support of the King, but the King's support was not enough when sufficient of the aristocracy had turned against a minister. Walpole's younger brother, Horace, was the celebrated diarist, letter-writer, and commentator from whom we learn much of the 18th century aristocratic mind. Painting by Arthur Pound. *Courtesy National Portrait Gallery, London.* See John Cannon, p98.

I: William Pitt the Elder, first Earl of Chatham, was the grandson of Thomas Pitt, who was of no eminent family, but was extremely rich. Wealth was and is one way of rising up the social and political ladder, and Thomas Pitt's sons and daughters were variously married into the nobility, were ennobled, or were ancestors of noble lines. The Elder Pitt, who sat as MP for that most famous of "rotten boroughs", Old Sarum, was one of the ablest politicians of the age and presided over the brilliant British victories over the French and Austrians during the Seven Years' War (1756-63) in Europe, India, and Canada. He obtained a peerage for his wife, Hester, as Baroness of Chatham in 1761 before he obtained his Earldom five years later, as he preferred to remain in the House of Commons. On his death in 1778, Parliament voted £4,000 a year to whoever should hold the Earldom of Chatham. Chatham's second son, William Pitt the Younger, became Britain's youngest prime minister, aged 24, in 1783, which post he held with a short interruption until his death in 1806. It was the administration of the Younger Pitt, who turned Britain's massive economic and naval might against, first, the French revolutionary armies and, then, Napoleon I, which set the scene for the eventual defeat of the French Emperor at Waterloo in 1815. On his death, Pitt the Younger left a debt of £40,000 which a grateful nation paid off for

him. Painting after Brompton. *Courtesy National Portrait Gallery, London*.
See John Cannon, p98.

J: John Stuart, third Earl of Bute KG, was Prime Minister to George III from
1762-63. Bute inveigled his way into the household of Frederick, Prince of
Wales, thanks, apparently, to a shower of rain at Egham races in 1747 which
kept Frederick in his tent and in need of a fourth player at whist. George II
could not speak of Lord Bute except with contempt, but he was so firmly
favoured by the Princess of Wales that, on the death of Frederick in 1756, his
influence on "the king-in-waiting" increased. Bute was an instance of the
truism that one needed royal patronage to become prime minister, but that
this patronage alone was not enough to sustain a man in office. Having
engineered the overthrow of the Elder Pitt, Bute pursued a peace policy with
the French, inimical to that of Pitt's administration and to much of the
sentiment in the country. Although he resigned in 1763, Bute's influence
with the King was so considerable that George Grenville obtained the
Sovereign's promise never to see the favourite again in 1765, the King being
tactfully advised that otherwise he would be unable to count on an
administration that could command a majority in the House of Commons.
He purchased Luton Hoo, Bedfordshire, where he formed a magnificent
library, a collection of astronomical, philosophical, and mathematical
instruments, and a gallery of Flemish and Dutch paintings. Bute had his
wife created Baroness Mount Stuart and his eldest son Baron Cardiff, who
was created Earl of Windsor and Marquess of Bute on the third Earl's death
in 1792. Painting by Sir Joshua Reynolds. *Courtesy National Portrait
Gallery, London*. See John Cannon, p98.

K: Arthur Wellesley, first Duke of Wellington KG, was the third son of
Gilbert, first Earl of Mornington. Unless an elder brother died, prospects for
younger sons of peers lay in marriage, the Church, or the military. Wellington
was probably Britain's most successful general, Waterloo being only his most
famous battle. There were many others: Salamanca and Vittoria in Spain
being pivotal in the Peninsula Campaign. Wellington was heaped with
honours and riches at home and abroad: two marquessates and a dukedom
at home; he became a duke and a Grandee of the First Class in Spain; a duke
in Portugal; and Prince of Waterloo in the Netherlands. He was prime
minister twice, though not successfully, Warden of the Cinque Ports, Constable
of England at Victoria's Coronation, Constable of the Tower. Spain gave him
an estate in the Duoro valley worth £20,000 a year, which the family still own.
A grateful British Parliament granted him £100,000 in 1812 to maintain his
new dignity of a marquessate; in 1814, he was granted a further £400,000 to
buy lands to support his new dignity of a dukedom; and in the following year
a further £200,000 - huge sums at the time. Though large, these sums were
probably considered insignificant compared with the cost of keeping armies
in the field under a less successful general. The Dutch and other nations
granted him estates. When he died, aged 84, in 1852, the nation mourned.
He was perhaps the aristocrat of aristocrats, personifying the abiding *raison*

d'être of any nobility: that of being the valiant conqueror of the nation's enemies. It was a role never quite to be emulated again, and a role put aside permanently by the aristocracy after the disaster of the First World War. Painting by R Home. *Courtesy National Portrait Gallery, London.* See David Cannadine, p109.

L: William Lamb, second Viscount Melbourne of Kilmore, was Home Secretary in the Grey administration which enacted the Great Reform Act of 1832, abolishing many of the "rotten boroughs" and granting parliamentary representation (subject to strict property qualifications) to the new cities of the Industrial Revolution: Birmingham, Manchester, Leeds, Bradford. The measure was forced through the House of Lords by William IV who promised to create enough peers willing to vote for it. But the Reform Act did not affect the aristocracy's hold on the levers of power, and the period 1832 to 1870 was another "golden age". Lord Melbourne was Prime Minister, except for a short break, from 1834-41. His wife was Lady Caroline Lamb, writer and termagant, who became besotted with Lord Byron, of whom she wrote that he was "mad, bad, and dangerous to know". Painting by Sir Edwin Landseer. *Courtesy National Portrait Gallery, London.* David Cannadine, p109.

M: Henry Temple, third Viscount Palmerston KG, was a member of some one's government from 1807, almost continuously, until he formed his first government as prime minister in 1855, in which office he died 10 years later. He was popular and, as foreign secretary and prime minister, laid the foundations of the formal Imperial Britain that was arguably to last until 1947 when India gained independence. As a peer of Ireland, he could sit in the House of Commons and, for the last 30 years of his life, was MP for Tiverton, Devon. It was less easy to be prime minister from the Lords by the 1850s. After the Second Reform Act of 1867, it was almost essential to be prime minister from the Commons as Disraeli and Gladstone found. Painting by John Partridge. *Courtesy National Portrait Gallery, London.* David Cannadine, p109.

N: The Rt Hon David Lloyd George, first Earl Lloyd-George of Dwyfor OM, who tried to keep the finances of the fading Liberal Party afloat after the First World War by selling peerages and baronetcies. It was Lloyd-George's People's Budget of 1909 - which raised taxes to pay for the first state pensions - that brought the last clash between Commons and Lords and finally determined the subservience of the unelected chamber to the elected one in the Parliament Act of 1911: peers could no longer stop money bills, which meant that the House of Commons could always overrule the Lords in contentious legislation by "tacking on" a money bill. Even Lloyd George, however, took an earldom in the last year of his life, he said, to please his second wife, Frances. Painting by Unknown Artist. *Courtesy National Portrait Gallery, London.* David Cannadine, p109.

O: Weetman Pearson, first Viscount Cowdray, founder and head of
S Pearson and Son Ltd, later S Pearson Longman, and now Pearson plc, one
of the most successful multinational companies based in Britain.   Pearson
owns *The Financial Times*.   With the Liptons, the Levers, the Basses, the
Cowdrays, the Pearsons were the commercial millionaires, finally recognized
in their own right as leaders in the nation in business, and not by virtue of
public office or military prowess.   Tsar Nicholas II was distressed at the
future Edward VII's familiarity with such commercial men, while the
German Kaiser Wilhelm II was reported to have said of Edward VII's
yachting in Thomas Lipton's *Shamrock* that the British King went sailing
with his grocer.   The Honours System, which had been largely designed by
the aristocracy for the aristocracy, was overhauled by George V in 1917 with
the creation of the Most Excellent Order of the British Empire which made
for the distribution of honours to a much wider group of people.   Painting by
Sir William Orpen RA, photographed by Jim Henderson.   *Courtesy third
Viscount Cowdray*.   See David Cannadine, p109.

P: Felicity, Baroness Lane-Fox of Bramham, West Yorks, was introduced
into the Lords by Lord Holderness and Lord Grimthorpe on 9 June 1981.
Overseeing the ceremony was the then Mr (now Sir) Colin Cole, Garter
Principal King of Arms.   Lady Lane-Fox is an excellent example of the value
of new creations to the House of Lords.   She has been Vice President of the
Royal Association of Disability and Rehabilitation; Chairman of Phipps
Respiratory Unit Patients Association (St Thomas's Hospital); Patron of the
Handicapped Adventure Playground Association and Patron of Design and
Manufacture for the Disabled.   Lady Lane-Fox is herself disabled. *Courtesy
Universal Pictorial Press & Agency Ltd*.   See Sir Colin Cole, p129.

Captions by Robert Smith

Foreword

The Lord Mackay of Clashfern, Lord High Chancellor

I am delighted to welcome the publication of *The House of Lords, A Thousand Years of British Tradition*, as the latest insight into one of the three parts of the legislature of the United Kingdom of Great Britain and Northern Ireland. I understand that, through the generosity of Mrs Celia Lipton, a lady who was born in Edinburgh, it has been possible to reduce the cover price of the book, and I hope that her sponsorship will, therefore, help the publication to reach a much wider readership.

The House of Lords is a dignified part of the British Parliament and a debating chamber in which the standard of debate is well informed and carefully argued. Although not all of the British constitution is written, a great deal of it is, and much of relevance to the House of Lords is embodied in important constitutional statutes. Members of the House of Lords have the time and ability to refine considerably Bills sent up from the House of Commons, as well as those initiated in the House before going to the Commons.

The House of Lords also represents an important part of British history. Arguably, as Professor Loyn says in the opening chapter, the history of the House of Lords can be traced to the Saxon Witanagemot of the late 10th century. That an institution has lasted for a millennium says at least two things about it: its survival powers must be immense and its ability to adapt to changing circumstances at least as great. A body that has lasted 1,000 years must have some special features worthy of remark.

The House of Lords comprises two types of peerage creations: hereditary peers and life peers. Many people think that life peers are the modern invention of the Life Peerages Act 1958. They are not. They were created by monarchs from the later middle ages well into the reign of Queen Victoria. Most Law Lords were life peers, as they still are.

In the late 20th century, the idea of an hereditary right to sit in a nation's legislature might seem to some people to be anachronistic. But it is part of the British constitution, which has emerged by evolution, not by revolution. As a result of that evolution, the powers of the House of Lords are limited in a manner that reflects the nature of its membership. I believe that it does work and the combination of talents and experiences that are brought together in the House of Lords makes it a unique and most interesting body which those who read this book will come to understand better.

A Note from the Sponsor

Celia Lipton-Farris

When I was approached to sponsor this book, having previously sponsored the 900th anniversary of Domesday book in 1986, I was deeply honoured. I wish to thank the Lord Chancellor, Lord Mackay of Clashfern for his kind mention of me, and I wish to thank Mr Robert Smith for inviting my participation.

As a child I was taken on school trips to the Houses of Parliament. What impressed me most was that someone named "Guy Fawkes" tried to blow it up. But what puzzled me even more was, why on earth we would want to celebrate this every year? Though I must admit I really did enjoy the fireworks!

What should be cause for celebration is the noble history of the House of Lords. To this day it serves as a symbol of tradition proving its worth. This inspiring book, *The House of Lords, A Thousand Years of British Tradition*, will provide the British people with invaluable historical information of which they can be justly proud. It will also inform those in foreign lands as to why the British system of government has so long endured.

I wish to applaud the contributing authors for their painstaking work and absorbing insights. My congratulations go to the Manorial Society of Great Britain and Mr Robert Smith whose vision made this significant book a reality.

Although my home is now in the United States, I shall always be the daughter proud of her mother land – Great Britain.

To all who presently serve in the House of Lords, and to all who will follow I extend my deepest and most sincere wish .... long may you prevail.

Preface

Robert Smith, Editor and Publisher

I AM certain, almost beyond peradventure, that there is no book which deals with the history and development of the House of Lords from, as it were, the beginning to the present. There are, of course, hundreds and hundreds of books about this event, or period, that minister, or Act: but none, that we have found, which treats chronologically with the institution from start to "finish".

In choosing 1042, the first year of the reign of Edward the Confessor, to open the book, no doubt some one will argue that we should have begun with the earlier Anglo-Saxon witans; but one of the the publisher's jobs is to start somewhere and it seemed sensible to me to start with the tail-end of the Anglo-Saxon Monarchy. Having said that and for the benefit of anyone thinking of picking up pen and paper to correct me, I am aware that there was no such thing as the House of Lords in the mid-11th century; indeed, no concept of a "second chamber" until well into the 14th century - some historians might argue even after that.

The eventual emergence of a "house of peers" (lords temporal and spiritual) does not appear to have been a planned development by English administrations. Rather, English kings, in the Anglo-Norman and early Plantagent periods (1066-1272), looked to the magnates (the owners of most of the land and, therefore, the richest and most powerful men in the kingdom) for their support. This support came in various forms, but principally in money and services, but also in advice. In the early part of the period, the services (such as appearing armed) or money *in lieu* of services were fixed by custom and recorded in documents, like Domesday Book, or the feudal grants of Henry I. At first, it was a fairly simple process: William the Conqueror, in confirming landholdings in Domesday, exacted fees and services from his magnates (or tenants-in-chief) in return for recognizing their holdings. This all seemed fair enough in the beginning because most of the holders of lands had come over with the Conqueror, or during his reign, and they acknowledged the debt. But as sons and grandsons inherited, or as some people alienated their holdings, so, with the passage of time, the memory of the debt receded and it became harder for the royal officers to collect traditional dues. Efforts were made in the 12th century to remind the magnates of their responsibilities in return for their land: Henry I's feudal grants and then Henry II's assizes in the 1160s are examples. Added to this were the Plantagenets' prodigious need for money, over and above that which they could traditionally expect, to pursue their truly imperial ambitions in France. *Ad hoc* assemblies were, therefore, summoned by Henry II and his successors in the 13th century of magnates in an effort to get them to cough up. A further problem for the English kings was that, increasingly, the land they had reserved for themselves in Domesday which was later called "ancient demesne", was insufficient to meet financial needs a century later, without including the cost of holding the French provinces. Partly, this was caused by the increasingly complex and consequently costly nature of government, but mainly by kings' willingness to grant away lands from the royal domain for loyal service: grants that were less and less balanced by the profits of justice or the acquisition of lands through forfeiture and escheat. By the reign of Henry III (1216-72), these *ad hoc* assemblies are sometimes being called "parliaments" (meetings for deliberation), but the word had not acquired its specialized meaning. Some of the parliaments assembled by Henry III seem even to have included representatives of the more important towns.

Edward I (1272-1307) is the King commonly associated with "parliament" and it is from his reign that we can start to talk of summonses to the towns and counties (the later "knights of the shire") who come to meet as the "commons". But most of Edward's parliaments are parliaments of magnates and/or clergy (abbots and bishops), some of them very sparsely attended indeed. Essentially, the separation of Lords from Commons emanates from these times and appears to have been accidental, but as the idea of an honorific peerage established itself during the 14th century - perhaps particularly in the reign of Edward III (1327-77) - the separation becomes prescriptive and complete, although it has to be remembered that both "houses" from an early date regularly met through "commissioners" of each body to discuss the king's demands and their responses.

On the continent of Europe, parliamentary development, for a variety of reasons, developed differently: there were usually three "estates", the clergy becoming a separate one; but the crucial difference between England and most of the rest of Europe was that the nobility in this country enjoyed no special privileges simply by being noble. In France and Germany, for example, nobility came to mean exemption from taxation. This never happened in England and so the interests of Commons and Lords, certainly as applied to taxation, were often identical, and commoners and noblemen frequently found themselves allied against the financial exactions of the Crown with all that this implies for the exercise of power.

Almost surely, if you were asked to draft a constituion for an imaginary country, you would not draft the English and later British constitution of a Crown, Lords, and Commons, the three legislative institutions. The British constitution is still largely prescriptive, but much of it *is* written down, except that, unlike many other later constitutions, it is not all written down on "one sheet of paper", so to speak. It is written down in Acts of Parliament, but also in judgments of the Courts: the Common Law, the legal conception of which, especially in the 17th century, is that good law emerges by practice and eventual acceptance, and bad law is rejected by practice. The great Lord Chief Justice, Sir Edward Coke, believed that all law emerged from the people and that Acts of Parliament, or the will of princes, were simply declaratory of law that was, in its practice, already accepted, or else such Acts or Royal Statutes would be repealed, or ignored, as being unacceptable. Magna Carta (1215) or the Petition of Right (1628) were not innovative, by this analysis, but merely declaratory of what was already Common Law and accepted time out of mind. The essence of our constitution and its principal value is, or perhaps (now that Britain has acceded to the European Communities Treaties) was, that everything is legal provided there is no law or judgment saying that an activity is illegal. The reverse is the case in much of the rest of Europe where something is legal if the law says so, and everything else is illegal. This "shading" of difference may not amount to much day to day, but it can be and has been critical in the development and enshrining of liberty.

And we have reached the important word: liberty. Can there be liberty in a constitutional arrangement which involves an unelected chamber in the legislature? (Indeed, the Monarchy is not elected, so this makes two out of the three legislative branches which have no democratic mandate). This question is not new, and the purpose of this book (and its two sequels which will be published next year, *The Monarchy* and *The House of Commons*) is to place this question in its historical context. While history in itself may contain no lessons, it does at least help us to formulate the questions intelligently.

Liberty is not the same thing as equality, and people have tended to confuse the two. There is no such status as equality, though we are led to believe in it and to pursue it by government and media, to the exclusion of liberty. In a modern democracy, the media has become of towering importance, thanks to technology, and there is certainly no equality, while the liberty to express views, to try to shape opinion rests with journalists, editors, and especially proprietors - not with readers. Democratic government must work with the media, and so has risen in the late 20th century a monolith which speaks of equality, but has little conception of liberty, other than its own, and denies the right of reply to the vast majority. Our rulers talk of equality in citizens' charters (the UK) and "town meetings" (the US); the media comment on such matters, indeed, like to think that they initiate such debates. This is not to say that newspapers and television stations do not have willing readers or viewers. The media must reflect their customers, like any other business, but when a proprietor can say that he is considering switching his newspapers from Conservative to Labour, then the myth is exploded. *The Sun* claims to have won the 1992 general election for Mr John Major. If this is so, then it may well win the next general election for Mr Tony Blair. Few of us would be foolish enough to imagine that this is liberty for us, or even for Mr Major and Mr Blair, who are no more than competing supplicants for the same favour. This is the way things have developed and this is the democracy that we have; as Socrates found when he was democratically sentenced to death, democracy can be as tyrannous as any dictatorship. Indeed, at some point in their existences, even dictatorships enjoy some consent.

As long ago as the 1850s, commenting on the United States, Alexis de Tocqueville thought that liberty was no longer the chief and constant object of our desires and that equality had become our idol. He said that it was a depraved passion which impelled the weak to try to lower the powerful to their own level, and reduced men and women to prefer equality in slavery to inequality in liberty. It is truer still today in America where 98% of people who stand for office are elected in succession to a previous office-holder of the party, or are re-elected in that party interest: Presidents Bush and Carter are exceptions that prove the rule. How different is this from an hereditary autocracy, or an autocracy of the sort conducted by the governing party of Mexico for the past 60 years? In our own case, we are in process of demolishing everything that has been built up and adapted over centuries, and served us well, in the name of equality as determined in the media with at least the tacit (if reluctant) consent of politicians.

It is unquestionably a privilege to sit in the Lords, but it is also unquestionably a responsibility, and I can think of no better example of the kind of selfless work that is undertaken in the upper house than the report, earlier this year, on euthanasia. Such balance and care is much harder to obtain from an elective chamber, whose members must always be thinking of re-election.

Mr Blair, the new leader of the Labour Party, has pledged to abolish the House of Lords in the interests of equality. This is not new. Every Labour Opposition since the Second World War has had abolition of the Lords on its agenda at one time or another, not least the late, much lamented, one-time Communist firebrand, Manny Shinwell, later Lord Shinwell, who came to love the place.

The House of Lords consists of hereditary peers and life peers, the latter being recommended by the Prime Minister to the Queen. One of the arguments put against the hereditary element is that there is no way you can guarantee against mediocrity; but if you look at the last century of parliamentary democracy, what prime minister, except Churchill, has been anything but mediocre? Who, in the century before that, except the Younger Pitt, was better than average, yet Britain enjoyed her greatest growth in that period? No one complains that music does not provide us with a Beethoven every four or five years. Why should we expect it of politicians? Our elected representatives are driven by democratic expectation, as enunciated in the media, to promise greater and greater achievements, new and better reforms, so that, increasingly, they depart from the concept of declaring law as it has emerged and been accepted, but to inventing it. And the media, voracious for novelties and ever starker revelations - to feed the appetites they have created and jaded - latch onto lobbies and pressure groups who, they think, will supply this fodder. We now believe that government can do anything to ameliorate our lot. In fact, governments have very little capacity to do good, and very great capacity to do harm.

In a democracy, it becomes difficult for us to preserve our independence against these aggressions of power. None of us is strong enough alone to engage in the struggle with advantage, so that only a general combination can protect our liberty. And the question is: who or what will protect us? It is not my purpose to arrive at solutions, any more than this is the purpose of the other historians in this book and the two next year. Our rôle is to trace the development of our legislative institutions and to suggest the questions for others to answer.

I have said that it is not the job of historians to offer solutions, but I will offer several prognostications. I am fairly confident that if Mr Blair accedes to power at the next general election, he will quietly shelve his programme for abolishing the Lords. So long as it is there, no one has to think of something else to replace it, and it is very useful to be able to make life peers of leading industrialists, educationists, trades unionists, experienced ex-MPs, and others - the best of the brains of the country, and get them to work for us for very little indeed. But if Mr Blair persists, he would be best advised not to replace the Lords, for no occupant of 10 Downing Street is surely going to make a second chamber elective, thus giving it as much legitimacy as the House of Commons. If any political leader were thinking of changing the structure of our legislature, we should all be clear in our minds what this would mean. If there were to be an elective upper house, as in America, it would have has much right to make or break law as the lower house. "Gridlock" for 50 years in the US Congress has prevented all American presidents from tackling the structural difficulties created by democracy, principally balancing the books, which is a price still to be paid by the American people. Our structures and institutions, while superficially similar to American ones, are different (that was what the War of Independence was all about), and the grafting on of a US-style senate may not suit. A unicameral parliament would make all the more complete a prime minister's will. Limited though the powers of the Lords are, they have, in the last 15 years, been able to revise and fine-tune legislation from what has been effectively one-party government to the general benefit of all.

And finally the abolition of the Lords means the abolition of the Monarchy, for one cannot stand without the other. A future political leader and the media will almost certainly tell us that the abolition of the Lords is another step towards equality, and that the Monarchy would remain unscathed. Do not believe them. The Monarchy may not go immediately, but its end would be nigh, just as the death knell of the French monarchy was struck, not in 1789, but in 1830 with a Citizen King. If this sounds like Citizen Queen and the "People's Palace", the comparison is not overdrawn. The House of Lords has lasted for a very long time, and something that has survived for so long must have something going for it. As for a Britain without a Monarchy, it would simply no longer be Britain as we know it.

A book of this sort has brought a mix of academics, chosen because they seemed to be the best in their fields of research. It is the result of a Conference held by the Manorial Society of Great Britain at University College, Oxford, in September 1992. My excellent colleague and Co-Editor, John Moore of Bristol University, thanks the contributors in his Introduction and it would be redundant for me simply to duplicate his praise and gratitude.

In these times publishing a book of single essays is rather costly. This would have placed a burden on the Manorial Society of Great Britain, so I turned to a friend whom I had met many years ago in London, Mrs Celia Lipton-Farris. With her generous support, Mrs Lipton-Farris has made this publication possible.

As I was to discover, years later, and as many readers will remember, Mrs Lipton-Farris is better known in Britain as Celia Lipton, and she began her career as a child artist during the Second World War. Rather than join the 800,000 children evacuated from London during the Blitz, she chose to remain and sing. Although born in Edinburgh, of a Scottish mother, Mrs Lipton-Farris was raised and educated in London where her father, Sydney Lipton, impresario and orchestra leader was well known for his recordings and weekly broadcasts on BBC radio.

Celia Lipton topped the bill at the London Palladium at the age of 15, and sang with, among many others, the Mantovani and Melachrino orchestras for the BBC. She played Lilli in *Lilac Time* at Her Majesty's Theatre, Prudence in *The Quaker Girl* at the Coliseum, besides taking part in the compulsory ENSA troop entertainment programme. At the war's end the U S O invited Celia Lipton to tour Europe and entertain the troops. Shortly therafter her careet took her to New York, where she appreared on Broadway at the National Theatre in *What Every Woman Knows*, a musical version of J M Barrie's *Maggie*. She also starred as Esmeralda in an NBC television production of *The Hunchback of Notre Dame*. It was during her stay in America that she met the man who was to be her husband until his death in 1985, Victor W Farris. Mr Farris was an inventor and industrialist, with 275 patents to his name, among them the Farris Valve, used in British and American warships. He also invented a machine that wrapped cellophane around cigarette packages and the American milk carton.

From Palm Beach, where she now lives, Mrs Lipton-Farris has devoted her not inconsiderable energy and talent in support of the Salvation Army, the American Cancer Society, the American Heart Association, and numerous other charities. Through her entertainment connections, she has organized events for scores of US and British causes, gaining the support through personal appearances of Elizabeth Taylor, Kirk Douglas, Michael Jackson, and a host of other household names. Nor has she neglected her singing, having brought out a number of compact disc recordings in the last few years, and her next project is in aid of the Great Ormond Street Hospital, London. When she was playing Peter Pan during the war, she visited patients at the Hospital dressed in her title role. Mrs Lipton-Farris's latest British cause is *The House of Lords, A Thousand Years of British Tradition*, and we are all very grateful to her for having made things so much easier.

I would also like to record my thanks for their support and encouragement to Lord Forte, Lord Sudeley, Sir Colin Cole (the last two members of the Governing Council of the Manorial Society of Great Britain), Miss Sheila Pearson, Mrs Rosamond White, Miss Christine McGeoch, and Mr Michael Blishen.

Finally, a tremendous vote of thanks to John Moore, my Co-Editor, especially for sorting out all the notes.

John S Moore

Introduction

"Throughout recorded time, and probably since the end of the Neolithic Age, there have been three kinds of people in the world, the High, the Middle and the Low. They have been subdivided in many ways, they have borne countless different names, and their relative numbers, as well as their attitude towards one another, have varied from age to age: but the essential structure of society has never altered. Even after enormous upheavals and seemingly irrevocable changes, the same pattern has always re-asserted itself, just as a gyroscope will always return to equilibrium, however far it is pushed one way or the other."[1]

George Orwell, satirizing much sociological writing in the "extracts" from Emmanuel Goldstein's *The Theory and Practice of Oligarchical Collectivism* incorporated into his *Nineteen Eighty-Four* (and, incidentally, writing far better English than most sociologists), nevertheless accepted, and indeed highlighted by his deliberate repetition of the passage, the fact that most societies known to historians have been hierarchical in their structure. It is one of the sad ironies of history that revolutions intended to produce more just social arrangements - the French Revolution of 1789 with its talk of "égalité", the Russian Revolution of 1917 inspired by the Marxist dream of abolishing "class" - have invariably led merely to the replacement of one ruling class by another. (Cynics and realists, like George Orwell, have argued that such replacement is the intended purpose of revolutions). In this as in many other ways, the British experience of revolution was rather different. The ruling class, having experienced the Civil War and the Cromwellian regime that ended by relying on the naked military force of the Major-Generals, was determined to maintain itself in power. When the aristocracy did decide on revolution in 1689, it was a very atypical revolution, memorably described by Bertrand Russell as the occasion when "[my] family, and a few others gave one king notice and hired another" (although, as John Cannon shows in chapter 7, it was more than just an aristocratic *coup d'état*).[2] By doing so, the aristocracy maintained its hold on power well into the 19th century and allowed the middle class to produce its own type of revolution, the Industrial Revolution, which in the long run has proved beneficial to most of the world's population.

What is not in doubt is that Britain was (and is) a hierarchical society, though the basis of that structure has changed over time, and it follows that any history that does not reflect the dominating part played by "The High" is bound to be misleading and incomplete. Neither I nor any of the contributors to this book would for a moment support a return to the old-fashioned "kings and battles" type of political history that once dominated British schools masquerading as "History" in its entirety. Equally, however, the rise of historical disciplines such as economic and social history and archaeology has too often been accompanied by an unhistorical anti-snobbery: the "common people" and their doings were all that mattered, and the rulers and élites could be (almost) written-out of the scene. Neither version, or rather perversion, should be acceptable to the modern reader, for whom history should be the past, so far as it can be recovered, of all the people - "High", "Middle", and "Low" - in a given area, whatever its size, from continent to town or village. It is, of course, perfectly legitimate to concentrate on a particular social level so long as the final product is not being put forward as "total history", and no excuse is therefore needed for a book on the English, Scottish and later British nobility. As John Cannon has written (p 99),

> "who would wish to hear about the doings of the nobility? The short answer is, anyone who is seriously interested in history since, whether one likes them or not - not a very relevant consideration - they wielded over many centuries very considerable power."

First, what do we mean by "nobility" or "aristocracy"? The terms are not synonymous with the "peerage", those entitled to sit in the English (and later British) House of Lords initially as the result of an individual writ of summons and subsequently by right of descent, or in the Estate of the Baronage in the Scottish Parliament until 1707. Basically, the nobility or aristocracy is a body of landholders (under feudal tenure, which still exists in Scotland, though, excepting copyhold, such tenure was in the main abolished in England in 1660) or landowners who possess rights over substantial areas of land. In earlier medieval England before the invention of the titles of Dukes (for persons not of royal blood) and Marquesses under Richard II, the principal divisions were the Earls, the Barons and the Knights. Earls and Barons generally possessed land in several counties, which they held from the Crown by knight service "in chief" (ie with no intermediate overlord) while knights rarely held land in more than two adjacent counties and typically held not from the Crown "in chief" but from an Earl or Baron, or more rarely an ecclesiastical overlord, a Bishop, Abbot or Abbess, by a "mesne" (intermediate) tenure. Knights and their increasingly civilian fellows, the gentry, were invariably lords of manors and would later be collectively termed the "squirearchy". Earls and Barons became the "Lords in Parliament" by right, whereas knights and gentlemen were only eligible for election to the House of Commons, despite a fiction that the county representatives were the "knights of the shires". In Scotland, as Adam Bruce shows (chapter 6), there was a roughly parallel division of the nobility between Earls and Barons, both of whom held their dignities and lands directly from the King, and "lairds" who were subtenants of the Earls and Barons.

The size of the nobility and its subdivisions varied over time and historians' estimates of size also vary since, while the size of the peerage can usually be determined within close limits, it is much more difficult to calculate the total size of the landed class. As John Miller comments (p 68), "it is difficult to see the peerage as a distinct social or economic "class" ... the peerage should best be seen as a small section of the landed élite, distinguished from the rest by the possession of titles of nobility. The peers were the major and the gentry the minor nobility."

In England Domesday Book enables us to calculate that in 1086 there were about 180 great secular tenants-in-chief, but since relatively few estates had yet been "subinfeudated" (granted to mesne tenants) and most knights were still maintained within their lords' households, the number of knights cannot be stated with certainty. In all, there were about 7,000 tenants-in-chief and undertenants in 1086, of whom perhaps 5,000 were knights.[3] The 1166 *cartae baronum* (returns of knight-service by barons) suggest that there were then about 300 great secular lords and about 5,300 knights;[4] in the 13th century there were about a dozen earls, around 160-200 barons and about 400-500 "fighting" knights; the total knightly class may have numbered 3,000.[5] By the later 14th century there were about 70 Parliamentary peers, perhaps 1,250 knights and less than 3,000 esquires and gentlemen.[6] For most of the 15th century there were 50-60 peers, a figure which exceptionally rose to 105 in 1454, while the nobility below the peerage in 1436 comprised about 1,000 knightly families assessed as having a yearly income of over £40, about 1,200 families of esquires assessed at over £20 of annual income, and about 1,600 men, mostly gentry and merchants, with over £10 a year.

In the 16th century, the peerage fluctuated between 51 and 57, while it is possible to calculate the approximate size of the landed nobility in 1522-25 using Cornwall's estimates, derived from the musters and lay subsidies, that those assessed at over £40 per annum constituted about 1-2 per cent out of a total population of 2.0 - 2.35 million, say 8,000 families in the 1520s.[7] In the 17th century, however, the peerage almost trebled from around 60 to 176 in 1715,[8] while the size of the landed nobility as a whole in the later 16th century and earlier 17th centuries comprised about 8,000 - 10,000 families; its size can be more precisely determined from calculations for England by Gregory King in 1688 and by Edward Chamberlayne in 1692. King estimated that there were 160 peers with an average annual income of £3,200 each, 800 baronets with £800 each, 600 knights with £650 apiece, 3,000 esquires with £450 each, 12,000 gentlemen averaging £280. Chamberlayne believed there were 159 peers with an average annual income of £8,000, 749 baronets with £1,200 each, 1000 knights with £800 apiece, and 6,000 esquires and gentlemen averaging £400 each. It seems likely that King's figures on social distribution are more likely to be correct, but Chamberlayne's estimates of average incomes may well be preferable.[9] Joseph Massie in 1759-60 estimated the size of the landed classes as follows: 10 families, with an average annual income of £20,000, 120 families with an average annual income of between £6,000 and £8,000, 480 families with an average annual income of between £2,000 and £4,000, another 640 families with about £1,000, and 2,400 families with between £600 and £800; on the margins of gentility were 14,400 families with between £200 and £400. In 1873, the landed nobility (Bateman's "Peers and Peeresses", "Great Landowners", each with an annual income of £3,000 or more, and "Squires, each with between £1,000 and £3,000 per annum) comprised 4,200 families together owning 18.5 million acres (53.7 per cent) of England and Wales, of whom 400 peers held 5.7 million acres (16.6 per cent).[10] Only after 1880, with the onset of agricultural depression, followed by the imposition of death-duties in 1894, did the economic position of the "landed interest" begin to decline.[11] Throughout its main period of dominance, before the Industrial Revolution, the landed nobility formed a tiny minority of the total population, as the following table shows:

THE LANDED NOBILITY AND TOTAL ENGLISH POPULATION:

DATE	ESTIMATED SIZE OF NOBILITY (families)	ESTIMATED SIZE OF TOTAL POPULATION (millions)	NOBILITY AS A PERCENTAGE OF TOTAL POPULATION
1086	7,000	1.75	2.0%
1166	5,600	2.5	1.1%
c.1300	3,300	5.0	0.3%
c.1400	4,300	2.5	0.9%
1524	8,000	2.4	1.3%
c.1600	10,000	4.1	1.2%
1690	16,500	4.9	1.7%
1760	18,000	6.2	1.5%
1873 (a)	4,200	21.5	0.1%
1873 (b)	13,800	21.5	0.3%

Notes:

Noble families have been assumed to be above the national average size and have been calculated as 5; the estimates for English medieval population are more speculative than the later figures, which derive from E A Wrigley, R S Schofield, *The Population History of England, 1541-1871* (London, 1981, repr Cambridge, 1989). The English population estimates need to be raised slightly before 1700 to allow for Welsh population, and more substantially after 1700 for Scottish population; likewise the Scottish nobility also needs to be included after 1700. It is not likely that these additions would substantially alter the figures in the final column. The 1873 (a) figure is the total of "peers and peeresses", "great landowners" and "squires"; 1873 (b) includes "greater yeomen", giving a total perhaps more comparable with the figures for 1760 and before.

And so this book is emphatically not a "dry-as-dust" constitutional history of the House of Lords or of the peerage alone; indeed, the House of Lords as an institution only came into existence in a recognizable form late in the Middle Ages, though it had recognizable antecedents in the Anglo-Saxon *witenagemot* ("assembly of wise men") and the earlier medieval *magnum concilium* or "great council".[12] It focuses on the families who formed the ruling élite, at national and county level, at different times in our history, whose power was based on the possession of land, of military power, of jurisdictional control over their localities, and of access to the King and to the "levers of power" in the developing central government. Nonetheless, while such factors were necessary to the acquisition and maintenance of power, they did not guarantee its permanence. For this a degree of political adroitness and sheer luck was also needed.

In an age when much real power still lay with the Crown, when the personality of the wearer of the Crown mattered, and when personal contact with the monarch and his or her favourites was a vital component of political life - true down till George III's reign - to fall out of favour with monarch or favourites was indeed to court disaster. As late as Queen Anne's reign, the power of the Whig coalition led by Godolphin and Marlborough largely depended on the Queen's friendship with Marlborough's wife Sarah; once the Queen withdrew her favour, their position was greatly weakened; the fall of George Grenville in 1765 is explained by a recent historian as resulting from "a crucial deficiency. He had none of the arts of a courtier. His relationship with the King ... was disastrous".[13] Equally, royal favour alone could raise a man of talent whatever his personal background - whether the "new men raised from the dust" deplored by the chronicler Orderic Vitalis in Henry I's reign, Thomas Wolsey, illegitimate son of a butcher who became Henry VIII's first chief minister, Archbishop of York, and Cardinal-Legate of England, or Wolsey's successor Thomas Cromwell, son of a Putney clothworker and alehouse-keeper[14] - and royal assent was always required for ennoblement: the Crown to this day remains the "fount of honour" even if other, non-royal, hands control the tap.

The need for other kinds of good fortune can be seen throughout our history. As several contributors emphasize, to be on the wrong side politically could be disastrous, and it was a matter for careful judgment whether to support the Montfortians rather than Henry III and "the Lord Edward", Thomas of Lancaster and his Ordainers rather than the eventually victorious Edward II, the Appellants and later Henry of Lancaster rather than Richard II, the Yorkists rather than the Lancastrians, the Tudors rather than the Yorkists, Lady Jane Grey rather than Mary Tudor. David Carpenter in chapter 2 points out that from the reign of Edward II onwards, the penalty for political failure was no longer merely disgrace or forfeiture but execution. As late as 1644, the Earl of Manchester still bitterly commented on Charles I,

> "If we fight a hundred times and beat him ninety-nine times, he will be King still. But if he beats us but once, or the last time, we shall be hanged, we shall lose our estates, and our posterities will be undone,"[15]

and the Civil War notably divided some élite families, as well as causing great heart-searching among members of the ruling class generally whether to support King or Parliament.[16] Political executions were still commonplace as late as the 1680s, but thereafter to go into opposition no longer resulted in personal danger: "the Earl of Bute, on his retirement in 1763, was able to devote more time to his botanical interests" (p 103).

After the Reformation, not to be officially Anglican was to incur political disadvantages often worsened by heavy fines for "recusancy": only one important aristocratic family, the Dukes of Norfolk, remained Catholic for most of the period from the Elizabethan religious settlement of 1559 to the Catholic Emancipation Act of 1829.[17] The political history of Scotland was equally disrupted by factional dissension among its nobility, and James VI of Scotland, having become James I of England, was justifiably able to boast in London, safely out of reach of the Scots aristocracy,

> "This I must say for Scotland, and I may truly vaunt it, here I sit, and govern it with my pen, I write and it is done, and by a Clerk of the Council I govern Scotland now, which others could not do by the sword".[18]

While it was politically necessary to be Anglican in England after 1559, in Scotland it was equally necessary to be Presbyterian after 1689: "Episcopalians" (Scottish Anglicans) were regarded as only a little above the hated Roman Catholics in official and popular esteem.

Other forms of good luck were also required even if the dangerous shoals of politics and religion were successfully avoided: the need to ingratiate one's self with superiors, the need to conciliate equals, and the need to attract inferiors all necessitated political acumen and personal charm, which by no means all nobles in every generation possessed or even saw the desirability of possessing. Given the size of landed estates, at the highest level usually extending into many counties and at lower levels often into at least one adjacent county,[19] as well as the number and large size of households maintained by most aristocrats,[20] a level of efficient administration was essential which in turn required the selection and retention of competent stewards and other officials. This at the top level of estate and households could only be achieved if the estate-owner saw the need to select such men carefully and had the wit to recruit them. Although, with the rise of the baronial council and the professional steward in and after the 12th century,[21] and later of the trust and the settlement,[22] others could assist with the selection of officials, the ultimate responsibility still remained with the head of the family. As contemporaries repeatedly observed, an estate was like a little kingdom, and the owner of an estate needed the same personal qualities in dealing with his territory as the king did in dealing with his kingdom. Otherwise, slackness, corruption, and inefficiency set in, and the more honest and enterprising servants looked elsewhere for their future rewards.[23]

Above all, biological good fortune was essential, since the first duty of every head of family, from the highest nobleman to the lowliest peasant, was to perpetuate the male line. Yet, as several contributors observe in their chapters, there was a natural tendency for noble family-lines either to die out completely or only to produce daughters.[24] This natural biological trend was not confined to the nobility, but it was likely to be enhanced by strategies for the expansion of the estate and the survival of the family which were much more common among the upper landed groups of society. In particular, the arranged marriage was used to acquire land in several ways. For most of the period covered by this book, a bride's family would give a "marriage-portion", normally land, for her maintenance after marriage which would pass to her eldest son on her death and would then be absorbed within the estate he had inherited from his father; such land would only revert to the bride's family if she died childless. Thus a family that produced more daughters than sons would be subject over several generations to a gradual attrition of its land to provide such "portions", though this would partly be counterbalanced by "portions" acquired with the wives of the family's sons. The net result would probably only be punitive for families in groups on the margins of gentility, especially the "poor knights" in the 13th century and the "mere gentry" of the 16th to 18th centuries, particularly in periods when the cost of maintaining gentle status was being increased by inflation, which applied to the 13th, 16th, and 18th centuries.[25]

But there was another adverse factor also at work. From the 16th century onwards, the size of "portions" was increasing because impoverished aristocrats were often having to compete against mercantile or professional fathers willing to give larger "portions" in order to obtain husbands of noble rank for their daughters and, by acquiring aristocratic "in-laws" as well as a landed estate of suitable size, to insert themselves into the charmed circle of aristocratic society.[26] Equally, provision had to be made for younger sons, since the emphasis from the Norman Conquest till the present day on "primogeniture" (inheritance by the eldest son) meant that the younger sons would not normally expect to succeed to their father's estates.[27] In the Middle Ages this responsibility could often be discharged by arranging for military training in the household of an overlord or the King, the expectation being that the young knight would then make his way by success in war or marriage or both. The model to be followed was William Marshal, younger son of a minor landholder, who rose to eminence through his military skills, and was rewarded by the king's grant of the marriage of Isabel de Clare, together with her vast estates and her father's old title of Earl of Pembroke.[28] An alternative path was by training for the Church: most bishoprics and ecclesiastical sinecures were monopolized by aristocratic offspring in the medieval and earlier Tudor periods: after the wealth of the Church was reduced at the Reformation, the parish clergy more and more became a graduate profession recruited from the younger sons of lesser gentry and the yeomanry.[29] Increasingly from the 16th century, younger sons were expected to earn their own living in the armed services (especially after the Restoration) or in foreign trade, banking, the expanding colonial empire or the professions, notably the Church, the law, and medicine, after they had served an apprenticeship. Edward Chamberlayne in 1669 thought that there were 16,000 younger sons of gentlemen,

> "who have small Estates in lands, but are commonly bred up to Divinity, Law, Physick, to Court and Military Emploiements, but of late too many of them to Shopkeeping",

while in 1756 Lord Chancellor Hardwicke observed in the House of Lords (where no one contradicted him),

> "Since Queen Elizabeth's reign, particularly since the Restoration, it has been thought no disgrace to the younger sons of the best families in the kingdom to engage in commerce."[30]

The position for a noble family was far worse if a father had no son to succeed him. His heirs were then his daughters, who, with their husbands, would divide their father's estate between them, the shares being absorbed into their respective husbands' paternal estates provided that the marriage produced an heir.[31] Over time, this would, and did, lead to the number of large estates shrinking while the estates themselves grew in average size.[32] Indeed, for reasons that have only become clear with modern genetics, there was a tendency for estates that had once passed in the female line for lack of male heirs to do so again at a later date, as the gene-combination predisposing towards the production of girls only reappeared in subsequent generations.[33] The immediate upshot of a noble marriage producing only girls was an undignified scramble to secure their marriages (and their estates) if they were unmarried at their father's death. Feudal overlords, led by the Crown, down to 1642 asserted their rights of "wardship" and "marriage" in order to arrange for the union of each heiress to one of their own younger sons, to a favoured retainer or client, or simply to the highest bidder of suitable rank.[34] Almost the only check on this process was that, since wives on marriage took their husband's rank and status, the rule of "no disparagement" meant that brides ought not to be allocated to grooms whose status did not at least equal their own previous standing.[35]

After the Restoration, matters improved, since the prevalence of the "strict settlement" coupled with "trustees to preserve remainders" allowed fathers to make provision for the maintenance of their daughters (and of their younger sons) by empowering trustees to do so, or, if there was no son, to divert the estate to another branch of the family with a suitable male to take control.[36] Similarly, as John Cannon shows (p 102), the device of peerage creations "with special remainders" made possible the transmission of titles in the male line avoiding problems presented by female heiresses. Such devices to control the descent of estates and of titles were facilitated by the disappearance or obstruction of control from above: the formal abolition of "knight service" in 1660 meant that the "feudal incidents" of "wardship" and "marriage" were abolished.[37] Only very gradually, however, did the Church's view that "free consent of the parties" was essential before a valid marriage could occur become accepted in landed society, while as late as 1753 Lord Hardwicke's "Act against Clandestine Marriages" had to be passed to prevent abuses in the marriage process, not least the danger that heiresses would be manoeuvred into marrying fortune-hunters.[38] Only in the 18th century did romantic love become respectable as a basis for choosing a spouse in the landed aristocracy and even then the selection of a spouse would be confined within a small group of "eligible" suitors.[39]

Primogeniture, of course, like all inheritance systems, only applied after a landholder's death, but there were other factors at work during a landholder's lifetime that reinforced the integrity of a landed estate. The first of these factors was yet another result of the Norman Conquest. Whereas Anglo-Saxons, both men and women, had apparently been able to bequeath land freely in the late pre-Conquest period, after 1066 land could no longer pass by will.[40] This situation did not radically alter until the rise of the trust and the "use" (a special form of trust) in the late medieval period, but the significance of these developments was limited by opposition from feudal overlords led by the Crown for reasons that will shortly become clear. The outcome was the provision in the Statute of Uses of 1536 that "uses" were only valid if the deeds of "bargain and sale" setting them up were enrolled in a "court of record" (either a county court or one of the central courts at Westminster). Since one of the main reasons for a "use" was privacy, which would be impossible with public enrolment, the "use" was discarded. Finally, pressure from the landed interest produced the Statute of Wills of 1540, under which two-thirds of a tenant's land held by knight service and all his land held by "socage" (freehold) tenure could be freely bequeathed.[41] But the social habit created by, and embodied in, primogeniture still remained strong among the landed nobility, and although an estate could after 1540 be dispersed among all sons and daughters by will, in practice this rarely happened. The importance of land was such (for reasons to be examined) that the bulk of estates still passed from father to eldest son after 1540 as before. Landlords still faced problems of providing for younger sons and daughters which, given the general illiquidity of most members of the landed group, could only be met by limited land-sales or borrowing, effectively without security and therefore at high rates of interest. As we shall see below, these problems were greatly eased after the Restoration by two legal innovations, the mortgage "with equity of redemption" and the "settlement", coupled with a fall in interest-rates: together, these meant that borrowing became safer and cheaper.

The second factor that worked to keep estates intact during a landowner's lifetime was the structure of feudal landholding that prevailed in England down to 1642 and was formally abolished, for the upper ranks of landed society, in 1660. (For copyhold tenants of manorial lords the structure remained in being until the Law of Property Act of 1922 unless it had been previously abolished by private agreement or "enfranchisement"). All feudal superiors or overlords would receive a "heriot" (death-duty) on the death of an inferior or vassal, while the vassal's heir (or co-heiress if there was no male heir) would pay a "relief" or "entry-fine" on succeeding to the estate. If the heir or heiresses were minors and unmarried, the even more lucrative rights of "wardship" and "marriage" would apply. Under the former right the estate of a minor would be at the disposal of his or her lord until he or she came of age, and it was a rare lord who did not indulge in what we would call "asset-stripping"; under the latter right, a lord could choose a spouse for any of his vassal's children who were unmarried minors and for the vassal's widow, again a right that could be lucratively exploited. Feudal superiors would therefore suffer from, and generally oppose, anything that affected their receipt of the "feudal incidents": heriots, reliefs or entry-fines every generation and the more occasional profits from "wardship", "marriage", and "aids" (one-off payments on specific occasions, notably the knighting of the lord's eldest son and the marriage of his eldest daughter). Hence, in the Middle Ages, a gift by a vassal to the Church, which, as a legal corporation, could not die – it held "in mortmain" (by a dead hand) – meant that the overlord and his successors would no longer receive heriots, reliefs, entry-fines or the more lucrative rights of "wardship" and "marriage". Given Roman Catholic piety, medieval overlords generally gave their consent in return for prayers for their souls.

More generally, overlords increasingly found from the 12th century onwards that the exaction of their rights, whether to knight-service in the case of the knights and gentry or to labour-services and rent in the case of peasants, was being impeded if the holdings of their vassals were divided. At the manorial level this meant that lords generally opposed any attempt by tenants to compromise the integrity of their tenements by subdivision or subletting, and the hierarchy of tenements found in manorial surveys - hides, half-hides, virgates or carucates and bovates - remained intact until the pressure on agricultural land radically eased as population fell in the later 14th century. At higher levels overlords, headed by the Crown, moved to limit conditional gifts by the statute *De donis conditionalibus* in 1285 and to abolish further subinfeudation (the creation of new subtenancies) in 1290 by the statute *Quia emptores*. Even the substitution of one subtenant by another on gift or sale required a "licence to alienate" from an overlord which had to be purchased: the Crown was still exacting payments for such licences down to the Civil War. In short, the structure of feudalism itself operated to keep the bulk of estates intact between the 12th and the 17th centuries.

Given the range of possible misfortunes that could befall a nobleman - and death in battle was a further eventuality that could not be ruled out, either in the Middle Ages or in the World Wars of the 20th century - how did the aristocracy survive? Several separate factors can be mentioned which, in

combination, help to explain its extraordinary durability. The first factor
points to the significance of landholding. For most of the period covered by
this book, down to the late 18th century, Britain was a "pre-industrial
society" in which the possession of land was the key to wealth, status, and
power.[42] Agriculture was the principal source of wealth; its prosperity
depended basically on the amount of land possessed and its successful
management and exploitation, given current agrarian organization and
current agricultural technology. Access to land determined whether the bulk
of the population starved, scraped by, or enjoyed modest plenty. It follows
from this that the landed aristocracy, who held directly, or controlled the
access to, much of the usable agricultural land in the British Isles, dominated
the economy and controlled most of its wealth either as profits from their own
agricultural operations (especially in the 13th century) or as rents from the
farms and cottages leased to tenants. The secular nobility's share of English
land was of the order of 49% in 1086, compared to 17% held by the king and
26% held by the Church;[43] the equivalent figures on the eve of the Reformation
were 45% (nobility), 4% (Crown), and 30% (Church).[44] By the end of the 17th
century, after the dissolution of the monasteries and chantries, a reduction
in episcopal and cathedral estates, and the sale of most Crown lands as a
result of royal indebtedness, the aristocracy owned about two-thirds of the
agricultural land in England and Wales;[45] in Scotland, ex-monastic land had
also ended in the hands of the nobility as "commendators".[46] After further
aggrandizement at the expense of smaller landholders in the two centuries
after the Restoration, 710 landlords, each holding more than 5,000 acres,
between them held a quarter of the British Isles in 1873, as radicals were
swift to notice.[47]

The effectiveness of the nobility's landownership was further increased by
two factors. The first was their willingness to invest capital in their estates.
In the period before the Black Death, when most landholders were directly
exploiting their "demesnes" (home farms), this investment mainly took the
form of building mills, both the water-mills which could grind corn but also
drive fullers' hammers and the windmills which were appearing in England
by the mid-12th century and may indeed have been an English invention;
since manorial lords could force their tenants to grind corn at their mills, this
was an investment with a guaranteed return.[48] Another method of increasing
lordly incomes at minimum cost was to license the extension of the farming
area onto previously uncultivated waste or woodland, the process known as
"assarting", wherever there would still be sufficient land left for the pasturing
of plough-beasts and other animals, the cutting of furze and timber and the
digging of stone, clay, and turf for the villagers' use.[49] Some lords, such as the
Berkeleys in Gloucestershire, were already starting in the 13th and 14th
centuries to consolidate their agricultural operations by purchasing freehold
land locally, buying-out rights of common pasture, and beginning to eliminate
open fields.[50] From the 16th century onwards the landlord class was
increasingly willing to invest capital in agrarian improvements, especially
the enclosure of both "open fields" and commons and wastes,[51] but also in the

"infrastructure", particularly turnpike roads and canals,[52] and in better agricultural methods on their tenanted farms, particularly "up-and-down" or "convertible" husbandry, the "floating" of water-meadows, selective livestock-breeding, and, above all, more complex and flexible rotation systems made possible by the elimination of the annual fallowing of arable land.[53]

The second factor was the nobility's increasing ability to raise money safely on credit for the improvement of their estates, initially resulting from the rise of the mortgage "with equity of redemption" during the 17th century, but enhanced by the rise of "settlement". This innovation brought the trustees of the settlement, many of whom were professional experts, especially lawyers, with useful knowledge, into close connection with estate-administration, which at the same time was benefitting from the rise of professional estate stewards and surveyors.[54] Since not all of an estate would be "settled", there was scope for raising money for improving or extending the estate as the opportunity arose. This increased ability to borrow safely was further enhanced by a considerable reduction in the rate of interest on secured loans during the 17th and early 18th centuries, so that by the Hanoverian period it was normally possible to borrow money at about 5% per annum.[55]

After 1750, of course, Britain began to industrialize, but this did not mean any immediate weakening of the power of the aristocracy. Its political control only gradually lessened during the 19th century after the first Reform Bill of 1832, and the greatest change did not come until the Parliament Act of 1911 severely curtailed the power of the House of Lords. Despite the undoubted rise of the middle classes after 1800, "deference" was a habit deeply ingrained in the English who proverbially "loved a lord" (the Welsh and the Scots were less deferential because the lords were mostly English or Anglicized). Moreover, the Industrial Revolution also offered economic opportunities to the nobility which, if seized, could be extremely beneficial, as David Cannadine emphasizes in chapter 8. Since the Revolution was "steam-driven", it was necessarily "coal-fired", while the continual growth of British population after the 1680s also meant ever greater demand for coal as a domestic fuel.[56] Since the Industrial Revolution was also characterized by mechanization of industrial processes and therefore by a switch from wood to iron and steel, landlords whose estates were sited on top of accessible coal-measures or iron-ore deposits were thus well-placed to benefit from "royalties", even if they did not wish to become more directly involved in the business of mining or processing.[57] Many landlords were, however, prepared to become directly involved in industrial management, including the Dudleys in Staffordshire and the Ashburnhams in Sussex, or in associated transport-facilities, notably the Marquesses of Bute in Cardiff, the Lowthers in Whitehaven, and the Devonshires in Barrow-in-Furness.[58]

Moreover, since the Industrial Revolution involved very great urbanization in England, South Wales, and the Scottish Lowlands to accommodate an increased population and a population moving from the countryside to predominantly new towns (although London grew into Europe's largest city by 1700 and into the world's largest city by 1800),[59] there was a constant demand for new housing and for land on which the houses could be built. By 1851, the Registrar-General announced after the Census that year that half the English population now lived in towns. The landed aristocracy, who had been profiting from the growth of London since the 16th century (eg the Russells), were again well placed to profit from the demand for building land, and even dukes joined in the movement (the Duke of Norfolk at Glossop and Sheffield, the Duke of Devonshire at Eastbourne). Not to be outdone, the Prince Regent in his capacity as Duke of Cornwall began to develop Kennington.[60] Other landlords benefitted from the demand for clay (for bricks, tiles, and pipes), stone, timber, and roofing-slates. If their estates were fortunately situated, even quite small gentry families, such as the Smythes outside Bristol and the Sneyds in North Staffordshire, could become disproportionately wealthy from minerals or urban building or both. In short, the Industrial Revolution strengthened the economic position of the landed nobility.

So much for noble wealth. But because of that wealth and its source, social status also depended on the possession of land. It was possible from the 14th century to make a large fortune from trade and finance in London, but to rise in the social scale necessitated the acquisition of land. The De La Poles did this so successfully that they rose to become Dukes of Suffolk. By 1600, the wealth of London aldermen was so great that some were richer than all but the greatest landlords; in 1691, one London merchant's daughter, Bridget Hungerford, was said to be the richest heiress in England when she married Robert, Lord Lexinton.[61] By the 18th century the price of land was being pushed above levels justified by the economic return from agriculture alone by the "non-economic" demand from "new men" who needed to buy an estate of sufficient size to establish themselves in landed society (or, if younger sons, to reestablish themselves),[62] though their wealth was now coming from diverse sources; the spoils of India (Clive), West Indian sugar (Codringtons and Jenkinsons), banking (Hoares), brewing (Whitbreads, Guinnesses, Tennants). Increasingly, these entrants into landed society were also being recruited into the peerage.[63]

Finally, land was the source not just of wealth (economic power) and status (social power) but also of military power (in the Middle Ages) and political power (in and after the 16th century). Even in 1086 it is clear that "manpower planning" lay behind the Domesday survey and that the context for the survey, the "invasion scare" of 1085, is vitally important in explaining why the survey was made.[64] This also explains why the survey so carefully enumerates all groups of the rural population. Throughout the medieval period and well into the 16th century, his manorial tenants were the obvious source from which a lord would raise the bulk of his forces, stiffened by any tenants by knight service; many tenants were also liable for "castle guard" at their lord's castle. Not until the "military survey" of 1522 and the subsequent Tudor "musters" for what became the militia in Elizabethan times did the state begin to assume responsibility for military training which had previously been a noble preserve.[65] With the increasing importance of the county electorate (because of the increasing importance of Parliament) from the 16th century, the nobility, and especially the peerage, also obtained a new sort of civilian power; men on their estates now meant votes, and this political power of the peers was increased by their capture of most borough seats in the 16th and 17th centuries. Both trends were facilitated by an effective reduction in the value of the forty-shilling freehold franchise, established in 1430, as a result of inflation in the periods 1500-1640, 1680-1715, and after 1750.[66] By the late 18th century, 210 out of a total of 558 seats in the House of Commons were controlled by the Lords, and a further 120 seats were held by Irish peers or the sons of English peers, so that the increasing political supremacy of the Commons did not mean a decline in the power of the peers. Even in the 19th century the effective power of the Lords was still very great, though its roots were being undermined by the Secret Ballot Act of 1872.[67] Nevertheless, the 20th century began with a British prime minister still sitting in the House of Lords (the Marquess of Salisbury).

So far, our explanations of the persistence of the nobility, their estates, and their power have concentrated chiefly on the importance of their estates as sources of wealth, status, and power. But there are also other factors which ought to be considered, even those verging on "dry-as-dust", the significance of which becomes clearer if we compare the English nobility with its continental counterparts. Since this book concentrates on the British nobility, most contributors have, rightly, not tried to supply any contrast with European conditions, though John Cannon notes in passing the difference between the position of the English Crown, increasingly controlled by Parliament after 1689, and that of most rulers in Europe, where representative assemblies were becoming powerless to the point of extinction (p 100). When the French Revolution began in 1789, archivists and other officials had to be put to work to discover how the Estates-General (which had last met in 1614) actually worked. By contrast, the English peers in the House of Lords formed part of a two chamber Parliament, meeting regularly, in which, by the middle of the 18th century, real power was passing to the House of Commons. Nevertheless, while most continental aristocracies enjoyed varying degrees of tax-exemption, British peers did not. Yet the differences between the English and continental nobilities went much deeper than just their relative access to formal political power or fiscal privilege.

Basically, despite the Norman Conquest, English society was much more open than its continental counterparts, and this openness increased over time. Henry I as a deliberate act of royal policy married Edith-Matilda, who next to Edgar the Aetheling was the senior representative of the old Wessex dynasty, and, according to a near-contemporary writer, he encouraged Norman nobles also to marry English gentlewomen.[68] Within a century of the Norman Conquest the author of the "Dialogue of the Exchequer" claimed

> "Nowadays, when English and Normans live close together and marry
> and give in marriage to each other, the nations are so mixed that it can
> hardly be decided, in the case of free men, who is born English and who
> is born Norman."[69]

There may have been some exaggeration, but if the picture had been wildly
overdrawn its didactic purpose would have been frustrated. With the loss of
Normandy in 1204, the "Norman" aristocracy increasingly regarded itself as
"English" and by the end of the next century was speaking English as its first
language. By the 15th century, nationalist writings such as the *Libelle of
Englishe Policye* openly asserted the superiority of England and all things
English to foreigners, especially the French, and such nationalism was
reinforced by the Reformation; most foreigners were Roman Catholic and
therefore by definition bad. The beginnings of what would later be described
as the "Whig interpretation of history" were in the making.

Nevertheless, a sense of common identity and common difference from
foreigners drew Englishmen of all social ranks together, and thus made
movement between the ranks easier. In England mainly because of the
factors such as primogeniture which kept estates intact as entities, there was
an important status difference from the continental situation; only the eldest
surviving son (or in default eldest surviving grandson) of an English peer
would inherit his father's status and parliamentary privileges. Younger sons
and daughters might have "courtesy titles", which were precisely that - titles
of courtesy which conveyed no legal rights, privileges or powers. Younger
sons and daughters were commoners, superior commoners may be, but
commoners nonetheless, whose personal status could only be maintained, in
the case of sons, by their efforts in a variety of professions or superior trades,
in the case of daughters, by successful marriage. In short, generation by
generation, there was a constant outflow of individuals from the peerage, and
indeed from the English nobility as a whole, in a downward direction, and
there was not, and could never be, a sharp division between peer and
commoner. By contrast, in most continental aristocracies, all the sons of an
aristocrat inherited their father's status, leading to an "inflation of honour"
counterbalanced only by the requirement that a noble too poor to maintain
his status had formally to resign his noble title.[70] Another consequence of this
European situation was an inflated sense of collective self-esteem - hidalgoism
in Spain, for example - that kept the nobility apart from the rest of secular
society, unresponsive to and largely uncomprehending the needs of that
society, and hence unable to adjust to changing circumstances. In France
there were even divisions within the aristocracy, as opposed to ascending
grades in England, between the *noblesse de l'épée* and the *noblesse de la robe*.
Few mourned the passing of the French "aristos" in 1789 or the Russian
dvorianstvo in 1917, because the rest of society could see few useful functions
being fulfilled by them, hence it was only too easy for their detractors to
portray them as mere parasites.

Because of the constant outflow of younger sons and daughters from the ranks of peerage and nobility in England, as well as the biological tendency for families to die out in the male line, it was obviously necessary for the ranks of the nobility at least to be replenished by recruitment from below (Crown policy, especially under Elizabeth I and James I, could and did affect the elevation of nobles to the peerage, as Steven Gunn and John Miller both show in their chapters). Social mobility, therefore, was absolutely essential for the survival of the nobility - which we have seen above was always a small group in the population as a whole - and this clearly could only produce new recruits to the nobility if there was no unbridgeable gulf between noble and non-noble. As early as Elizabeth I's reign, it was obvious, even to a conservative-minded lawyer like Sir Thomas Smith, that

> "... whosoever studieth the lawes of the realme, who studieth in the universities, who professeth liberall sciences, and to be shorte, who can live idly and without manuall labour, and will beare the port, charge and countenaunce of a gentleman, ... he shal be taken for a gentleman ... (and if need be) a king of Heraulds shall give him for mony [a coat of] armes newly made and invented ..."[71]

Once an Englishman had joined the ranks of the landed nobility, it was not too difficult to find a Buckingham, a Walpole or a Lloyd George from whom a peerage could be purchased if he was so minded. (Only a few eccentrics like Ralph Sneyd of Keele turned down the offer of a peerage, in his case on the grounds that, being of good Anglo-Saxon descent, he would not demean himself to accept a title from the descendant of a Norman bastard.) In fact, from the 16th century onwards, there was, as we have seen, an increasing inflow into the nobility - a "multiplication of the gentry" in Christopher Clay's words - from a variety of sources; successful farmers rising from the yeomanry, merchants especially from London, Indian "nabobs", West Indian slaveowners, bankers, army and navy contractors, industrialists, successful military and naval officers, even successful privateers such as Sir Henry Morgan, some of whom were "new men" but many of whom were younger sons reclaiming what they saw as their rightful place in society. As Harold Perkin and the Stones suggested in two famous books, the English landed aristocracy formed an "open élite".[72]

This social mobility had considerable repercussions for the rest of the English population and for English history as a whole. Unlike, say, Russia, most of eastern and central Europe, and Spain, where, before the 20th century, there was virtually no mercantile and industrial middle class between the landed aristocracy and the depressed mass of peasantry, and where, as a result, there was, equally, no chance of rising from "low" to "high", the English aristocracy drew from and responded to a growing and evermore prosperous middle class composed of urban professional men, bankers, foreign traders, wholesale merchants, and industrialists and rural entrepreneurs and yeoman farmers who were increasingly articulating their demands through county society and the House of Commons. Not only did such men form the seed-bed from which the new generation of aristocratic recruits would rise, but their demands, especially in economic and above all commercial matters, were being translated into national policies, with considerable benefit to the whole country. Political and financial stability, and the rule of law, were seen as necessary conditions for the economic growth that alone could produce widespread prosperity throughout the nation.[73] While the continental varieties of "mercantilism" involved increasingly bureaucratic regulation of trade and industry typified by Colbert in France, Restoration England abandoned domestic economic regulation, partly because such regulation seemed economically no longer necessary and partly because the political price, the continuance of the centralized "prerogative" government of the Tudors and early Stuarts, was deemed unacceptable.[74]

What was substituted in England was "protection" for overseas trade against foreign competition and the erection of a captive overseas market, the "old colonial system".[75] As a result of the growth of overseas trade, which produced increased employment at home because of greater overseas demand for English goods and a wider range of mass-consumption goods, the British standard of living in the early 18th century was already a source of amazement to European visitors who saw even the "common man" well-clothed and shod, eating meat and white bread, drinking tea with sugar, smoking Virginian tobacco, using pewter cutlery and pottery tableware.[76] By contrast, most of central, eastern, and southern Europe was populated by impoverished serfs, and even in France and Germany most peasants went barefoot, ate brown or black bread and rarely touched meat, while tobacco and even necessary salt was heavily taxed. Only in the Netherlands were living standards generally at or near British levels.

The necessary conditions for much of this achievement were, as we have already seen, political and financial stability, and the rule of law. Though all these conditions had been established by the earlier 18th century initially in the interest of a ruling class which disliked arbitrary rule and arbitrary taxation, the benefit applied to all. A British nobleman who dared to oppose a king, a powerful minister or even the king's mistress, would not find himself, as his French counterpart would, en route under the authority of a *lettre de cachet* to the Bastille where he might rot for years: as noted earlier, at worst he would be forced only to retire to his roses. In England the rights of the individual had long been respected, even as far back as Magna Carta in some respects. For Magna Carta was not simply a charter of baronial liberties and ecclesiastical exemption (though it was mainly that): several clauses affected the "common man", such as 9 (debts not to be levied on land if there were sufficient chattels), 13 (ancient liberties of London), 15-16 (limitation of "aids" from free men; no increase in free services), 20 (reasonable amercements [fines] on free men and villeins), 30-31 (protection of horses, carts and timber from royal exactions), 38-40 (rule of law; access to justice), 41 (freedom for merchants), 43-44, 47-48 (freedom from "evil customs" of the forest).[77]   And the ruling class by the later 17th century had perceived, correctly, that it could not expect respect for the law if that law did not respect the rights of all individuals: *Habeas corpus* was a legal remedy available to all.   Hence William Blackstone in his *Commentaries* pointed with justified pride to the contrast with the continent:

> "The idea and practice of this political or civil liberty flourish in their highest vigour in these kingdoms, where it falls little short of perfection ... the legislature, and of course the laws, of England being peculiarly adapted to the preservation of this inestimable blessing even in the meanest subject. Very different from the modern constitutions of other states, on the continent of Europe ... which in general are calculated to vest an arbitrary and despotic power, of controlling the actions of the subject, in the prince [ruler], or in a few grandees."[78]

This was not simply Blackstone's alleged incurable optimism: two years earlier, the "great commoner" himself, William Pitt the Elder, had made the same point even more dramatically in a debate on the Cider Bill of 1763:

> "The poorest man may in his cottage bid defiance to all the force of the Crown. It may be frail; its roof may shake; the wind may blow through it; the rain may enter - but the King of England cannot enter; all his forces dare not cross the threshhold of the ruined tenement."[79]

Compare this sense of security and protection under the law with France where any display of modest prosperity by a peasant would swiftly be followed by visits from the local tax-collector and the seigneur's steward. While there was, undeniably, a dark side to Georgian and early Victorian England - the ferocious game-laws, the ready resort to capital punishment and criminal transportation - it was still a better place for the "common man" to inhabit than almost anywhere else in Europe.   One of the reasons, paradoxically, is that it was also a better place for most nobleman to inhabit. British nobles were not at the beck and call of their sovereign who could not command their attendance at a royal palace for years on end as the Bourbons could compel the *noblesse* to reside at Versailles. The London "season" was devised by the nobility for the nobility: royal banquets and levées would be fitted into an aristocratic schedule rather than being the central *raison d'être* as in France. The London season began when the nobility returned from hunting and harvesting and ended when the nobility left for a spa such as Bath or for hunting in the shires: its start and its finish had nothing to do with Crown precepts. The social fact thus reflected the political fact: in France the king ruled; in England Parliament, and through Parliament the landed élite, ruled. While Britain after 1689 became more constitutional, most of the continental powers emulated France, competing to produce clones of Versailles and of the political system it embodied. This helps to explain how Britain and its aristocratic government weathered the Revolutionary storms in and after the 1790s better than any other European state and successfully managed the transition to a more democratic form of government in the 19th century; unlike its continental confreres, the British nobility were not out of touch with opinion or with political realities: they knew when to yield, and how to yield gracefully, most notably in 1832 and again in 1910-11.

And so from past to present and future: although the House of Lords has lost most of its former political power, as Lord Sudeley shows (chapter 10) the Lords have still a valuable function to perform. Not least is their revising function which was already singled-out by Lord Hardwicke in the 1750s as the essential counterpart to a House of Commons already overbusy:

> "our statute books are increased to such an enormous size that they confound every man who is obliged to look into them ... now ... almost every new law is first drawn up and passed in the other House, so that we have little else to do ... but to read over and consent to the new laws they have made: nay, some of them are sent up so late that we have hardly time to read them over ... the other House by their being so numerous, and by their being destitute of the advice and assistance of the judges, are too apt to pass laws which are either unnecessary or ridiculous, and almost every law they pass stands in need of some new law for explaining and amending it ... it is high time for this House to ... resolve to put a stop to it, by resolving not to pass any Bill ... that comes from the other House unless it comes up so early in the session as to leave us sufficient time to take the advice and assistance of the judges upon it, and to consider every clause of it maturely".[80]

It is a function which will remain necessary in the future, as Enoch Powell predicts (chapter 11). What, then, of the nobility itself? Here is a final paradox: while the nobility down to 1914 vaunted its power and influence in a very visible display of wealth in the form of its estates, its great houses in London and the countryside, its often extravagant mode of living, it has survived since by becoming discreetly invisible or by becoming part of a poor aristocracy's survival show.[81] Yet the landed nobility is still alive and well, indeed in some cases still very wealthy, as is shown by the latest *Times* survey of the "Top 500". This list of those individuals in Britain estimated to be worth over £20 million each includes 61 members of the landed aristocracy (12 dukes, 7 marquesses, 6 viscounts, 18 earls, 10 lords, 3 knights and 5 commoners) whose wealth is principally derived from their estates and the contents of their country houses.[82] The rich, as well as the poor, are still with us today, but the primary basis for new wealth is no longer the land: where land is held by the "new rich", it is owned simply in order to provide a gracious setting for a leisured life away from business. By contrast, among the peers only sixteen names - the Viscounts Hambleden, Leverhulme and Rothermere, the Earls of Inchcape and Stockton, Lords Cayzer, Forte, Hanson, Iliffe, Laing, McAlpine, Palumbo, Rayne, Rothschild, Weinstock and White - represent new wealth. With these exceptions the names of the peers, or the names of their families, would have been familiar to a British reader in 1893 and also in 1793. To end, as I began, with George Orwell,

> "... the essential structure of society has never altered. Even after enormous upheavals and seemingly irrevocable changes, the same pattern has always re-asserted itself, just as a gyroscope will always return to equilibrium, however far it is pushed one way or the other".

Moving from the peerage to the landed nobility as a whole, we may ask if it still fulfils a useful function. Or is gentility, in Lord Burghley's famous sneer, "but old riches"? (He was, of course, "new rich" himself). My own answer would derive from an example in my home area of south Gloucestershire (*alias* North Avon), where the late Earl of Ducie, an Australian sheep-farmer, succeeded to the run-down estate, centred on Cromhall, of his childless cousin in 1952. He spent forty years in restoring the estate and earned the respect and affection of his tenants and neighbours in doing so. He died at a meeting in his estate office while considering further improvements. After his death, it was found that he had arranged for land to be given to a self-build association to provide more houses for the inhabitants of Cromhall. That, I would argue, is genuine nobility: it is a practice still quietly followed by many landowners and manorial lords where their financial circumstances permit. Nobility, in the final analysis, is derived from personal character and behaviour, not from birth or wealth: "port" and "countenance" are more important than "charge".[83]

The footnotes to this Introduction are to be found on pages 179-87.

1: H R Loyn

From witenagemot to concilium:
the antecedents of the House of Lords: 1042–1215

AN EXAMINATION of the antecedents of the House of Lords, its prehistory so to speak, takes us straight back to Anglo-Saxon days, to the Witan. We have seen a great swing back and forth in historical opinion on this theme. To the 19th century, in continuous and vigorous line from the lawyers of the 17th, the witan, or *witenagemot*, was the institutional cornerstone of the inspiring notion of Anglo-Saxon freedom opposed to Norman tyranny, an essential part of the picture of a free community, free farming folk, local courts, a central assembly, a witan, gathered together around a king empowered to take advice from his responsible local leaders, free yet subordinate.

This picture was highly imaginative, supported scarcely at all by hard evidence, and there was a natural reaction. Even so, it came as something of a shock to many of us when we looked hopefully in 1943 to the index of that great book, *Anglo-Saxon England*, by Sir Frank Stenton, only to find under *Witan, Witenagemot*, "see Council, the king's."[1] And this even though Felix Liebermann, a scholar justly admired by Stenton, had published in 1913 what was (and to some extent still is) an authoritative account of *The National Assembly in the Anglo-Saxon Period*, ie the witan.[2]

In some respects, it has been left to the present generation to give us back our witan, and a good thing, too. In the 1950s a young Canadian scholar of Icelandic origin, Tryggvi Oleson, presented an interesting monograph on *The Witenagemot in the Reign of Edward the Confessor*.[3] It was not as well received as it should have been, and indeed was inadequate in the handling of some of the charter evidence, but it helped to shift discussion back onto the right lines. More important and immediate is the work of Simon Keynes, rich in texture and in depth of diplomatic study.[4] Two of his conclusions are direct to our interests. First there is his surprisingly effective analysis of the charters that have survived from the reign of one of the least regarded of later Anglo-Saxon kings, Eadwig (956-59). Some 60 or so diplomas (charters) are known from the year 956 and Keynes has been able to show that they fall into distinctive groups, highly suggestive of construction and issue at four productive meetings, January, February, the summer, and November.[5] The inference is clear that their issue coincided with the meetings of what we may legitimately call the witan. On Ethelred (991-1014) his analysis is even more trenchant, and we are left with the realization that central assemblies were held regularly, and that an element of power struggle was mirrored in the composition of assemblies at which charters were issued. To take an example of outstanding importance, it seems evident from the pecking order in subscription of great men to the charters that Eadric Streona, the true wicked man of the reign, took over an important role in affairs from about

1005, and that some if not most of the subsequent disasters can be laid at his doorstep.[6] The witness lists to charters betray the composition of central assemblies which were indeed not only great ecclesiastical feasts. They were also concerned with routine business, the issue of charters, humdrum everyday matters, the supervision of a geld system - a land tax that worked.

It was at these witans also that declarations of law could best be made. There was a long tradition of such activity in Anglo-Saxon England, with perhaps the most conspicuous and complete example coming from the reign of King Alfred (871-99). I have long held that the proem to his laws should be taken seriously, long extracts from the Old Testament leading to his assertion that Christ came not to destroy the law but to fulfil it, and the negative Golden Rule that "one should not do unto others that which you would not have them do to you".[7] There follows a substantial account of the law-declaring process in which the witan plays a full part:

> "Then I, King Alfred, collected these together and ordered to be written many of them which our forefathers observed, those which I liked: and many of those which I did not like I rejected with the advice of my councillors and ordered them to be differently observed. For I dared not presume to set in writing at all many of my own, because it was unknown to me what would please those who should come after us. But those which I found which seemed to me most just, either in the time of my kinsman, King Ine, or of Offa, King of the Mercians, or of Ethelbert, who first among the English received baptism, I collected herein and omitted the others. Then, I Alfred, King of the West Saxons, showed these to all my councillors and they then said they were all pleased to observe them."[8]

Similar sentiments recur throughout later legislation: "All that had been established at Grately at the great assembly at which Archbishop Wulfhelm was present and all the nobles and councillors that King Athelstan could gather together"; at Exeter where councillors complained that the Grately decrees had not been properly observed. Later kings, Edgar, Ethelred, and supremely Cnut, follow the precedent of issuing laws with the advice of their councillors. Archbishop Wulfstan of York (1002-23) played a prominent part, taking on responsibility for much of the written version of the laws of Kings Ethelred and Cnut.[9] The Anglo-Saxon Chronicle for 978 even gives us one precious glimpse of such an assembly at work, precious and also disastrous:

> "In this year, all the chief councillors of the English people fell from an upper storey at Calne, except Archbishop Dunstan alone who remained standing upon a beam: and some were very seriously injured and some died."[10]

Declaration of law was special, an assertion of the spiritual as well as the secular authority of the king over the whole community. What of the more prosaic political occasions? If we take simply the generation before the Norman Conquest, there are many occasions when consultation with a council was evident, directly or indirectly: the recall of Edward the Confessor from exile in 1041, 12 months before the death of his half-brother Hardicnut; the exile of Sweyn, eldest of Godwin's sons; the decision not to fight a civil war in 1051; the summons of Edward Atheling from Hungary; the election of Harold Godwinson as Harold II in January 1066.[11] Such high political activity supplements our knowledge of the routine business that was also clearly the concern of the witan.

Yet terminology was still vague. "Witan" could be used, and was, of shire courts or of a meeting of several shires. One is conscious of analogies and contrasts with Scandinavia where the term "Thing" was used generally of local courts, never except in the Icelandic "Althing" of national assemblies. But from the conversion of the English to Christianity (St Augustine at King Ethelbert's court or Edwin's Council in the 620s) right through to the election of Harold in 1066, great public meetings of the high-born of the community were known and in many respects spoke for the whole community, more the ancestor of the House of Lords than Parliament!

The Normans, therefore, inherited a tradition of great assemblies. My own generation was brought up in the belief that the Great Council of the early Norman kings was in effect a feudalized witan. It was also brought up on the constitutional tack, believing that separate from it was a smaller council, the *curia regis*, as it is sometimes called (as if the language were synonymous with substance) consisting of the king, some of the royal household, the *familiares*, one or two great officers with fancy titles. This smaller *curia* was the body through which royal decisions were made and by which the practical acts of government were enforced. Provided that the terminology was accepted, the two beliefs were valid. On the feudal question, Stenton again was a powerful guide. He called his influential book on the period 1066-1166 *The First Century of English Feudalism*.[12] There could be no feudalism without a fief; and from 1066 to 1215 the great tenants-in-chief were expected to attend the Great Council when summoned as part of their feudal duty.

One hazard, however, faces us as we approach the 12th-century problems, and that is the temptation to confuse government and administration. Administrative developments were relatively straightforward with identifiable general patterns. For finance, the reign of Henry I was a critical period with the evolution of the Exchequer. For our legal institutions, it was the reign of his grandson, Henry II, and the germs of permanent courts that were to become the King's Bench and Common Pleas.[13] But the Great Council itself was a very different proposition, and anyone who expects to find there evidence of a deliberative assembly, lumbering towards a collective decision is in for a rude shock. For we deal with an active monarchy throughout this period. The king governed, helped by an inner group. The tough, often ruthless, men got away with it: the Williams and the Henrys. The nice men ran into trouble: Robert of Normandy or King Stephen. One of the most revealing comments in the later stages of the Anglo-Saxon Chronicle, fearsome when the full implications are considered, concerns Stephen who is described as "a mild man and gentle and good - and one who did no justice".[14]

What then were the functions in Norman days of the Great Council, heir to the witan and immediate ancestor of the House of Lords? Three possible lines of investigation are opened up by the evidence, its relationship with the king, its composition, and its range of activities. The first of these can be dealt with swiftly. Stenton was basically right to stress that this is the King's Council. The king governed, and only rarely did the council take on an independent life. Even the question of succession and election of a new monarch grew more tenuous as primogeniture became the rule, though even towards the end of the period the election of Richard I to the neglect of possible claims of Arthur, the young son of his elder brother, and the rallying around Henry III, John's nine-year-old heir, were matters in which the council played an important role.

The composition of the council presents many complex problems. In Anglo-Saxon days, there was indeed an enormous range from a few ecclesiastics and noblemen in direct allegiance to the king to vast national assemblies attended by Welsh princes and heaven knows who else, perhaps up to as many as 500 people in all.[15] The formality of post-Conquest feudalism simplified and clarified affairs. Great tenants-in-chief – the earls and barons – were expected to attend, a good proportion of bishops and abbots, and named great officers such as the Chancellor and the Marshal as their offices became more rigorously defined. Three times a year at the chief religious festivals of Christmas, Easter, and Whitsun, William I wore his crown, and the Chronicler recorded many of these meetings and those of his successors.[16] Gloucester for the winter session, Winchester for spring, and Westminster for summer were the favoured locations, though personal and political circumstances made it impossible for such movement to be established as permanent. The great councils held on these occasions involved not only social but business sessions: and absence without reason or excuse from the greatest men would surely be noticed. By the reign of Henry II, the ecclesiastical element was growing less impressive. Meetings were often held, for example, in October away from the main religious feasts.[17] The climax came with the flood of meetings that preceded the issue of Magna Carta and the charter itself defined the composition of its ideal council in the following terms:

> "For obtaining the common counsel of the realm for the assessment of aids (other than the three cases aforesaid) or of scutage we will cause to be summoned severally by Our Letters, the archbishops, bishops, abbots, earls and great barons. We will also cause to be summoned generally by Our sheriffs and bailiffs all others who hold directly of us to meet on a fixed day, but with at least 40 days' notice, and at a fixed place. In all letters of summons we shall explain the cause thereof. The summons being thus made, the business shall proceed on the day

appointed, according to the counsel of those who shall be present, even if not all the persons summoned have come."[18]

The limitations of function of this council have often been noted, its concentration of the assessment of aids and scutage, but its description of the composition with its clear separation of the important men summoned separately and the others summoned generally remains invaluable. Magna Carta shows a sophisticated concern for finance, but this was far from the only or indeed principal element in the story of the Anglo-Norman councils. A series of snapshots from dramatic material, some of it very familiar, may help to indicate the complexity of the conciliar background in the 11th and 12th centuries. The planning of Domesday Book took place at mid-winter at Gloucester, and the Anglo-Saxon Chronicler described events in the following terms:

> Then at Christmas, the King was at Gloucester with his *council*, and held his *court* there for five days, and then the archbishop and clerics had a *synod* for three days. There Maurice was elected bishop of London. and William for Norfolk, and Robert for Cheshire - they were all the King's clerks.[19]

We note that the three separate terms for an assembly are used, witan (council) court (*hired*, which can also mean household), and synod. We note also that it is after all this that the Domesday Book discussion took place, and "the King had much thought and very deep speech with his witan about this land, how it was settled and with what type of men". This council was no idle receptive body, summoned merely to receive royal dictates. Thoughtful debate took place, leading to administrative action and the creation of Domesday Book.

Other snapshots are more ambiguous. A full account, made in the 12th century, has been preserved of a great meeting held at Old Sarum on 2 November 1088. This was strictly a court rather than a council but a reminder in itself of the thin line that divides these institutions in the early medieval world. The issue was King William Rufus's authority over the recalcitrant Bishop of Durham. Many bishops were present to whom the Bishop of Durham, William of St Carilef, appealed unsuccessfully. He withdrew temporarily, leaving the King "with his bishops and magnates and sheriffs together with his officials, huntsmen, and other servants". On his return, he made a dramatic appeal to Rome, but the King and his advisers concentrated on feudal aspects, the castle at Durham. The King himself is said to have summed it all up (giving an insight into his own character and sense of reality) when he glowered at the bishop and said, "although you will not accept the judgment of my court you will give me your castle".[20] Councils, of course, even if royal, could occasionally be held in the king's absence, notably when the king-duke was active in Normandy itself. In 1124-25 there is one grim and fearsome entry in the Peterborough Chronicle which tells of such a council. King Henry I sent orders from

Normandy to Roger, Bishop of Salisbury, his lieutenant, *secundarius a rege*, ordering all the moneyers in England to come to Winchester at Christmas. When they got there, they were taken out one by one and each deprived of his right hand and castrated. All this was done before Twelfth Night, and the Chronicler adds, "it was done justly because they had ruined all the country with their false dealing: and they paid for it".[21]

The crisis of the controversy between King Henry II and Thomas Becket, Archbishop of Canterbury, gives further close evidence of conciliar activity. In January 1164, the matter of criminous clerks and royal customs, how they should be observed and seconded, was raging and the proceedings, often heated, lasted three to four days. More than 50 bishops, abbots, earls, and great magnates were present, including the two archbishops, 12 bishops (the elect of Worcester among them) and 10 earls. Others included some of the leading feudatories: the Warennes, the Lacys, the Bissets, the Malets, the Cheneys, and the Maudits.[22] This was truly an active council and the proceedings, the "constitutions", we are told, were drawn up by the great men themselves in the presence of the Lord Henry (the eldest son of Henry II) and of the King himself.

Many other glimpses could be given of the king in council, the drama of Anselm and Becket locked in formal disputes that ended in their exile; the recognition of Matilda as heir to her father, Henry I, at a great council held in 1127; the detailed discussions of Henry II in councils at Clarendon itself or at Northampton; the Coronation of Richard I (attended by at least 60 named great men); the difficulties under the justiciars in Richard's absence and with John in the background; the deposition of the "chief justiciar" and chancellor, Longchamp, when, in the words of a recent shrewd commentator "the council had taken a first step towards its future claim to speak for the community of the realm".[23]

From all the 12th-century evidence, it is possible to tease out some generalizations to describe the function of the council at a time when the shape of the House of Lords was slowly emerging. Four principal probes seem to come naturally from such evidence. The first is purely a matter of commonsense. For great political occasions, in an age when communications were poor, councils were essential. At ecclesiastical feasts and feudal convocations for war, the king needed to take advice. Under Henry II, the conflict with Becket, the coronation of the young king, Henry, in June 1170, the campaigns of 1176 and 1179, prompted the summons of great councils: and such meetings in turn prompted central governmental activity. Then again, the legal attributes of the council remained powerful, constituting with the king present the unquestioned highest court in the land. In a famous case in 1164, Henry of Essex was arraigned for treason and failed in the resulting trial by battle.[24] Thomas Becket at one stage was placed in the King's mercy.[25] In 1194, at Nottingham, John was charged with treason against Richard and threatened with complete forfeiture.[26] And side by side with the legal function of the council can be found the germs of a legislative activity. This was a prominent feature of the reign of Henry II when the institution of the great assizes and legal reforms were directly linked to meetings of council, though the main line is still clear. Council was not needed. The power to govern rested with the king. Lastly, comes recognition that the council might indeed have a say in the election of a new king, though again this is not always straightforward as the sorry episode of Stephen and Matilda and indeed the succession of Richard I demonstrate.

Political, legal, even legislative functions can be disentangled or hinted at, and so can the hint of a right to be consulted at the election of a new monarch, but limitations are equally obvious. Only very rarely is there the least suggestion of initiative on the part of the council. Even the deposition of Longchamp turns out on closer investigation to have been triggered by royal decree from Normandy. But habit and convention prove more potent. As society grew more complex, so also did the range of functions expected from the king and with it the need to institutionalize. As with administrative development, the Exchequer and Law Courts, so now with the constitutional balance. The long centuries of advice and rough formality, honed down by Church practice, ultimately bore fruit. The reign of John, and supremely Magna Carta, represent the time of ripening in an age increasingly concerned with literacy and permanence.

Footnotes to this Chapter may be found on pages 187-8.

2: D A Carpenter
From King John to the first English duke: 1215-1337

THE YEARS between the loss of Normandy in 1204 and the outbreak of the Hundred Years' War in 1337 were the most formative in the whole history of the English nobility. The Anglo-Norman baronage was transformed into the English peerage and a large amorphous body of "knights" became the gentry - the basic structures familiar down to modern times. The nobility sponsored programmes of constitutional reform which shaped the future of England's polity - Magna Carta in 1215; the Provisions of Oxford in 1258-9; the Ordinances of 1311. The appearance of knights representing the counties in Parliament marked the beginning of the House of Commons. Politics also became more violent, with the penalty for political crime death - as it continued to be down to the 18th century. And at last, a powerful image of the nobility emerges in its heraldry and in the effigies upon its tombs. It is with "image" that this chapter begins.

If we ask how the nobility wished to be regarded, the answer can found be in numerous parish churches, abbeys, and cathedrals. Take the church of Waterperry in Oxfordshire. There, in the south aisle, beneath an elaborate canopy, rests the effigy of a knight in armour, the Lord of the Manor, Sir Robert Fitz Elys, who died in the 1340s. The details of the armour, the scabbard, sword-belt, and sword are exquisite.[1] How splendid, yet also how inappropriate. What have arms and armour to do with a penitent death and the hope of life thereafter? Would it not be more fitting, as indeed became the fashion later, for the sepulchral effigy to be emaciated and worm-eaten, covered, if at all, by a winding sheet; the message stark, "as I am now, so you will be".[2] The message of the Fitz Elys tomb is quite different: "as I am now, so you will never be". Such effigies, often erected during life, were designed not to encourage pious preparations for the next world, but to make arrogant assertions about this. To that end a military effigy was essential. Anyone can appear in a winding sheet, but only a noble in a suit of elaborate and expensive armour. It mattered not at all that Robert Fitz Elys's effigy was very similar - down to the details of the face - to that of his fellow Oxfordshire knight, John of Broughton at Broughton (they are clearly by the same craftsman).[3] The whole point was to show that you had the latest armour - like the latest Rolls-Royce - and there was no status in a face. Indeed, in two of the earliest effigies, those preserved at Furness Abbey in Cumberland, the face was concealed altogether, the knights being depicted with their helms on, the eyes glaring through the slits as though going into battle: a unique impression of the power and menace of the medieval knight.

The one feature of the effigies which was personalized - like a personalized number plate - was the coat of arms depicted on the shield and surcoat. The 13th and 14th centuries were the great age of heraldry - when the coats were young and simple, not yet divided into quarters, eighths, and sixteenths by generations of family alliances. The Fitz Elys arms were a bend between six fleur-de-lys.[4] Like so many coats, they thus punned on the family name - Elys - and hinted at its ancient lineage, for the surname had been born continuously since the 12th century Lord of Waterperry, William Fitz Elys.[5] The simplicity of these early coats makes another important point. They were designed for recognition in battle. Indeed, at Bannockburn, although the Scots determined to capture and ransom Gilbert de Clare, Earl of Gloucester, they killed him by mistake since he went unrecognized, having failed to don his surcoat with the famous three chevrons of the Clares.[6] Arms and armour, therefore, were for use as well as status. Robert Fitz Elys was extremely busy in Oxfordshire's local government - he finished up as Sheriff in 1342-3. Yet he was also employed raising troops from the county and, in 1322, campaigned in Scotland.[7] To have arms and not use them in tournaments or on campaign was like having a fast car and keeping it in the garage. One has only to handle a medieval sword - like that of Henry V at Westminster Abbey - and feel its wonderful, almost weightless balance, to surge with the desire to stab and slash with it.

The context in which arms and armour were used, however, changed radically in this period. Warfare and politics became more violent. The bloodless centuries give way to the centuries of blood. The Battle of Lincoln in 1217 was second only to Hastings as a critical battle in English history. It secured the Throne for King John's nine-year-old son, Henry III, and prevented England being ruled by the Capetian kings of France. Yet, at this decisive battle, only one person of any consequence was killed - the Count of Perche - and so rare were such fatalities that, for a moment, no one could believe that he was really dead: surely he had merely fainted.[8] The pattern was little different in May 1264 at Lewes, again a momentous battle which determined that Simon de Montfort would rule England with Henry III a prisoner in his hands. Here a mere handful of knights died in the course of the fighting. Next year, at the Battle of Evesham, practice was altogether more lethal. Simon de Montfort himself and approaching 30 knights were done to death on the field of battle.[9] A decisive change had taken place, one which foreshadowed the mass slaughter of nobility in the Wars of the Roses.

At Evesham, however, civilized conduct cracked, but did not shatter. Not one of the knights captured during the battle or picked up wounded from the field after it was executed. This mercy was of a piece with political conduct in England for over a century. Indeed, between 1135 and 1307, not a single member of the Anglo-Norman or English high nobility suffered corporal punishment - death or mutilation - for a political crime, not even during the 1215-17 civil war, vicious and embittered though it was. All this changed during the reign of Edward II (1307-1327). In 1312, Piers Gaveston, Earl of Cornwall, was beheaded. Gaveston was merely the son of a Gascon knight, but he was still the first holder of an English earldom to be executed since Waltheof in 1076. The *Vita Edwardi,* the best chronicle of the reign, was well aware that something remarkable had taken place.

> "In slaying Piers, the earls of England had undertaken a difficult task,
> unlike anything that has happened in our time. For they put to death
> a great earl whom the King had adopted as a brother".[10]

This solitary execution was followed by a bloodbath. After the Battle of
Boroughbridge in 1322, Thomas, Earl of Lancaster, Leicester, Derby, and
Lincoln, grandson of Henry III, by far the greatest noble seen since the
Conquest, was, in the words of the *Vita Edwardi*, "led forth from his castle
of Pontefract and mounted on some worthless mule was led to the place of
execution. Then the Earl stretched forth his head as if in prayer and the
executioner cut off his head with two or three strokes."[11] Lancaster's
execution was accompanied by that of 23 other nobles.[12] The pattern was set.
From 1322 onwards, however high the noble, however pathetic his situation,
the penalty for serious political crime was most often death. In 1330, it was
the turn of the Earl of Kent. "This Earl," recorded the Anonimalle Chronicle,
"was the son of the (late) King (Edward I) and uncle of the present King
(Edward III). And so, out of pity because no one wanted to behead him, he
stood outside the door of Winchester Castle from the hour of prime, when he
was sentenced, until vespers, when a menial retainer of the King's marshalsea
was ordered to behead him."[13] The clement centuries had given place to the
centuries of blood.[14]

Why, then, was there so long a period when battles for the nobility were
bloodless and rebellion exacted no corporal penalty? Why did the situation
change? A starting point here can be made with armour. It was for show. It
was also for effect. Indeed, by the early 13th century, it was so effective that,
in the normal cut and thrust of battle, while a knight might be bruised and
battered, he would rarely be killed. At the Battle of Lincoln, the Count of
Perche was unlucky; a lance, a chance in a thousand, was jabbed through the
eye piece of his helm and pierced his brain; he brought three great blows down
on the helm of William Marshal (the dents were clearly visible afterwards)
and then fell dead from his horse.[15] At the Battle of Boroughbridge in 1322,
the Earl of Hereford was similarly unlucky; he was speared between the legs
(one area unprotected by armour) by an unsporting pikeman hiding beneath
the bridge.[16] The killings at Evesham, therefore, were highly deliberate. The
knights were unhorsed, flung to the ground, disarmed, and stabbed to death.
Hence one chronicler spoke of "the murder of Evesham for battle it was
none".[17]

Normally, things did not get that far. When a knight was surrounded or
unhorsed, he simply held up his hand and asked to give up. At Evesham, by
contrast, offers to surrender were not accepted: according to the chronicler,
Langtoft, the royalists had sworn "that they would take Simon and his sons,
and, without accepting ransom, would put them to death". "Have you no
mercy" Montfort cried in his last agony.[18] But on other occasions, surrenders
were routine. At Lincoln, the Count of Perche was killed, but 47 nobles
surrendered.[19] There were obvious reasons for clemency. One was the
prospect of ransom; for which, as we have seen, the Scots would have spared

Gilbert de Clare at Bannockburn, had they recognized him; another was the civilizing force of chivalry. While recent discussion of chivalry has stressed its compatibility with shrewd calculation and ruthless brutality, it has ignored the targets of that brutality.[20] The greatest knights could wage the dirtiest of wars, but their victims were not their fellow nobles, but the lower orders; it was they who died in the battles or starved when their crops were burnt. The three pits found at Lewes, each containing "by estimate" 500 bodies, were filled not with knights but with peasant footsoldiers.[21] Among the aristocratic élite, by contrast, there was a real sense that warfare was a great game where the aim was not to kill your opponent, but to impress him with deeds of gallantry and daring. At Lincoln, both sides applauded Sir Richard of Samford, who, having taken his wife up onto his horse, was about to make his escape when a knight shouted out, "leave her, you can't take her".

> "Immediately he put her gently to the ground, and turning on the knight he unseated him with a blow from his lance in the chest, then took up his wife again and saved her".[22]

Likewise in 1263, even his baronial opponents admired the brave defence of Gloucester Castle made by the royalist castellan Matthias Bezille. There was no question of his execution afterwards. Rather it was the lower orders who suffered. Thus

> "they took a carpenter, who, they said, had shot the shot (which killed a squire of John Giffard)
> And led him to the tower on high, and made him hop to the ground
> He hopped, and was bruised and died speedily".[23]

In chivalry there was assuredly one law for the nobles and one for the rest.

Ransoms and chivalry, however, cannot be a complete explanation for the period of aristocratic immunity. Ransoms, after all, were just as lucrative and chivalric courtesies just as affecting in the 14th century, as the first phase of the Hundred Years' War was to show. Nor is there a purely military explanation for the increasing casualties in battle, for example, the use of massed ranks of archers.[24] It was against the horses, not the armoured knights, that the archers were most lethal; and, in any case, the slaughter had begun at Evesham in 1265 before the new archery tactics had been evolved; death by dagger rather than by arrow.

Some historians, therefore, have suggested another reason for the transformation in this period. The years of immunity are ascribed to the very narrow concept of treason which existed in the early Middle Ages - confined to plotting to kill or killing the King - and to the baronial right of *diffidatio* which formally severed the allegiance between vassal and lord, thus legitimizing the former's rebellion and protecting him from punishment. All this was altered, so it is suggested, by Edward I (1272-1307), in his state trials of Welsh and Scottish rebels. There he broadened the scope of treason to include rebellion and warring against the King, thus making the feudal *diffidatio* effectively redundant. "The savagery of 14th Century politics," it has been claimed, "owed much to this change".[25] But was there really a change? It is difficult to believe that treason, before Edward's reign, was confined to plotting against the King's life and excluded making war against him. In truth, the explanation for the change in practice does not lie in a change in theory.

Whether treason was described as *proditio*, *seditio* or, in Roman Law terms as *laesa maiestatis*, a key element in it was always the Germanic concept of breach of faith.[26] That the punishment for this was corporal was universally accepted. "Geoffrey and Odard...have broken faith with me, and thus deserve to be punished by death or mutilation," declared Henry I in about 1125.[27] That waging war could easily be viewed as a breach of faith and thus as treasonable is shown by Henry III's letter before the Battle of Lewes in 1264. It was evident, he declared, that Simon de Montfort and his accomplices did not observe "the due fealty to us or care in any way for the security of our body". In other words, they had committed treason. How was it evident? Because they had raised "general war and disturbance in our kingdom".[28] That the penalty was, therefore, death was made clear by Henry's son, the future Edward I, who demanded that the Montfortians surrender with halters round their necks for drawing and hanging.[29] There was nothing very surprising about rebellion and warfare being regarded as treasonable in this way. The law books of Glanvill and Bracton, written in the 1180s and 1220s, both defined treason, *laesa maiestatis* as "the killing or betrayal of the person of the King or the kingdom or the army", a definition so wide that it could stretch to a whole multitude of political crimes.[30] Thus, in 1232, Hubert de Burgh only just escaped a corporal sentence (it was drawn up but never pronounced) on the same type of charges - misappropriation of royal funds, usurpation of royal power - which brought many a Tudor minister to the block.[31]

The idea that potential rebels could escape the consequences of their treason through a formal act of *diffidatio*, like that performed by the Montfortians in 1264, is ludicrous. The *diffidatio* cleansed the Montfortians of *seditio* in their own eyes, but in the eyes of no one else. "Old traitor, old traitor, it is impossible any more for you to live," chanted the royalists as they closed in on Simon next year at the Battle of Evesham.[32] When Henry himself defied the Montfortians before Lewes it was not because he wished to place the war on a gentlemanly footing in which both sides fought according to some Marquess of Queensbury Rules – quite the reverse. He wished to be freed from all rules. The Montfortians were now his "enemies" whom he could attack and kill without let or hindrance. The medieval *diffidatio*, therefore, led, in theory at least, into a lawless jungle where warfare and politics could be nasty and brutish, not into a neat playing field where they were sanitized and controlled.

If we wish to find the reason for the long period of aristocratic immunity and its disintegration, we should turn away from theory, and focus instead on practice. What emerged after 1066 was a unique political situation which steered rulers away from exacting harsh penalties for treason. That situation had its origins in Normandy. Violent judicial punishment flourishes in political societies which are tight-knit and enclosed. Normandy, before and after 1066, was the reverse of that.[33] Families held lands in the duchy from the duke and outside it from other lords. Potential rebels always knew they would find safe haven with Normandy's overlord, the King of France. The latter, in particular, became a master at fomenting discord within the Norman and Angevin ruling houses. Duke Robert, William Clito, the sons of Henry II: there were nearly always French-backed standard bearers round whom the disaffected could gather. In these circumstances, executions and mutilations seemed increasingly futile. They would rarely be the end of the story when the kinsmen of the punished could find it so easy to escape and revolt. After 1066, the creation of an Anglo-Norman baronage, with lands in the kingdom and the duchy, meant that these features of Norman politics embraced England as well, in the process becoming more pronounced. What was the point of executing a noble in England, when that might merely provoke the rebellion of his kin in Normandy? As the Norman realm expanded, so it became less and less "an empire entire unto itself". Fundamentally, Anglo-Norman and Angevin politics remained permanently open. There was no way the king-duke could slam home the bolts and settle accounts behind closed doors.

These basic conditions of politics were powerfully reinforced in the key periods after 1066 when kingdom and duchy fell under different and warring rulers, each seeking to control the other's dominions. This was the case between 1087 and 1106, when Robert, Duke of Normandy, fought successively against William Rufus and Henry I, and between 1135 and 1154 when Henry I's daughter, the Empress Matilda, fought against King Stephen. It was essentially in these periods, when rebellions were most frequent, that the practice of clemency hardened into custom. The separation between England and Normandy created appalling problems for the Anglo-Norman baronage. If a family had divided its properties with, for example, one son holding the Norman lands and another the English, then the brothers found themselves on different sides in a civil war. If, alternatively, the lands were still united under a single lord, then he had to choose between treason in England and treason in Normandy. This was the stuff of Anglo-Norman politics, and why rebellions were so numerous. But to have punished the rebels with execution would have been counter-productive. It would merely have increased the support of the rival across the Channel and threatened everyone with a revenger's bloodbath.[34] Thus, as Orderic Vitalis shrewdly noted, Rufus showed mercy to those who had conspired against him in England in 1095, "out of respect for their exalted kinsfolk who might have sought vengeance in Normandy".[35]

After 1066, therefore, despite the large number of rebellions, first executions and then mutilations became unknown. William I's one important execution was already the exception which proved the rule, for it was of an Englishman, Waltheof, whose death had no Norman consequences.[36] Thereafter, Rufus hanged one noble and mutilated some others.[37] Henry I was guilty of a few mutilations, but executed no one.[38] And then, remarkably, during the civil war of Stephen's reign, there were no executions or mutilations at all. For the most part, the penalty for rebellion became simply forfeiture. The large number of feuds which resulted showed how wise the rulers were not to add execution as well; at least these were feuds over land, not over blood.[39]

By the end of Stephen's reign in 1154, therefore, a virtuous cycle was already in motion and was strengthened by Henry II's clemency to the rebels of 1173-4.[40] One act of mercy begot another. Despite the theory, in practice there was no corporal penalty for noble treason. Ultimately, the cycle proved strong enough to survive the collapse of the Anglo-Norman world out of which it had grown. The conquest of Normandy in 1204 by the King of France was quite different from the earlier separations of the kingdom and the duchy. Then the Anglo-Norman baronage had survived. In 1204 it was destroyed, since nobles who retained their English estates lost their lands in Normandy. As a consequence, English politics became more enclosed and intense. The King could execute without repercussions elsewhere in his dominions.

With its original foundations knocked away, at each political crisis after 1204, the virtuous cycle came under increasing strain. Once it disintegrated there would be no easy restoration. Rather the waters would flood into an altogether different cycle - a vicious and far more enduring one of killings tit for tat. Nonetheless clemency survived for over a century after 1204. That was partly because it was now sanctioned by custom, as we have seen; and partly because the noble themselves saw that they had every interest in seeing it continue for it was they who would suffer once the tit for tat killings started. If the policy of rulers had begun the years of clemency, the self-interest of nobles ensured that they continued. This point was highlighted, and the prospect of revenge killings graphically described, in 1215. In that year, King John had wanted to execute the rebel garrisons of Tonbridge and Rochester castles, although the latter was full of nobles. On both occasions, he was stopped by the same argument, powerfully expressed by Savari de Mauléon, one of his leading captains.

> "My Lord King, our war is not yet over; therefore you ought carefully to consider how the fortunes of war may turn; for if you now order us to hang these men, the barons, our enemies, will perhaps take me or other nobles of your army, and, following your example, hang us."[41]

In 1265, the pattern of clemency came under even more strain and was at last eroded. Incensed by a whole series of humiliations, the royalists murdered the Montfortians on the field of battle. Had Evesham been less of a decisive victory, had a Montfortian party ever recovered power, then the revenge killings described by Savari de Mauléon would doubtless have begun. Indeed, in a sense they did, for it was precisely in revenge for his father's death that Guy de Montfort murdered Henry III's nephew in the church at Viterbo, Italy, in 1271, a crime for which he was placed by Dante up to his neck in a boiling stream in Hell (*Inferno*, canto xii, 118-20).

There were, however, no executions after Evesham, in part because the nobles were determined to keep down the slaughter, as they had been throughout the 1264-5 civil war.[42] The real turning point came, as we have seen, in the reign of Edward II, and it was the nobles themselves who brought it about. Forgetting Savari de Mauléon's advice, they executed Gaveston, thereby pronouncing their own death sentences and pulling the last support - noble self-interest - from the virtuous cycle. Gaveston's execution required no new theory. In 1311, he had been sentenced to exile; if he returned he was to be treated as a "public enemy" and it was as such - precisely the status which Henry III had conferred on the rebels in 1264 - that he was executed.[43] But what impelled the earls to put theory into practice in this unprecedented way? It was partly the unprecedented provocation of Gaveston himself; a foreigner and an upstart; a man of intolerable insolence and arrogance who mesmerized the King and lorded it over everyone else.[44] It was partly too the influence of Edward I, not of his theory but of his practice. Edward's threats to the Montfortians before Lewes presaged not merely the murders at Evesham but also actual executions of the high nobility, not to be sure in England, but in Wales and Scotland. The execution of the Welsh Prince David in 1282 was particularly felt to break new ground. David was drawn, hanged, beheaded, eviscerated, and quartered. It was a death as the Oseney Abbey chronicler put it, "unheard of in past times".[45] Yet, in fact, there were precedents for this multiple punishment for traitors.[46] What was new was the victim coming from the high nobility. In 1306, a Scot of equivalent status, the Earl of Atholl, was likewise executed.[47] Inflicting the same fate on Gaveston seemed all the easier to contemplate. From that death, the execution of Thomas of Lancaster and his supporters assuredly followed. As the Lanercost Chronicle noted:

> "The cause brought forward (for Lancaster's execution) was that he had borne arms against the King... but those who knew best the King's mind declared that the Earl would never have been summarily beheaded... had not that other cause prevailed (revenge for the execution of Gaveston) but that he would have been imprisoned for life or sent into exile."[48]

By the end of Edward II's reign, therefore, the practice was for nobles to be executed for political crimes, a practice reinforced by a fresh cycle of revenge killings later in the century, in the reign of Richard II. By the 15th century the wheel had spun a full circle since the early 13th. The cry in battle, the practice after it, was "kill the nobility, spare the commons". The letting of noble blood continued into the 18th century.

Politics, therefore, became more violent, but politics about what? Nobles, of course, were often driven by hard material grievances over the King's distribution of patronage, financial exactions, and direction of policy. Yet what is remarkable about this period is the way nobles also sponsored constitutional programmes which attempted quite genuine reform of the realm. In Stephen's reign each noble had extracted his own individual charter conceding him land and rights. In John's reign the nobles together extracted a general charter dealing with the grievances of many sections of society: Magna Carta.[49]

There is, of course, a widespread view that the Great Charter is simply a narrow baronial document. Indeed, when Mrs Thatcher reminded the French, during the 200th anniversary celebrations of the Revolution in 1989, that we had been there long before with our Magna Carta, she was berated on her return even by the Tory press. The Charter, she was told, looked after the sectional interests of the great barons. What had it to do with the rights of man? How could it hold a candle to those great principles of "Liberté, Egalité, Fraternité"? Mrs. Thatcher was guilty of both bad history and bad manners! In respect of the second, perhaps, the Tory press was right. But over the first they were very far from it. In those two great chapters of Magna Carta - 39 and 40 - which are still on the statute book today, still part of the fundamental law of this country, no *free man*, not just no baron or no bishop, is to be deprived of his property, outlawed, exiled or imprisoned, save by the "lawful judgement of his peers or by the law of the land". No one at all is to be denied right and justice. There was nothing isolated about chapters 39 and 40. The truth is that the Charter, to a greater or lesser degree, catered for the grievances of all sections of society: barons, ecclesiastical institutions, knights, townsmen, freemen, even peasants. In so doing, it asserted one great principle which has remained a fundamental bar to tyranny ever since: the king's government was subject to the law.

The same wide range of concerns was evident in the two great programmes of reform which followed Magna Carta: the Provisions of Oxford in 1258-9 and the Ordinances of 1311. Both were more radical than the Charter in that they sought to wrest control of appointments and patronage from the king, thus foreshadowing the constitutional demands of the 17th century. Both were concerned to carry through a wide ranging reform of the realm. In 1258-9 local government was overhauled with the sheriff being made an important county knight and given a salary. A justiciar was appointed to tour the country and give "speedy justice no less to poor than to rich"[50]. In 1311, the Ordinances dealt with grievances over purveyance (the king's right of compulsory purchase), over the maltote (a tax on wool exports), and the royal forest.[51]

A great noble, in this period, in a different way widened politics beyond the merely baronial. To say that Simon de Montfort was the founder of Parliament, or more exactly of the House of Commons, seems a facile simplification.[52] Yet the fact remains that during his period of power in 1264-5 he *did* expand the political community in a way never done before. In 1258, the Provisions of Oxford had still envisaged a narrow oligarchical parliament. It was to meet three times a year, but the only representative element was supplied by 12 magnates chosen by "the barons" to represent the "whole community of the land". That community, it was confidently affirmed, would be bound by the Twelve's decisions.[53] In June 1264, by contrast, Simon de Montfort ordered each county to choose four "prudent and law-worthy knights" to come to Parliament to discuss the business of the realm. To the Parliament of January 1265 he ordered two burgesses from the major towns to come as well.[54] The parliament of 1265 thus became the first at which knights and burgesses sat together; the House of Commons in embryo. In summoning knights and burgesses with increasing frequency to his parliaments, Edward I was merely following where Simon de Montfort had led.

If politics, therefore, became more brutalized, they were also more constructive. The nobles were concerned for themselves and for the realm as a whole, and that for two reasons, by no means mutually exclusive: idealism and self-interest. The idealistic explanation of noble conduct goes in and out of fashion among historians; yet it is firmly grounded in the contemporary sources. Take again the case of Simon de Montfort. With his friend and spiritual councillor, Robert Grosseteste, the greatest reforming bishop of the age, he had almost certainly discussed the Aristotelean distinction between just rule and tyranny; the just ruler devotes himself to the welfare of his subjects, the tyrannical merely consults his own interests. With the friars at Oxford - their regent, Adam Marsh, was another personal friend - he had probably contemplated the whole nature of the State, viewing it, like them, as a human body in which the prince was the head and the labourers were the feet. The need to consider the interests of all parts of the body was thus an imperative, and accordingly in his will, drawn up in 1259, Simon expressed especial concern for "the poor people of my land... namely its tillers", whom he might have oppressed.[55]

Yet if Simon's friends revered him as a saint, his enemies chopped off his arms, legs, and head and hung his testicles on either side of his nose.[56] For them he was a greedy, power-crazed traitor. And certainly, Simon's career can also illustrate how a wider concern for the realm might be the product not merely of ideals but also of self-interest. Simon's grievances, like those of so many medieval magnates, were essentially over patronage: he had not received enough of it from the King. In particular, while he had married Henry III's sister, he had received her without an adequate landed endowment. Essentially, Simon hoped that the revolution of 1258 would put these matters right. But once the revolution had taken place, it was vital to make the new regime popular and well supported. The King had been coerced. The new regime had originated not in consent but in violence. On 30 April 1258, in an electrifying démarche, the barons had marched in armour into

Westminster Palace and confronted the quailing monarch: "What is this my lords, am I wretched fellow, your prisoner?", Henry had cried.[57] In terms of political power, Henry had indeed become a prisoner, and like all prisoners he wished to escape. Against his attempt to do so, Montfort and the other revolutionaries knew that their chief security lay in the popularity of their regime; hence the general reform of the realm.

That reform also reflected a wider truth about the greater nobles' position and power. They did not rule in lordly isolation. They had to reach out to towns (especially London), to freemen, and above all to the lowest section of the nobility itself, the section formed by what historians, without risk of anachronism, can call by the end of the 13th century, the gentry. The rise of the gentry was part and parcel of general changes in the structure of the nobility. To these we now turn.

Between 1204 and 1337 the higher nobility of England was transformed, in terms of nationality – from Anglo-Norman to English – and in terms of definition – from feudal baron to parliamentary peer.

The change in nationality was caused by the loss of Normandy in 1204, which meant that for the first time since the Conquest the high nobility was as English as the rest of the population. Down to 1204, there had been an élite of about 100 barons who held land in the kingdom and the duchy.[58] Many cannot have been born in England at all – the basic criteria for being English. Twelfth-century noblewomen, pregnant in Normandy, did not hurry across the channel so that their sons could play for England, much less for Yorkshire. Even when a nobleman was born in England, his Norman possessions profoundly affected his pattern of life and outlook. Probably, like the Norman kings, he spent as much time in Normandy as in England; and probably as a consequence he felt a kind of dual nationality. Even as late as the 1220s these distinctions created fault lines within the nobility and divisions between it and the rest of the population. William Longespee, Earl of Salisbury, born in England and with no Norman interests, spoke happily of "all we native-born men of England". But his friend, William Marshal, Earl of Pembroke, born in Normandy on the family's extensive estates there, could make no such identification. He spoke of "all the native-born men of England". He was not one of them.[59]

The loss of Normandy in 1204 soon enabled all the nobility to share in Longespee's Englishness, for henceforth they lived only in England and were always native born. There were internal and external consequences. The narrowing of horizons created the context for the intensity and violence of later medieval politics already discussed. Yet, at the same time, with the power of the nobility at last behind them, national feelings exploded outwards into wars of conquest - under Edward I against the Welsh and the Scots, under Edward III against the French.

By the time the Hundred Years' War began in 1337, England's nobility had been virtually redefined. This was at least the case at the very highest level - throughout the 13th century there were about a dozen earls, each with incomes of more than £1,000 a year. But beneath the earls, the feudal barons became the parliamentary peers. Early in the 13th century, tenure by barony still defined an élite within the nobility. A prime concern of Magna Carta in 1215 was to fix the relief (or inheritance tax) of a baron at £100; barons, or at least the most important of them, were to receive personal summonses to great assemblies – the assemblies soon to be called parliaments. Most barons had incomes of several hundred pounds a year.[60] Between 1086 and 1327, 210 baronies are known to have existed.[61] In practice, however, to define the upper nobility by tenure by barony was becoming increasingly anachronistic. This was because baronies were subject to a constant process of division, largely through failure of male heirs. In practice, many baronies became so divided between co-heiresses that they ceased to exist. Others became concentrated in the hands of a single lord. Since very few new baronies were created after the immediate post-Conquest period, the number of individual barons steadily declined. Alongside them there were many wealthy "new men" who did not hold baronies at all. Not surprisingly, therefore, Edward I's practice in issuing personal summonses to Parliament (perhaps derived from that of his father Henry, III for whom evidence is wanting) bore no relation to Magna Carta's theory. Of the 53 laymen summoned to the Parliament of 1295, as many as 22 did not hold by barony.[62]

Edward I's summonses, however, had as yet no role in redefining the nobility for the list of those summoned varied from one parliament to the next.[63] The decisive change took place between 1307 and 1330 when the list became much more standardized. In the second half of the 14th century, the number of parliamentary peers became fixed at about 70; the right to a personal summons became hereditary; and new men appeared only when they had obtained the lands of a previous person on the list.[64] In 1215 a personal summons to the embryo parliament had been the prerogative of the "greater baron", but that was a vague term and there is no sign that possession of a summons came to define a grade within the nobility. Indeed, clearly it did not for otherwise the reforms of 1258 which abolished summonses altogether and allowed the barons simply to elect 12 parliamentary representatives would have been inconceivable.[65] A hundred years later, a standardized list of summonses very definitely marked off a parliamentary peerage from the lower ranks of the nobility.

Among those lower ranks there had been a transformation even more significant; the rise of the gentry. In the first half of the 14th century, it is easy to describe typical members of the class. Robert Fitz Elys, whom we have already met, is a good representative of its upper levels: the Lord of Waterperry in Oxfordshire (a large and valuable manor), and of Worminghall and Oakley nearby in Buckinghamshire; an income from these lands of perhaps £100 a year; a knight and a fighting one at that; a holder of numerous local government offices culminating in that of sheriff; all that is missing is that he was never, apparently, an MP.[66] At a lower level were Robert's neighbours, the Quatremains (one Thomas Quatremain followed another for most of the 14th century) They were lords of two small manors at Ascot and North Weston in south Oxfordshire with an annual income of perhaps £30. Unlike their ancestors in the 13th century, they were esquires rather than knights, but they could still be busy in local government and still armigerous and active militarily - at any rate the Thomas who died in 1342 is depicted with his son on a later brass in Thame parish church in full armour surrounded by the Quatremain arms - gules, four hands or, a fess azure.[67] There were perhaps 50 men of the type of Robert Fitz Elys and Thomas Quatremain in a medium-sized English county in the 14th century.[68] Of course, lords of one or a few manors had been active in county affairs in the 12th century as well. Yet the intervening years had seen significant changes in such men's status and activity.

In the 1320s, the sheriff of Oxfordshire, in response to an order from the government, made separate lists of the *milites*, *armigeri,* and *homines ad arma* in his county. His ability to do so reflected the emergence of the three groups into which the later medieval gentry was to be divided; at the top the knights (*milites*), in the middle, the esquires (*armigeri*), and at the bottom the gentlemen, although that title became common only in the 15th century.[69] In the 1200s, there was no sign of a threefold division. There was simply a large, amorphous group of knights, perhaps as many as 4,000, running from lords of several manors down to men who held small parcels of land and were not lords of manors at all. For that very reason, knighthood carried very limited social prestige.[70] In the course of the century, all this changed; the number of knights declined and the honour became confined to the wealthy. To become a knight in this period was described as "to take military arms" - *ad arma militaria capienda*. Although it is far from clear how this was checked, it was certainly necessary to possess those arms before the knighting; and, as they became increasingly elaborate, as one also had to equip an increasingly numerous entourage, and throw an ever more elaborate party on the day of the ceremony, so the initial capital cost involved in assuming the rank rose dramatically. Consequently, first descendants of non-manorial knights ceased to assume knighthood, and then those of lesser manorial lords like the Quatremains. Ultimately, by the early 14th century, the honour was was becoming confined to those, like the Fitz Elys's, with three manors and above.[71] The number of knights was down to perhaps 1,250 and getting smaller.[72] In consequence the honour now carried a prestige it had quite lacked 100 years before.

The decline in the number of knights in the 13th century created the rise of the esquires in the next. Already in the 1320s, as we have seen, the Sheriff of Oxfordshire felt able to distinguish the esquires (armig*eri*) from the knights above them and the men at arms (*homines ad arma*) below. In other counties, the sheriffs were less sure, lumping esquires and men at arms together. But ultimately the desire for status among those who could no longer afford knighthood meant that the triumph of the squire was assured. This process, in its turn, created the gentlemen of the 15th century, a title invented essentially to stress the noble or gentle status of lords of manors who did not become esquires, either through lack of funds or lack of military aspiration. Historians have quite fairly lumped together as "the gentry" knights, esquires, and all manner of gentlemen (*gentils*) beneath the rank of knight, as it was put in 1363,[73] for they had much in common. By and large they were all lords of manors, all might hold local government office, if at different levels - the knight as sheriff, the gentleman as coroner; and all, increasingly, might have coats of arms. Nor was there any permanent divide between knights and the rest. Many esquires and men at arms in the 1320s' lists became knights later in their careers. Likewise, families often moved in and out of knighthood, and indeed of squirehood, over generations. Between 1264 and 1370, the Wace family of Oxfordshire produced in succession an esquire, a knight, a lord with no military title, and a knight.[74] What had happened was none the less important. The decline in the number of knights in the 13th century set in train a process which stratified the late medieval gentry by making social distinctions more defined.

What had also changed was the way of life of manorial lords. In the 12th century, they had certainly been active in local affairs, but the plethora of local government offices held by the likes of Robert Fitz Elys and Thomas Quatremain - coroner, escheator, tax collector, justice of assize, gaol delivery, oyer and terminer, JP - were essentially created in the years between 1190 and 1350. If the office of sheriff was much older, only in the 13th century did it become dominated by local knights. The whole pattern of local government had changed, thereby transforming the lives of the local lords who came to run it; thereby, to a degree, creating the gentry. An equally important change had taken place at the national level through the summoning of knights, representing the counties, to Parliament. We have already seen how the years between 1258 and 1265 constituted a watershed in this process. In the first half of the 13th century the great magnates in Parliament had felt able to speak for everyone in important matters like the granting of taxation. After 1265, no tax could be granted without the consent of the knights.[75] By the early 14th century, they were becoming essential for the holding of a valid parliament. New too were the political views articulated by the gentry. In part these were a response to the heavy taxation which began in the 1290s, prompting the knights in parliament to propound radical schemes for the reduction of royal expense. The knights also urged the reform of local government, demanding above all that it be run by local men, or, to put it another way, that it be run by the gentry. As early as 1215, indeed, Magna Carta had stipulated that the king's judges, visiting the shires, should sit with four knights elected in the county court.[76]

The gentry, then, had risen, and, up to a point, it had risen by royal command. The king had created the new local government offices and commissioned the gentry to fill them; the king had needed taxation and summoned knights to

Parliament to grant it. Yet he had not been an entirely free agent. He employed the gentry in local government yet he also distrusted them. The movement towards "self-government" in the shires was one he had frequently sought to check.[77] Its ultimate triumph owed a good deal to the demands we have mentioned above, and to the power of the gentry that was making them. Likewise the necessity to summon representatives to grant taxation indicated the power of the gentry and, in particular, its new-found independence from the upper nobility.

The power of the gentry derived ultimately from the solidity of its material position. This view has not gone unchallenged. Indeed, it has been argued that in the 13th century the knightly class passed through a severe social and economic crisis; hence the falling number of knights was the result of decreasing resources as well as rising costs; hence too the political demands of the class were generated by despair not by confidence. In this perspective, the gentry of the 14th century was essentially the body which was left after a long process of winnowing over the previous 100 years.[78] It is certainly true that a significant number of knightly families in the 13th century ran into debt (often to the Jews) and were forced to sell up, most frequently to religious houses or prosperous royal officials. On the other hand, a much larger number of families, with one manor and above, maintained the bulk of their properties intact, and sometimes increased them, whatever temporary difficulties they passed through.[79] Indeed, many of these families showed tremendous energy and resilience in facing the supposed cause of the economic crisis, a period of inflation, especially acute between 1180 and 1220, and lasting thereafter down to 1260. Thus the Quatremains retained the same basic properties throughout the century, and by 1279 had them in excellent condition with extensive demesnes, ideal for producing a large corn surplus which could be sold each year on the market, thus proofing the family against inflation. The Fitz Elys's, meanwhile, had decisively improved their position. In the early 13th century, Emma Fitz Elys had lamented her "great need", but her need was to finance litigation which turned out to be highly successful, securing her Oakley, and two other manors, later used to endow a junior branch of the family. Then, in the early 14th century, the family advanced again when Robert Fitz Elys's marriage secured him Nethercott in Wilshire.[80]

This material strength and enterprise were linked to social changes which brought the gentry increasing independence from their tenurial lords, changes often related to the break-up of feudalism. Some of the factors which operated here can be seen in the history of the Fitz Elys's. Their chief manor, Waterperry, had been held from the greatest baronial family in Oxfordshire, that of d'Oilly; and in the late 12th century they were still close to their d'Oilly lord.[81] But any exclusive allegiance to the family was weakened by the Fitz Elys's also holding from other lords - Worminghall from the Earl of Gloucester, and Oakley first from the King and then from the Earl of Cornwall.[82] A great deal, in these circumstances, would depend on the personality of the incumbent d'Oilly, but Henry, the last of the line, who held the barony from 1175 to 1232, was a pious nonentity. After his death, the barony passed through marriage to two different families in the next 11 years.[83] The Fitz Elys's can no longer have felt much allegiance to a tenurial lord. No great baron could answer for them in Parliament or anywhere else. True, feudal bonds quickly metamorphosed in bastard feudalism. The tie of tenure was replaced by that of cash or simply of "good lordship". In the 1220s, William Fitz Elys may well have had bastard feudal ties with the greatest potentate in Oxfordshire, the sheriff Falkes de Bréauté. A hundred years later, Robert Fitz Elys served first Roger Mortimer of Wigmore and then Hugh Despencer, Earl of Winchester.[84] Yet such allegiances, as Robert's shift from Roger to Hugh showed, were often fluid: lordship lasted "only so long as it was found to be *good* lordship or until it was ousted by better";[85] even when allegiances did endure, those retained were not automatons; and, in any case, there were also many knights and esquires who were independent of any lords, as seems the case with the Fitz Elys's for most of the 13th century.[86] These men were just as noble as any parliamentary peer; just as proud of their lineages and their armour. The effigies of Robert Fitz Elys at Waterperry and of his fellow knight, John of Broughton at Broughton, are almost interchangeable with the effigy of Edward III's brother, John of Eltham, Earl of Cornwall, in Westminster Abbey.[87]

The period between 1215 and 1337 was, therefore, utterly formative in the history of the English nobility. The basic structures then created survived almost into modern times. Macaulay thus sketched the country gentleman of the late 17th century.

> 'He was the member of the proud and powerful aristocracy... He knew the genealogies and coats of arms of all his neighbours... He was a magistrate... He was an officer in the train bands and his military dignity ... raised his character in his own eyes and those of his neighbours. Nor indeed was his soldiership justly a subject of derision. In every county there were elderly gentlemen who had seen service which was no child's play'.[88]

Macaulay might have been talking of the world of Robert Fitz Elys.[89]

Footnotes to this Chapter may be found on page 188-93.

3: John Fines
The nobility in the later Middle Ages: 1337-1485

THE STORY of the House of Lords has been chronicled with great distinction by two other contributors to this volume.[1] Their doings leave us amazed, but we cannot know the detail, for only two or three fragments of their journal survive, and even they read more like attendance registers. A place in the Lords was a fine thing indeed, but it was hard, expensive, and inconvenient to plod up to London roughly once a year, and many never came. The Parliament summoned for 7 June 1344 netted an archbishop, three bishops, the Earl of Huntingdon, and a handful of abbots and barons. The King was furious and three days later, after considerable whipping, they raised the number to an archbishop, seven or eight bishops, two abbots, two priors, eight earls, and five other lay magnates.

The question, however, remains, who were these people who wanted the honour and all that came with it, but were so undutiful in attendance? We get brief pictures of them coming into Westminster Hall by the North Door, on through Little Westminster Hall and into the Painted Chamber (having first shown their writs to the guard on the door). After 1362, business was in English (French being *trop desconue*) and the lords spiritual and temporal withdrew deeper into the royal palace to the White Chamber to consider in private what the Lord Chancellor (or sometimes the Chief Justice) had asked in the opening speech. The Commons went off to the Abbey Chapter House, but the two houses would meet in committee to agree their position before returning to the Painted Chamber to give their responses. Meanwhile, the triers of petitions had been meeting privately, as had the Court of Chivalry. On occasion, as trial by peers and the role of the upper house as the highest court of justice developed, they tried great cases, mainly of royal officers no longer in favour. To find out who they were we must begin at the beginning of our period, a time of acute crisis between the king and his nobility.

In 1326, Edward II endured what the *Polychronicon* politely called a "vile and opprobrious" death at Berkeley Castle. He had fought off the Lords Ordainers and Lancaster, but to his shame, it was his Queen and her lover Roger Mortimer, Earl of March, who finally killed him, and who went on to rule the country for three years in the name of his son, Edward III. Then, crawling along a secret passage, young Edward with the nobles who had conspired against his father, entered Nottingham Castle to arrest the Earl, as the Queen screamed for mercy for her "gentle" companion. So low had the monarchy fallen, and it must have seemed as if it could never rise again, yet 14 years later, Edward decreed the setting up anew of the Round Table, and immediately spent £500 on the building of an apartment at Windsor to house it. Arthur and his loyal knights were to live again.

It is hard for us to know what the legend meant to them, for we read it through Tennysonian and pre-Raphaelite eyes, or even further back through the eyes of Sir Thomas Malory who wrote a century after Edward III's excited announcement. Yet, whatever their vision, it was at least a beginning of that discovery of the fictive, of tragedy and comedy, of the sometimes subtle, sometimes violent contrast between hope and despair, honour and dishonour, love and hate, high chivalry and desperate chicanery, rejoicing in the pageant of a court *en fête* and the struggle through a winter wasteland.

It is perhaps a modulation from the pure legend of Arthur to the practical realization of a naughty world that badly needs rules that is the heart of medieval chivalry that marked the change from the intended Round Table in four short years to the foundation of the Order of the Garter. For although Ashmole could not believe such an improbability, it was the lovely Joan of Kent's loss of a garter at a ball that provoked the royal *Honi soit qui mal y pense*. The foundation of the Order was a staging post in the history of the English nobility and was to have a considerable influence on its future history. Its exclusivity (only twenty-six members, including the king) ensured the importance of the upper nobility, and its insistence on brotherhood, on the ties that bound its members together in loyalty to one another, and to the Crown made for much needed stability. The court with its rules of precedence and order inhibited internecine strife, but it also provided a venue in which dynasties might meet centrally (not threatened in their own power bases) and interconnect and ensure continuity by means of marriage. We are talking of some 50 to 60 titles sported by an even smaller number of families in which at this time the male line died out on average in the third or fourth generation.[2] There needed to be a mechanism, a system, an accepted code, and above all a meeting place in which the continued existence of this delicate organism, the higher nobility might be ensured.

Yet we should not forget that the Order of the Garter was one of many religious orders of knights (Ashmole lists forty-six in his *History*). The patrons were the Holy Trinity, the Blessed Virgin Mary, St George (these were fighting folk in reality) and St Edward the Confessor (they followed a king into battle). They were to support 13 canons and 26 veteran knights; they were to meet every year, wearing a common uniform, and when a brother died 1,000 masses were to be said for his soul. In the establishment of the order was the hope for the reestablishment also of the honour of the nobility and its sovereign.

It worked, for a time, because the Hundred Years' War required such a fighting team. At Calais in 1347, Hugh le Despencer, son of Edward II's favourite, hanged in 1326, served alongside Roger Mortimer, grandson of that Earl of March who had been dragged to his death in 1330, a minor but as a banneret carrying a pennon for the Prince of Wales. The war gave a reason for working together, enriching the nobility by pay, by ransoms and by loot.[3] In this it provided suitable conditions for warfare, by which all the damage of war was done on alien territory, and English nobles could take over offices of profit in captured lands. It seemed to present profit without risk. At Crécy, 50 English nobles died, while on the French side, the losses were one king, eleven princes, 80 great barons and 1,200 knights, and it was not long before ransom negotiations for the King of France himself were under way, after Poitiers in 1356.

Nevertheless Edward, who seemed in the middle part of his reign to promise so much success to his kingdom, was building already the framework of future disaster. His good health and the bad luck of his son meant that he reigned too long, leaving the Throne to a 10-year-old boy, and his fertility, and that of his children (not least the prolific John of Gaunt) built up a reserve of possible contenders for the Throne. The nobility was thus enlarged by a herd of royalty.

At the start of the 14th century, nobility had been easy enough to define. In 1307, there were six earls. In 1337, Edward III gave the previously kingly title of duke to his son the Prince of Wales and soon many other members of the Royal Family had it too. Richard II began his reign with panache, creating earls of his 11-year-old playmate and his French tutor. In 1385, he invented the title of marquess for life for his favourite, Robert de Vere, Earl of Oxford, and the following year made him the first duke not of royal blood in the male line.[4] The bounds were now broken - Richard followed the pattern of his great grandfather in trusting favourites rather than the established nobility, making Michael de la Pole, son of a rich merchant of Hull, Earl of Suffolk and his Chancellor. As before, the old nobility rose in revolt and at the end of the century it was an essentially noble revolution that placed Henry IV, John of Gaunt's eldest son, with very little right indeed upon the Throne, putting his claim to the question in Parliament before seating himself. Richard was assassinated at Pontefract, Yorkshire.

Just as Richard II had repeated the errors of Edward II, Henry IV's son, Henry V, repeated the successes of Edward III, providing his followers with opportunities for adventure, honour and loot, and in return being able to require of them obedience and loyalty. Yet there was a reverse side to the successes of war, for in emphasizing the qualities of aggression and in optimizing the role of leadership of a war band, the King was building yet another generation of dangerous nobles. In 1422, when Henry died, leaving an heir of nine months to the joint Thrones of England and France, he also left him a fighting troupe of great uncles and uncles who had only that narrow self-interest in view (except possibly for Bedford).

The struggle saw some mighty falls, not least that of Humphrey, Duke of Gloucester, who appears to have died of shock at his failure in 1446. There remained the leading contender for power, Richard, Duke of York, heir to the vast Mortimer estates[5], and great grandson of Edward III's third son and grandson of his fifth. Yet despite his claim, he could not manage the nobility when he became governor of the Kingdom- in 1454 he had to introduce fines for non-attendance at the House of Lords - £100 for a duke, £75 for an earl, and £40 for a baron. Despite the fines, of the 105 lords summoned only 45 came. Yet the position was still much desired, even by people who could not claim by ancient right of a (feudal) barony which had always had a place in the upper house. In the mid-century, the habit of creating baronies by patent (invented by Richard II) became common as when in 1441 the Crown created the new chamberlain, Sir Ralph Boteler, Lord Sudeley. Three years later, it was allowed to the Earl of Warwick to wear a coronet in presence of the King, a right previously restricted to dukes (although earls had used crowns for long enough - Arundel left three in his will in 1375).

The following year (1455) York took up arms and the Wars of Roses officially began. Six years on, his son ascended the Throne as Edward IV, aided principally by the heir of the Neviles, the immensely rich Earl of Warwick. When Warwick was resident in London, six oxen were roasted for breakfast (but it was decreed that no one should be allowed to take away more meat than could rest on the point of a dagger - thus the oxen were all needed). Warwick the King-Maker was soon rejected by Edward IV, who chose to promote instead the clan of relatives of his wife, Elizabeth Woodville. In 1465, John Lord Maltravers, 15-year-old husband of the Queen's sister, was knighted, and the next year the 11-year-old son of Lord Herbert was created Lord Dunster on his marriage to another of the Queen's sisters. Warwick was angry. In the struggles that ensued, many lives were lost and many estates were forfeited, providing means to reward those nobles who remained loyal.

The chaos that succeeded Edward's death is well recorded, but we might note just two points here. Richard III, Edward's brother, built his claims on accusations of bastardy, of the royal princes, and indeed of his dead brother. This, above all, was to hit at the very heart of the system - inheritance by the line of blood. No wonder he only held Buckingham for a few months, and took so few nobles with him to Bosworth Field in 1485 where he was killed by Henry Tudor. It was not killing children that people minded so much, it was the undermining of the one respected element of security, nobility by birth.

After blood, there were possibly four other elements to nobility in this period: wealth, above all (in 1478 George, Duke of Bedford, was deprived of his title on the grounds of the insufficiency of his lands); position, particularly in his own locality, for the noble's own territory was his kingdom, the king's own rights excepted; display, which proved all this; and the bonds of marriage that preserved it for the future. Wealth was a necessity for a lord who needed to support a great house and many retainers. Richard Fitzalan, Earl of Arundel and Surrey, left £11,000 in his will, written in 1375, yet when his executors came to check they found nearly £30,000 in the high tower at Arundel, £18,000 at St Paul's and nearly £11,000 on his Marcher estates[6]. During the crisis of Henry VI's insanity in 1454, it was said that Buckingham had prepared 2,000 badges bearing the Stafford knot, and inn signs up and down the country today witness to the symbols of loyalty to a local lord.[7] McFarlane quotes a livery roll of Edward Courtenay, Earl of Devon, for 1384-

5 which shows the shape rather than the size of a noble household. There were five other male Courtenays, seven knights, 40 esquires, 52 yeomen, four minstrels, eight parsons, three *damoiselles*, six pages, and 14 men of law.[8] Wealth came from land, of course,[9] but it also came from fees for positions held, and, in good times of warfare, from ransoms and loot and booty. It came, in large sums, from peculation. In 1455, Ralph, Lord Cromwell, left £5,481 6s 8d, as restitution for conscience sake, a huge sum representing the annual income of the greatest lords of the period.[10] It was never paid by his trustees.

Position was increasingly supported by institutions and regulations. The kings of arms and the Court of Chivalry were instituted in the reign of Edward III, and Richard III, belatedly understanding the need for security of this sort, founded the College of Arms by charter in 1484. The Court of Chivalry was most needed, of course, in establishing precedence for members of the upper house who wanted, above all, to sit in a good position. The questions put to the lords were answered in reverse order of precedence, with the most important answering last. Henry V made considerable efforts at regulation, ordering the Sheriff of Southampton in 1417 to check all those coming to join the expedition to France to see whether they bore arms by ancestral right, proper gift, or simply by having been at Agincourt two years before. If they could not prove their right, the arms were to be destroyed and their wages withdrawn. Further controls covered what a man might wear. Sumptuary legislation is as much to do with uniform as is legislation covering liveries, and the right to wear cloth of gold tissue (restricted to dukes) was as much a badge of recognition as the livery worn by one of the 299 members of the Duke of Clarence's household in 1469. By the following century, when the Duke of Buckingham spent £1,500 on his costume for the wedding of Prince Arthur (eldest son of Henry VII) and Katherine of Aragon, things had already got out of hand.[11]

Display was an important feature of the successful noble's life and, increasingly, display meant a great house where comfort and riches were shown against a background of order and ritual. The great brick mansions with their broad glazed windows and fireplaces with chimneys represented a new dimension in comfortable living.[12] The walls hung with tapestry, the tables covered with gold and silver, books and music beginning to take their place, and a degree of privacy (even in private there was display, Thomas of Woodstock's best bed was worth £180[13]) as against the hurly-burly of the hall, where, as in that most elegant of romances, Sir Gawain and the Green Knight, the court could quickly descend to an horrific kind of football with the Green Knight's head. Controls of precedence were always needed. John Russell, former marshal to Humphrey, Duke of Gloucester, wrote a manual on the subject called *The Book of Nurture* in the mid-15th century, explaining how to "set each person fittingly without amiss according to birth, property, dignity..." He also tells how to present and serve foods (wrapping bread being a particularly difficult task), how to dress the lord in well-warmed clean clothes, brushing him down before he leaves the room. There are instructions on keeping the bedroom and lavatory, neatly covering the hole with a cushion and supplying "blanket/cotyn/or lynen to wipe the nether ende". There are careful instructions on stocking and keeping a good wardrobe, on bathing the lord, and on putting him to bed. Such a good servant would deserve reward. Certainly Humphrey, Duke of Gloucester, had good servants and brave ones. His doctor wrote a careful statement on his health in his 45th year, noting his "daily morning cough" which he put down to over indulgence. He urged him to avoid north winds after a warm sun, sleep after dinner, exercise after society, frequent bathings, strong wine, much fruit, pork, and - not to put too fine a point on it - sex.[14] Indeed, there was a strange balance between the medieval and Renaissance world to be observed in the 15th century nobility. John Tiptoft, Earl of Worcester, spent three years studying in Italy, where he built a fine library and a good reputation for sound scholarship. Yet when he returned to become England's Constable under Edward IV, he used his knowledge of civil law to organize treason trials which ended with the full horror of English executions *plus* the nasty continental habit of impaling. When he was executed, he was accused as "the butcher of England".

To climb the greasy pole required a sure hand in those days. A good example among many is James Fiennes (whom Gibbon proudly claimed as his ancestor) who began as a second son at Herstmonceaux and made his way initially as a captain with Henry V. He was Sheriff of Kent in 1437 and added Surrey and Sussex two years later. In 1440, he was given £100 pension as esquire of the body to the King. In 1445, he was granted a £20 pension by the Earl of Warwick. In 1447, he was made (at his own request, on the fall of Humphrey, Duke of Gloucester, in whose death he was rumoured to have had a hand), Constable of Dover and Warden of the Cinque Ports which brought in another £200 a year plus wrecks and admiralty fees. In the same year, he was made Lord Saye and Sele in the rather distant right of his grandmother having bought out the senior heir who had ruined himself paying a large ransom. He was also made Royal Chamberlain and Constable of the Tower (another £75 a year). He exercised such a fine control that he read over court sermons before they were delivered. On the death of the Duke of Suffolk, he claimed that he would turn Kent into a deer park, but instead he fell victim in 1451 to Jack Cade and his rebels, who had him beheaded "half shriven" at the Standard in Cheap. Yet it would be a mistake to see all nobles of the period as bad barons. We should recall Henry, Duke of Lancaster, who wrote of himself in 1354 as "a foolish wretched sinner" who calls himself "Ertsacnal ecud irneh" penned the *livre de Seyntz Medecines* comparing physical ills with spiritual ones and recommending the cures of doctor Christ and his assistant, the "Douce Dame".

Even more impressive is the daily routine of Edward IV's mother, the Duchess Cecily, in 1485. She rose at seven and said matins and heard low mass; had breakfast; went to chapel and two further low masses; on to dinner where she listened attentively to devotional literature being read aloud. She then gave audience for an hour, taking a nap for a quarter of an hour afterwards. Then she took some wine or ale before proceeding to evensong. At supper, she repeated word for word what she had heard read at dinner. There followed a time of "honest mirth" with her ladies, and she took a cup of wine. Then she went to her chamber for private prayers and to bed by eight.

The preservative of nobility was marriage - if you wanted to build your estates and titles and hand them on to your successors, good marriages were essential. No family practised the art of marriage with more skill than the Neviles. The children of John, 3rd Lord Nevile's first marriage form a good sample: Ralph married first a daughter of the Earl of Stafford and then a daughter of John of Gaunt. Thomas married the heiress of Lord Furnival. Elizabeth let the side down badly by becoming a nun, but Alice married William, Lord Deincourt; Mathilda married William le Scrope and Eleanor Ralph, Lord Lumley. Many women played a substantial part in their husbands' bids for position and power. In 1441, Eleanor Cobham was charged with having used a witch to make love potions to entrap her husband the Duke of Gloucester, and with having hired an astrologer and a canon of Westminster to melt a wax image of the King in Hornsey of all places, in hopes of his death and her husband's succession.

Yet there was true love also. William de la Pole, Earl of Suffolk, writing his will in 1448 referred to his "best-beloved" wife, whom he trusted "above all the earth". Similarly, in the *Pageant of the Birth Life and Death of Richard Beauchamp, Earl of Warwick, KG 1399-1439*, no picture is more affecting than number 50 which shows how in a great storm at sea he ordered himself to be bound to the mast with his wife and son, so that if they foundered he would be recognized by his coat armour and they should be buried together. In fact, his final resting place is well worth a visit. His chantry chapel at Warwick cost him £2,481 and took 21 years to complete. In the centre is the remarkable statue of the Duke completed from a portrait by a London carver, assisted by a barber-surgeon to make sure the anatomical detail was correct. A specialist gilder from the Low Countries charged £200 for his work. The woodcarving, the painting was to be of the very best, as was the glazing, to be done with glass from "beyond the seas and with no glass of England; and that in the finest wise, with the best, cleanest and strongest glass of beyond the sea that may be had in England, and of the finest colours of blue, yellow, red, purple, sanguine and violet...".

What glory! Yet it was nearly all over. William Worcester, writing his *Book of Noblesse* in 1475, compared the education of nobles in Edward III's day with that of Edward IV's: then they "exercised in... usage of a school of arms, as using jousts, to learn to run with a spear, and handle an axe, sword, dagger and all other defensible weapons, wrestling, skipping, leaping and running to make them hard, free and well-bred" so that they may be ready to serve the king and their country when needed. Now they "set themselves to singular practice... to learn the practice of law or customs of land, or of civil matter, and so to hold courts, to keep and bear out a proud countenance at the holdings of sessions and shires…"

Footnotes to this Chapter may be found on pages 193-4.

4: Steven Gunn
Off with their heads: the Tudor nobility: 1485-1603

THE TUDOR period was one of dramatic and destabilizing change. Between the accession of Henry VII in 1485 and the death of Elizabeth in 1603, England's population doubled and food prices quadrupled. London rose to a new commercial and social dominance within the country, and the powers of central government expanded. The national church became Protestant, and humanist ideas and the new medium of printing worked great changes in education and culture, to the point where, for example, some 80% of London craftsmen were literate by the 1600s.[1] The social and political position of the peerage could hardly remain untouched by such developments; yet, as so often in its history, the English nobility proved surprisingly resilient and adaptable to the forces apparently working to undermine it.

Such a conclusion might not surprise us, but would, it seems, have surprised the secretary to the Venetian ambassador at Henry VII's court, who penned this obituary on the peerage of his day:

> In former times the titled nobility ... were extremely profuse in their expenditure, and kept a very great retinue in their houses (which is a thing the English delight in beyond measure); and in this manner they made themselves a multitude of retainers and followers, with whom they afterwards molested the Court, and their own countries, and in the end themselves, for at the last they were all beheaded.[2]

To be fair, this distant ancestor of Sellars and Yeatman probably had the great comital and ducal houses of Lancastrian England, rather than the entire "titled nobility", in mind. Many of these dynasties had lost one or more representatives in the welter of battles and executions between 1450 and 1499, and some lines - notably the Nevile Earls of Salisbury and Warwick and the Beaufort Dukes of Somerset - were indeed extinct by the time he wrote. Yet the Staffords and Percys, the De Veres and Fitzalans, the Courtenays and even the senior but less prominent line of the Neviles all survived to face the challenge of the new century, as did several dozen families of less antiquity or grandeur.

One lesson we might draw from our Venetian commentator is the danger of generalization; for the variety of the Tudor peerage was enormous. Noblemen's incomes ranged from the several hundred pounds a year which would not have been unusual for a substantial knight, to the £4,000 or £5,000 a year of the few richest families. Their interests ranged from hunting (the lowest common denominator for all those not mentally or physically incapable) to the highest of intellectual pursuits. John, Lord Berners (c1467-1533), translated Froissart's Chronicles into English, and Henry Howard, Earl of Surrey (c1517-47), was one of the leading poets of the age. Henry, Lord Stafford (1501-63), was a dedicated antiquarian, John, Lord Lumley (c1533-

1609), the greatest collector of paintings in Elizabethan England, and Henry Percy, Earl of Northumberland (1564-1632), such a devotee of alchemical experiments that he was known as the "wizard earl".

The range of commitment to national politics among the peerage was equally wide. By Elizabeth's reign, four generations of Howards had taken a leading role at court, in war and on the council since Edward IV's reign, as had three generations of Dudleys since the time of Henry VII. In the process, each family rose from the gentry and ramified, in the Howards' case to fill the duchy of Norfolk, the earldoms of Arundel and Nottingham, the viscountcy of Bindon, and the barony of Walden. Yet each also suffered grievous losses: two Howards were executed, two died in prison, and two were killed in battle; three Dudleys ended their careers on the block.

Such statistics make more understandable the utter detachment with which three successive Lords Ogle regarded the business of central government under Henry VIII. None ever appeared at court or in the House of Lords, though for the latter they had some excuse since the clerks sometimes even forgot to summon them. At least they made the bureaucrats' jobs easier by choosing the name Robert for the head of the family in all three generations.[3] Between the Ogles and the Howards lay a vast range of responses to the opportunities and dangers of political life, conditioned by the inevitable differences in ambition and competence among individual noblemen as well as by the resources and contacts available to different peerage families. Even in Henry VIII's reign, a more congenial environment for noble political activity than his father's or his daughter's, only a small inner ring of peers was very active on the national political stage, and only this small circle won substantial reward from the King; yet this situation was not so different from the later medieval norm as we might think.[4]

Though the peerage was thus an assemblage of very disparate individuals, it was also a recognizable group within Tudor society. Superficially, it was a remarkably stable body: there were 57 peers in 1485, 51 in 1547, 57 in 1558 and 55 in 1603. These totals hide a constant turnover, just as in the 14th and 15th centuries when a quarter of the peerage families died out in the direct male line every 25 years in a pattern barely disturbed by the political mortality of the Wars of the Roses. Indeed, Elizabeth's social conservatism and the lack of fluidity in the governing élite of her reign left the peerage as a whole more antiquated in lineage by her death than it had been in 1400. At that date 10 of the 17 existing earldoms had been created in the previous 50 years, while in 1603 only 2 of the 16 earldoms were of such recent creation. These figures conceal the flurry of new elevations under Henry VIII and the mid-Tudors, for in 1558, 46% of the peers were first- or second-generation noblemen, whereas by 1603 only 19% were such *arrivistes*. Yet even Henry tended to promote within the peerage as much as introduce entirely new blood. At his death nine of the 14 earls held titles less than 50 years old, but seven of the nine were the holders of inherited baronial titles.[5]

What was remarkable about the Tudor peerage was the speed with which the favoured few progressed through its ranks. It had long been the case that the richest gentry families were the natural candidates for elevation to the peerage, that their riches were sometimes the product of successful careers in the law, as in the case of the Scropes, Bourchiers and Howards, and that the timing of their creation was often determined by their service to the Crown. But in Henry VII's reign the interaction of these factors was accelerated, as the lawyers who dominated his council rapidly built up large landholdings, or even married noble heiresses, to project their immediate heirs into the peerage under Henry VIII as, for instance, Lords Bray and Mordaunt and John Dudley, Viscount Lisle.

For the ministers of Henry VIII the process was compressed into a single generation. Thomas Cromwell (c.1485-1540), son of a Putney alehouse-keeper, moved upwards and outwards in a geographical sequence with modern resonances, first to become Lord Cromwell of Wimbledon, then to the Earldom of Essex. Cromwell's protégé Thomas Wriothesley (1505-1550), the son and grandson of heralds, joined the world his family had chronicled as Lord Wriothesley, and later as Earl of Southampton. Legal and administrative skill took the Audleys, the Pagets and the Riches from social obscurity to the House of Lords in one jump, while those who started as gentry might reach the heights of the Brandons and Seymours as Dukes of Suffolk and Somerset, or of the Paulets as Marquesses of Winchester. Henry's impenetrable blend of self-confidence and suggestibility was one key to this acceleration of promotion, but there were others: the growing complexity of government and prominence of lay lawyers and financial administrators among the Crown's chief ministers, the ready availability of monastic land to endow new peers, and the interlude of royal weakness under the minor King Edward VI, when the Seymours, Dudleys, Herberts, Paulets, Wriothesleys and Parrs helped themselves to more elevated titles and estates to match. The change was not to last, however, and Elizabeth's parsimony with peerages matched that of her grandfather, Henry VII: even her chief minister William Cecil (1520-1598) had to wait until 1571 before he was created Lord Burghley, and never became an earl.

Elizabeth's conservatism probably strengthened the nobility's sense of group identity, if it had ever been put in doubt by the Henrician and Edwardian game of snakes-and-ladders. The functions performed by the peerage *en masse* no doubt did the same, as they attended in the House of Lords to add weight to parliamentary consultation and legislation, and graced the court to add lustre to the monarchy's magnificence. Yet, in the long term the peerage as a group was losing much of its prescriptive right to influence within government. Henry VII was the last ruler to make regular use of the Great Council, an afforced session of the House of Lords which could offer advice on great issues of State without the constrictions of parliamentary tradition. Henry VIII's reign saw the emergence of a Privy Council of clearly defined and limited membership, as the small administrative council of the later Middle Ages, supplemented by the most politically active peers, took an almost exclusive grip on the political role of counselling the monarch in affairs of state. This change deprived most noblemen of access to the decision-making machinery of government, an access previously recognized in their status as the king's "natural councillors" and their accepted role in advising the king informally at court, or formally in the Great Council or House of Lords, or in councils more loosely defined than the late Henrician Privy Council.[6]

It would be easy to overstate the degree of change involved. Under the Tudors individual noblemen continued to be powerful councillors, not least since membership of the Privy Council began to be tied to the tenure of great offices normally held by noblemen. The balance between peers and commoners among the king's innermost advisers did change, but this was partly an optical illusion produced by the replacement of clerics by lay commoners at the Reformation: even in the 15th century only a minority of noblemen had been very actively involved in central government, but they had worked alongside bishops and other churchmen as well as knights from the king's household, whereas their successors found themselves surrounded by lawyers, courtiers, and gentlemen bureaucrats. For most of Elizabeth's reign, between a third and a half of her privy councillors were peers, probably a higher proportion than in most of the administrative councils of the 15th century.

Yet change there was. Half or more of Elizabeth's titled privy councillors were first-generation noblemen, and the great regional magnates - Derby, Shrewsbury and Pembroke - tended to be poor attenders. Most peers were excluded entirely, and this was symbolic and symptomatic of wider developments. The idea that ancient wisdom might be inherited along with ancient riches was unpersuasive at a time when legal and financial matters were becoming increasingly central to the process of government, and when the Privy Council was expected to coordinate an ever more complex system of financial and judicial institutions. There was also less need to take the advice of noblemen because, as we shall see, their natural power at the local level was no longer as great as it had once been, and their role in executing the king's decisions in the localities was equally diminished. Even in war, their role was less preponderant than it had been. Henry's invasions of France in 1513 and 1544 were the last occasions on which the peerage turned out *en bloc* as they had for the Agincourt campaign, and changes to the mobilization system between the 1540s and 1560s made the army no longer a collection of noble retinues, but a force based on the obligation of all able-bodied men to serve in the county militia. In Elizabeth's war with Spain - as indeed in the earlier stages of the English Civil War - there was still an expectation that the highest commands would be held by peers: Leicester and Willoughby in the Netherlands, Essex and Mountjoy in Ireland, Howard of Effingham in the fleet. But it was a sign of the times that during the invasion scares of 1588 and 1596, non-noble military experts, familiar with the latest innovations in firearms, drill, and fortification, were appointed as regional superintendents over the heads of the predominantly noble Lord Lieutenants who commanded the militia. In war as in government, the combination of increasing technical sophistication with the currency of humanist thought with its meritocratic tendencies loosened the peerage's hold on power.[7]

The social superiority of the peerage was for the moment more assured. Privileges such as freedom from arrest for debt were maintained, and new marks of quality such as classical education, foreign travel and study at the universities were taken up with alacrity. Yet the privileges of the English nobility were weak compared with those of their continental contemporaries. They paid taxes, enjoyed minimal levels of independent jurisdiction within a legal system composed almost entirely of royal courts, and exercised comparatively paltry powers over their tenants because of the general withering of serfdom in England in the century after the Black Death. Their ability to exercise power thus rested more on their relationship with the Crown than did that of a French, Spanish or even a Scottish nobleman. The contrast was noted by the Spanish ambassador in 1555, when he described England as a "democratic" kingdom "in which nobility has no other authority than that entrusted to it by the king, possessing no rights in the exercise of criminal justice and little enough in the ordinary courts."[8] Those who set themselves in direct opposition to the king had long courted destruction, and even monarchs who mishandled affairs badly enough to end up deposed - like Edward II or Richard II - eliminated one wave of dissidents before being swept away by another. There was thus no need for any deliberately anti-noble policy for rulers like the Tudors who wished to assert tighter control over their country and its politics, nor any sense in diehard resistance to royal aspirations among the nobility. The relationship was one of service and mutually beneficial cooperation, on terms open to subtle negotiation on both sides.

It was a game in which the Crown held the stronger cards, but in which the players' priorities were not identical. While the Tudors' ultimate concern was to dominate national politics and manage international politics with sufficient assurance to stay on the throne, most noblemen were more interested in the protection of their own and their successors' influence in local affairs than in prominence on the national stage. Most, indeed, were remarkably uninterested in attending the House of Lords or the royal council even in the later Middle Ages when their role in national politics was more assured.[9] To evaluate the power of the Tudor peerage in the terms closest to most noblemen's hearts, it is the changes in their position at the local level that we must address.

That position rested above all on the ownership of land. Despite a decline in total landed wealth towards the end of the century, peers remained the greatest individual landholders in Tudor society. They were rivalled only by the bishops, whose collective landed income even in cash terms (with no correction for inflation) fell by one-third as a result of the Reformation, a far steeper decline than any afflicting the peerage.[10] On the other hand, the peerage as a body had not held a large proportion of the the country's total landed wealth even before the Dissolution of the Monasteries and the changes in the land market to which it lent impetus. Taxation returns of the 1520s suggest that the gentry then held an average of about one-third of the land in each county, whereas the peerage's share ranged from 1% to 7%; figures from 100 years earlier likewise suggest that the gross landed wealth of the gentry considerably outweighed that of the peerage.[11] Such figures help set the flurry of alienations of land by peers after 1558 - the economic foundation for Lawrence Stone's celebrated view of a crisis of the aristocracy - in their proper context. There was undoubtedly a rush to sell land by financially embarrassed peers, concentrated especially in the period 1590-1610, and its effect on the total landholdings of the peerage was marked. Debatable though the precision of counting manors as a measure of landed wealth may be, the fact that a large sample of peers held, on average, only 71% as many manors in 1602 as they had held in 1558 must mark a real decline in all the forms of power that landholding brought. Yet it is not self-evident that a decline of this sort - from a rather larger to a rather smaller minority share in the national stock of land - could have had the devastating effects on the nobility's social and political dominance that are sometimes suggested: it is not as though collective preponderance in landed wealth and local power shifted suddenly from the peerage to the gentry in the half century following the accession of Elizabeth. The decline followed a period in which many peers had exploited the Dissolution to expand or to consolidate their landholdings, and it is arguable that the greatest families at least - the Stanleys in the north-west are the classic example - were so rich in comparison with any possible rival for local dominance that even a marked decline in landed income did their social and political position relatively little harm.[12]

It was also the case that the most spectacular of these financial disasters were nearly always the result of wildly extravagant expenditure, far more reckless than could possibly be justified by the need to maintain social standing by conspicuous consumption more striking than that of the increasingly opulent London merchant class and the more pretentious county gentry. Roger Manners, Earl of Rutland (1576-1612), managed in the late 1590s to spend £11,000 or more a year, more than twice his income; £1,000 a year of this went on clothes and £1,000 or even £1,500 on gambling. That his problems were avoidable he helpfully demonstrated to posterity by emerging from his imprisonment after the Essex rebellion of 1601 a reformed character. By about 1606, his finances were stabilized and his debts paid off. Fecklessness with money was as great a problem for some peers under Henry VII and Henry VIII: Richard Grey, Earl of Kent (c1478-1524), sold off his inheritance to sustain his enjoyment of early Tudor court life, while the princely pretensions of Edward Stafford, Duke of Buckingham (1478-1521), were driving him towards bankruptcy even before they tempted him into the treasonable disaffection that brought him to his death. The problem was generalized by the set of young Elizabethans who clustered around the dashing Essex in the attempt to reclaim aristocratic predominance in the State, for whom devil-may-care over-spending seems almost to have been a badge of allegiance; but the soberer peers of the generations that followed generally managed to restore their houses' financial fortunes in preparation for the landowners' heyday of the 18th century.[13]

More significant in the longer term was the changing relationship between landholding and authority. As prices rose under the impact of population growth and Europewide inflation, there were difficulties for peers in extracting cash income from their estates. Rents were less flexible than prices, and economically realistic renting policies ran the risk of alienating the tenant loyalty that made landlordship so much more than a mere source of income: this scissors effect helps to explain the short-term problems experienced even by the more prudent late Elizabethan aristocrats. Those who coped best were the peers who diversified their activities into large-scale farming on their own demesnes for sale on the open market, thus exploiting price inflation, and those who fostered industrial development on their estates. Roger Manners' uncle, Edward, Earl of Rutland (1549-87), did both, deriving some 15-20% of his income from demesne farms, and modernizing the Rievaulx ironworks with the first recorded blast furnace in the north of England. Nonetheless, all peers were large-scale rentiers at a time when economic circumstances favoured merchants, graziers, grain-growers and clothiers, with the result that new money tended to catch up with, though not yet equal or outstrip, the old. Such new money tended to be spent on the symbols of prestige, in what could only be construed by aristocrats as a challenge to the social preeminence represented by a gilded coach or an embroidered suit. The only means by which they could reassure themselves, and continue to exert the influence over their inferiors which went with visible magnificence, was to spend ever more freely. At the extreme end of the spectrum, as we have seen, this produced the maniacally extravagant adolescents of Essex House; among the more balanced it produced some additional financial strain and a slow decline in the unquestioning reverence of the rest of the population for the peerage, as noble consumption became not so much more conspicuous than that of the élites of city and county.[14]

Buildings illustrate the point. Where bishops had led the country house boom under the Yorkists and Henry VII, noblemen and richer courtiers - many on the way to peerages - took up the lead under Henry VIII. Their greatest constructions are now often lost or ruined - Bradgate, Cowdray, Kenninghall, Mount Surrey, Old Somerset House, Sheffield Manor, Westhorpe - though Layer Marney and Thornbury Castle, neither finished by its builder, survive to suggest the grandeur to which new and old peers alike aspired. Under Elizabeth, however, the construction of great houses seems to have been at once a more open and a more closed activity: many a substantial gentleman had the means and the ambition to put up a far more impressive house than his ancestors would have dreamed of, yet the really spectacular prodigy houses were built almost exclusively by a very narrow circle of leading councillors and courtiers. The bulk of the peerage was thus simultaneously submerged by scores of Chastletons and left behind by a Holdenby or a Theobalds.[15]

Later medieval noblemen had translated income into authority not only by impressive building, but also by spending a significant proportion of their income - averaging a tenth or less, but for some great peers at times of political tension reaching as much as a third - on retaining fees to gentry and yeomen to secure their support in local affairs. First Edward IV and then Henry VII prohibited such retaining by statute, though each seems to have been trying to regulate the system in the Crown's favour rather than to destroy it at a blow. The law must have been sufficiently irksome to be worth evading, for peers responded by expanding their households and creating supernumerary stewardships and other offices on their estates (since the holders of household and administrative posts might be legitimately fee'd under the statutes). Retainers in this sense survived into Elizabeth's reign, as did small retinues maintained under royal licence by councillors and leading peers. But the old style of indenture between lord and retainer for life service in peace and war had disappeared for good, and the Crown supervised the relationship between peers and gentry more closely under the Tudors than it had been able to in the past, limiting the political and even military independence that a well-fee'd retinue might offer.[16]

Rather later than the retinue, the third main vehicle of the late medieval nobility for translating wealth into influence also went into decline. Noble households had long functioned as important social, political and cultural centres at the regional level, but from the early 16th century, their significance gradually declined along with their size. Their role in educating young gentlefolk was usurped by the grammar schools, universities and Inns of Court; their role as centres of distinctive regional cultures was undercut by the diffusion of a more homogeneous high culture, disseminated in print and centred on London: their rationale as centres for the exercise of a lavish hospitality, binding together the social orders under the leadership of the local lord, was dissolved by new ideas of Italianate civility, Stoic individualism, Ciceronian prudence and public relief of the poor; and their natural importance as the setting for the many varieties of social interaction through which a lord's power was articulated in local society decreased as, for many other reasons, that power itself diminished. Under Elizabeth, the greatest peers, especially those in the more conservative areas of the country such as the Stanley Earls of Derby and Somerset Earls of Worcester, still maintained large household staffs, drawn at the upper end from the local gentry; but by her death the downward trend in the size and significance of the great household was firmly established.[17]

The last and most direct link between landholding and authority sprang not from the deployment of landed income, but from each lord's relationship with his tenants. Even in the heyday of the indentured retinue, it was the tenantry that had provided the backbone of the military force at a lord's disposal. It was the tenantry that sat on juries to provide verdicts favourable to a lord's interests, or at its richer end provided biddable voters in parliamentary elections. Tenant loyalty to landlords, willing or coerced, was still a strong force in the Tudor period, as it continued to be for several centuries; but it was being weakened by simultaneous assaults from two directions. Attempts to increase estate income to meet the economic challenges of the period - by enclosure, drainage or other forms of "improvement", or simply by raising rents, if needs be altering the terms of tenure to do so - aroused considerable discontent and resistance, breaking the bonds of respectful obedience owed to landlords who kept to the paternalist model. Some lords did aspire to the ideal. One admirer of Ferdinando Stanley, Lord Strange (c1559-1594) wrote of him:

> Not markes and pounds, but hawkes and houndes,
> Is ever his desire:
> He lays not gether poores mens groundes,
> He is no countrey stroyer:
> He lives in love, of riche and poore,
> Sufficient he doth call his store.

Yet to call one's store sufficient in the inflationary 16th century was to deny oneself the ability to spend on maintaining one's standing in other ways.[18]

Meanwhile the use of tenants and other associates to bring armed force to bear in local disputes, or to pervert justice when sitting on juries, came under sustained attack from the Crown. Henry VII had so little faith in the jury system that he provided means of trial without jury for a number of offences, and the council courts whose work burgeoned in his reign made a speciality of rebuking great men for riotous behaviour or perversion of justice. Something like half the peers appeared before them in Henry's time, usually as defendants, and Cardinal Wolsey and his successors in Star Chamber continued the drive. Such central tribunals, notably the Court of Requests and the equity side of the Exchequer, were also quite prepared to decide disputes between landlords and tenants in favour of the tenants, for reasons of conscience (showing care for the poor) as well as of prudence (avoiding popular disorder) and jurisprudence (the tenants could often provide better evidence of local tenurial customs than the lord, especially when estates had changed hands). As in the operations of Star Chamber, there is also more than a suspicion that to be a great man in itself counted against one, that kings and their ministers were always predisposed to suspect those with influence in local society of using it to the detriment of justice, and that they were none too keen to reinforce a peer's local dominance when they had the chance to leave it in question. As Elizabeth's councillor, Thomas Sackville, Lord Buckhurst (1535/6-1608), told Gilbert Talbot, Earl of Shrewsbury (1552-1616) in 1592, "Your Lordships must remember that in the policy of this Common Wealth, we are not over ready to add encrease of power &

countenance to such great personages as you are". Indeed, Earl Gilbert and
his father Earl George (c1522-1590) fell foul of the Crown in exemplary
fashion in both these areas. In the 1570s and 1580s, the Privy Council backed
George's tenants against the Earl's attempts to increase his income from his
estates in Glossopdale. Then in the 1590s, Gilbert used his tenants to attack
the parks and fishweirs of his local rivals the Stanhopes, only to find the
tenants heavily fined in Star Chamber and himself excluded by a suspicious
government from his ancestors' traditional influence over the administration
of Nottinghamshire.[19]

The Talbots' experiences illustrate the ever increasing importance of royal
favour in the maintenance of a peer's position. Even in the later Middle Ages,
no nobleman could exercise great power in the teeth of royal opposition, but
few needed to try, for kings had by and large to recognize and work through
the local influence held by peers in order to secure effective government. As
the Crown's ability to intervene directly in local affairs increased, so the
terms on which king and nobles negotiated began to alter. Edward IV and
Henry VII greatly expanded the Crown lands, giving themselves a direct
territorial stake in local politics all over the country; the Dissolution carried
the process further. Central supervision of the local judicial system through
the council courts and the assize judges, and careful manipulation of the
membership of the commission of the peace, were matched by a growing flood
of litigation from local courts into the central courts, first Chancery under the
Yorkists, then Star Chamber and Requests under Henry VII and Henry VIII,
then the reviving King's Bench and Common Pleas from the mid-16th
century. Meanwhile, the Council of the North and Council in the Marches
of Wales brought more effective royal justice to the regions hardest to rule
from Westminster.

As the Crown's powers and the benefits it could confer expanded, so the quest
for access to those powers and benefits became ever more concentrated at
court. Peers became not only more dependent upon royal favour for the
maintenance of their own local supremacy, but also more dependent for
access to royal favour upon those with influence at court and in the council.
Already under Edward IV and Henry VII, royal confidants such as William,
Lord Hastings (c1431-83), and Sir Reynold Bray were paid fees by a number
of noblemen anxious to tap into their influence with the monarch; their
successors Wolsey, Cromwell, and Cecil were besieged by begging letters
from peers, often written in the most cringing terms. Contemporaries, for
example, Wolsey's critics, certainly expected noblemen to resent the need for
such subservience, but only a stiff-necked handful resented it sufficiently to
refuse to cooperate with such low-born ministers, and their careers ended on
the block.[20]

One obvious solution was for noblemen to become courtiers. Up to a point,
this met the interests of kings and nobles alike: peers had access to the centre
of power and prestige, and kings had courts made more impressive by a

galaxy of great men. Court culture with its jousts, music, poetry and romantic intrigue attracted and diverted noblemen, while subtly associating them with the Crown's propaganda, as they rode into the lists in outfits covered in Tudor roses from pavilions topped with imperial crowns. Yet most peers wished (and could afford) only to be part-time courtiers, and comparatively few noblemen by birth achieved the ideal combination of a mutually reinforcing influence as a court patron and as a regional magnate: already by Henry VIII's reign, the easiest route to such eminence was to begin as a courtier, as John, Lord Russell (c1485-1555), and Charles Brandon, Duke of Suffolk (c1484-1545), demonstrated. Under Elizabeth, Leicester, Cecil, and Buckhurst confirmed the trend.[21] Those who inherited titles could certainly build a career in royal service at court, in war, and on the Privy Council if they set their minds to it. Henry Courtenay, Marquess of Exeter (c1498-1539) did so under Henry VIII, Henry Fitzalan, Earl of Arundel (1512-80), under Henry, Edward, Mary, and Elizabeth, and Robert Devereux, Earl of Essex (1566-1601), in the last decades of Tudor rule. But the vagaries of politics could destroy all they had achieved, and their family's future too, at least in the short term: Essex and Exeter were both executed and attainted, and their sons had to wait three years and 14 years respectively for restoration; Arundel spent a year of Edward's reign in prison, and was in disgrace for the last 10 years of his life after supporting Norfolk's bid to marry Mary, Queen of Scots. For those whose success was less dangerous, but more moderate, such as Thomas Radcliffe, Earl of Sussex (c1525-83), the rewards of royal service barely covered its costs. For peers who were less successful than these, court life was often a sorry tale of political frustration and financial embarrassment. One in three of those of Elizabeth's peers who had inherited their titles held some office in the royal household or central government, but few of these posts brought real influence, or even sufficient income to balance the costs of life at court.[22]

The Reformation complicated matters further. Already under Henry VIII, some noblemen who opposed his policies in religion were omitted from the commissions of the peace, to which peers were usually appointed as a matter of course in the counties where they held significant landed interests. In the decades that followed, central and local politics alike became increasingly polarized along religious lines, to the point at which perhaps one in three Elizabethan peers refused to conform to the Church of England by 1580 and thereby severely limited the trust the Queen might place in their service. Some conservatives in religion were so powerful that even Protestant regimes could not avoid using them to supervise the implementation of policy, with all the implications the decision had for foot-dragging and the tolerance of noncooperation: yet again the Stanleys are the best example. But for other peers, religious disaffection interacted with the political frustration it brought in its train to bring on rebellion and disaster, for the Protestant Henry Grey, Duke of Suffolk (1517-54), under Mary, as for the Catholics Thomas Percy, Earl of Northumberland (1528-72), Charles Nevile, Earl of Westmorland (1542/3-1601) and Leonard, self-styled Lord Dacre of Gilsland (?-1573) in the Northern Rising of 1569 against Elizabeth.[23]

For all this, it was still in the royal interest to be able to rely on a single competent and trustworthy manager of local affairs in each area of the country, especially when such a person could build, in his exercise of delegated royal authority, on the natural authority in local society which broad landholdings, high social status, and a family tradition of local leadership could provide. Thus Henry VII, often characterized as the anti-noble king *par excellence*, ruled through noblemen he trusted in regions where such men were available: Thomas Stanley, Earl of Derby (c1435-1504), in the north-west; John De Vere, Earl of Oxford (1442-1513), in East Anglia; Jasper Tudor, Duke of Bedford (1431-95) in Wales, Giles Lord Daubeny (1451/2-1508) in Somerset; George Talbot, Earl of Shrewsbury (1468-1538) in the North Midlands, and so on. Henry VIII deliberately established Russell and Brandon as regional magnates in sensitive areas, and from Edward VI's reign, lord lieutenants of counties were appointed with increasing regularity to lead the militia and coordinate local government more generally. Twenty four of the 30 lord lieutenants serving in 1569 were peers, 19 of the 22 serving in 1587, though many of the noblemen appointed were also privy councillors.

Some came from the great houses whose local dominance was such that their selection could hardly be avoided: the Stanleys in Lancashire, the Talbots in Derbyshire. But others represented the insertion of a courtier and councillor without a landed base (without even the management of a significant Crown estate in the area) into the structure of local politics, in a way inconceivable in the later Middle Ages. Thus Elizabeth's cousin, Henry Carey, Lord Hunsdon (1526-96), was Lord Lieutenant of Norfolk and Suffolk from 1585 to 1596 even though he held almost no land in either county and was often away on royal business in the north. From their earliest days, the regional councils offered similarly ambiguous opportunities to peers. There were a number of noble presidents, especially of the Council in the North: but those chosen, from John de la Pole, Earl of Lincoln (c1462-1487), under Richard III to Henry Hastings Earl of Huntingdon (1536-95) and Thomas Cecil, Lord Burghley (1542-1623), under Elizabeth, tended not to have lands or local interests in the area of the council's jurisdiction. There were exceptions, such as the northern presidency of Francis Talbot, Earl of Shrewsbury (1500-60), or that of William Herbert, Earl of Pembroke (c1506-70), and his son Henry (c1538-1601) in the Marches, but even they each held significant territories in areas outside Yorkshire and Wales. Noble presidents of the regional councils were undoubtedly powerful men, but the power they exercised was in general less personal and more passing than that of the great regional lords they replaced.[24]

On the councils, and as lord lieutenants supervising their deputy-lieutenants, Tudor noblemen had to work with and through the gentry. This was nothing new. The third great key to noble power in the later Middle Ages, besides landownership and royal favour, was a peer's relationship with the knights, esquires, and gentlemen of the area where he hoped to hold sway. His ability to offer them the kind of leadership they would respect and cooperate in was probably a greater test of his competence than his ability to draw income and influence from his estates, or his ability not to offend the king. From the 14th century, it was the gentry that ran local government as justices of the peace, sheriffs, and escheators, and in the Tudor period their role became ever more important as the responsibilities of the JPs increased, *ad hoc* royal commissions such as those for the Dissolution multiplied, the prerogative courts commissioned gentlemen to interview witnesses or arbitrate settlements between litigants, and the growing stature of Parliament made seats in the Commons ever more desirable. At the same time, the "good lordship" of noblemen became less indispensable to the gentry because the expansion of the Crown estate, the growth of the court, and the extension of the royal administration provided ever more opportunities for direct service to the monarch for the ambitious (often legally-trained) gentry who had been a central element in bastard feudal affinities. Moreover, the rise of the prerogative courts devalued noble lordship to the gentry in two ways: the support of armed force in disputes was of considerably less benefit if its only result was a summons to the Star Chamber, and the resolution of disputes among gentlemen by the arbitration of a great lord - one of the primary peace-keeping devices of the later Middle Ages - was of less vital necessity. Finally, the refusal of monarchs from Henry VII onwards to conduct national politics largely by the arbitration of differences between noblemen, leaving them to represent the interests of the areas of their lordship, decreased the representative value of such lordship to the gentry. The result was that peers who wished to exercise local political power under the Tudors had to deal even more skilfully with their gentry neighbours than had their ancestors, and in general they managed to rule only as *primi inter pares*.

Three classes of peers provided partial exceptions to this generalization. First, there were the most prominent courtiers and councillors, whose power in the state reinforced their local leadership, as that of the Cecils did in Elizabethan Hertfordshire. Second, there were those of the landed regional magnates who were sufficiently flexible to continue to exercise the consultative and representative leadership that marked the best of late medieval good lordship, who drew into association with themselves those who would in any case have been the leaders of gentry society: yet again the Stanleys are the best studied instance. Third, there was a new breed, what we might call leaders by ideology, the forerunners of the parliamentarian and Whig peers of the century to come. The Elizabethan Earl of Huntingdon in Leicestershire and the north swayed more hearts as the figurehead of the godly Protestant interest than his acres or his offices would warrant, just as the Rich Earls of Warwick did in early Stuart Essex.[25] Most alarming for the Tudor regime, but probably most brittle, was an alternative variety of ideological leadership, that espoused by the ill-fated Earl of Essex. This promised reform of government by the reassertion of an aristocratic supremacy based on intensifying antiquarian research into medieval English politics, and on classical republican models of incorruptible senatorship; it opposed its adherents' quest for honour and anti-Spanish militancy to the cool legalism of its *arriviste* opponents, typified by the Cecils. Yet it was more than a factional platform, for it seemed to aspire to a renegotiation of the Tudors' relationship with the nobility. As Essex put it, "to serve as a servant and a slave I know not".[26]

The Essexians' politics were unrealistic and their history was not much better. It tended towards the varieties of myth espoused by such aristocratic republicans of the next century as Algernon Sydney, who thought that medieval noblemen had been powerful but responsible checks on bad rulers until the Tudors had seduced them into effeminacy to neutralize them as an obstruction to despotism.[27] The truth, as usual, lay somewhere between his good barons and the Venetian ambassador's secretary's bad barons with whom we began. But both observers' reports of the death of the late medieval aristocracy were premature. The nobility's role had undoubtedly changed between 1485 and 1603, and in some ways changed to the detriment of noblemen's power and self-respect. Essex could not have enticed seven other peers, including nearly a quarter of the earls of England, into his conspiracy if it had not. But most peers adapted themselves to changing times with some success. Deprived of unchallenged local hegemony, they made more use of their places as JPs. Deprived of access to the Privy Council, they attended more regularly in the House of Lords.[28] Deprived of automatic command in war, many of them sought the experience or education to prove themselves worthy of it. Deprived of unquestioned and visible social superiority, they cultivated the virtues necessary to demonstrate it. They were, as succeeding chapters will show, by no means a spent force.

Footnotes to this Chapter may be found on pages 194-6.

5: John Miller

The English kill their kings – from Divine Right to parlimentary monarchy: 1603-1714: the Stuarts

WHEN ONE tries to conjure up an image of the Stuart peerage, no clear picture comes to mind. For the 15th century, one has the great bastard feudal magnate - say a Warwick the King Maker (or a Richard of Gloucester). The centre of a great household and a great affinity, the possessor of a string of castles, such a magnate wielded great power over men, a power that could take military form, but which also permeated local government and especially the administration of justice. For the 18th century, one has an equally clear, but very different image. Now the archetypal nobleman is a Whig aristocrat, with massive landed estates and great country houses, designed for elegance and comfort rather than defence. The power of such a magnate - of a Duke of Newcastle or Bedford or Devonshire - rested on a solid foundation of landed wealth, but was expressed through the medium of control of parliamentary seats and access to the much enlarged patronage resources of the State.

Clearly, 18th century noblemen wielded great power. Equally clearly, that power was very different in kind from that of their 15th century forebears. The period in between had seen important changes in the nature and role of the nobility, changes which had required a measure of adaptation. This may explain why it is not easy to conjure up an "archetypal" Tudor or Stuart peer.[1] Indeed, if the 17th century calls to mind one image more than any other it is the execution of Charles I - which was, of course, followed by the abolition of the Monarchy and of the House of Lords. These events should not, however, lead us to assume that there was widespread hostility to either the Monarchy or the peerage. The abolition of Monarchy and Lords was in each case a pragmatic response, the first to the fact that those in power deemed the King too dangerous to live, the second to the fact that the number of peers actually sitting in the upper house had now dwindled to farcical proportions. Even before Pride's Purge, on 6 December 1648, attendance averaged about a dozen; after the Purge, it fell to as few as three. With the abolition of the upper house, peers were eligible to seek election to the Commons; three - the Earls of Salisbury and Pembroke and Lord Howard of Escrick - actually did so.[2] Although the Rump Parliament resolved in 1649 that "the House of Peers in Parliament is useless and dangerous and ought to be abolished" not all of England's new rulers were dogmatically opposed to the peerage. Pride's Purge and Charles I's execution were carried through by a small minority, centred on the New Model Army, which was highly untypical of those who had opposed the King in the First Civil War: indeed, Pride's Purge was a direct response to the refusal of the majority in Parliament to break off negotiations with the King. Oliver Cromwell was eager to persuade friendly peers to sit in what became known as the Nominated (or Barebones') Parliament and in 1657 agreed to the creation of the "Other House", with its own, Cromwellian peerage.[3] Even among the small minority of hardline republicans, some had ambivalent attitudes towards the peerage. Algernon Sydney was bitterly critical of monarchy: the courts of kings (he claimed) encouraged fawning, flattery, and corruption. But he was also immensely proud of his noble blood - he was a younger son of the Earl of Leicester - and above all of his descent from Sir Philip Sydney. He argued that republics allowed men of true nobility, true merit and virtue (like himself) to achieve positions of power, unhampered by royal favouritism, and that republics (like the Dutch) were particularly successful in that traditional preserve of the nobility - war.[4]

Having said all that, no study of the Stuart peerage can ignore the Civil War, nor do I intend to do so. The basic issue I wish to address is the transformation of the nobility from a military to a civilian élite. Between the Hundred Years' War and the 18th century, the main criterion for entry into the nobility changed from military service to political and administrative service, and nobles came to exercise power not through brute force, but through manipulation - and above all their access to the power and patronage of the State. The nobility remained a service élite, but the nature of that service changed, as service in an increasingly large and complex governmental machine came to eclipse military service as the most common avenue of access to the peerage. Insofar as military service still offered a way into the peerage, it was service in the armed forces organized and directed by the Crown, not, as in the Hundred Years' War, as semi-autonomous *condottieri*. In the process, the nobles' power came to depend more on the central government and less on their own landed and other resources in the localities and the powers of coercion and intimidation which those resources gave them. If politics in the 15th century centred on the relations of the king and a restricted group of magnates, who alone could maintain some kind of order in the localities, by the 18th century, politics, freed from the threat of armed insurrection, centred on the court, the administration, and Parliament.

In this chapter, I shall address two main issues. First, the changing composition of the peerage: who became peers and why? Second, how did the nature of aristocratic power change in the Stuart period?

I want to begin by considering those who held English peerages between 1603 and 1714, with particular reference to two issues. The first is relatively straightforward: the number of creations and promotions and the effect of these on the overall size and balance of the peerage. There are three possible complications. (i) Restorations and confirmations: I have counted these as new creations, partly because they added to the existing number of titles, partly because they are not always easy to distinguish from new creations. For example, after Viscount Stafford had been executed for treason and attainted in 1680, James II created his son Earl of Stafford - in principle a new creation, but clearly with a strong measure of restitution for what James regarded as an injustice. (ii) Creations for life: I have not included these, on the grounds that they were temporary. (iii) Members of the Royal Family: I have excluded legitimate members of the Royal Family partly because the title of (say) a prince of Wales was only temporary, partly because many of these peers were very short-lived: no less than four sons of the future James II were created dukes of Cambridge; none lived beyond four years. Illegitimate royal children are included because they had the opportunity to found new noble houses and because, at least in the case of Charles II's bastards, they had an important impact on the overall shape of the peerage - and especially its upper reaches. Two final points: where holders of Scots or Irish peerages were raised to the English peerage, I have treated these as new creations; where one individual received a series of promotions (for example, the first Duke of Leeds) I have counted each of them.

Figures for peerage creations and restorations cannot tell the full story, however. Because in most peerages, the title passed by primogeniture, many were short-lived, ending when the male line failed. K B Macfarlane calculated that in the 14th and 15th centuries roughly a quarter of peerage titles became extinct every 25 years. Nor did this situation change very much in the 17th century: about a third of peerages became extinct between 1649 and 1685.[5] In other words, in looking at the peerage we are looking at a constantly shifting group of families, including a few who have been around for a very long time and many more who are first or second generation peers. Many of these will, of course, have ancient pedigrees, real or fabricated. But the proportion of genuinely ancient peerages will at any given time be small and the proportion of newcomers will be high. For this reason, it is difficult to see the peerage as a distinct social or economic "class". Well over half the peerages extant in 1642 had been created since 1603. In terms of wealth, culture, and way of life, the peerage should best be seen as a small section of the landed élite, distinguished from the rest by the possession of titles of nobility. The peers were the major and the gentry the minor nobility.[6] In the words of Trevor Roper:

> Peers and gentry had, on their different levels, the same problems, the same ambitions, the same conventions, the same tastes. Both were landlords....They built - according to their capacity - similar houses; they were buried in similar tombs. It was an aristocratic age and the gentry accepted - in general - the standards of value and conduct of the aristocracy.[7]

The large areas of common ground between peers and gentry have led historians to use the term "aristocracy" ambivalently, sometimes meaning the peerage alone, sometimes meaning the peers and greater gentry. Here, for convenience of analysis, I shall be talking only of the peerage.

This brings us to the second principal theme of this section, which attempts to be qualitative rather than quantitative: what sort of people were these newcomers to the peerage? This is often not an easy question, because several different factors may come in to play. First, there was the question of pedigree, and of noble (or at least gentle) blood. To quote Francis Bacon:

"New nobility is but the act of power, but ancient nobility is the act of time".[8] On one hand, this meant that the elevation of a mere "sheepmaster", like the first Lord Spencer, or a merchant like Cranfield, could be seen as devaluing the peerage. Anthony à Wood complained that it was ridiculous to praise the birth of Lord Crew, whose father had been "an ordinary gent. and a grand rebel and Presbyterian".[9] On the other hand, some creations were clearly designed to continue (or revive) peerages which had failed in the direct male line or followed the inheritance of an important noble patrimony: thus John Holles, Earl of Clare, was created Duke of Newcastle in 1694 after inheriting many of the lands of the previous (Cavendish) Duke. Other examples of titles' being continued or revived include the Baronies of Ferrers, Conway, Lansdowne of Bideford, and Windsor.[10] Similarly, a number of peerages were created to honour the most distinguished members of the nobility: note, for example, the peerages (the Baronies of Butler of Moor Park and Butler of Weston) bestowed on the sons of the first Duke of Ormonde (though the two are better known to historians by their Irish titles of the Earls of Ossory and Arran).

A second vital consideration was wealth. Edward Chamberlayne, whose reference works became best-sellers, wrote that all peers "should have a convenient estate and value of lands of inheritance for the support of their honours and the king's service".[11] Spencer and Cranfield had no problems on that score, but others had. It was expected that a newly ennobled peer should be able to live in a style appropriate to his rank. In many cases, this created no difficulties: the chosen individual already possessed massive estates or had built up a tidy fortune from government service. Others needed some help, from the Crown. Naturally, Charles II took care to provide for his natural children, but most monarchs felt the need to endow distinguished public servants with modest means or to help out members of the nobility who had fallen on hard times. Thus William III granted land to Lord Chancellor Somers and Queen Anne did the same for Chancellor of the Exchequer Bingley, to enable them to support their newly acquired titles. Charles II continued the pension of £500 granted by his predecessors to Lord Hunsdon.[12] Perhaps the saddest comment on the need for wealth came from the fourth Earl of Marlborough. His father had made a career in the law and had risen to the post of Lord Treasurer. Now the Earl claimed that his relations had sold off all the family estates, so that he had no land and only a thatched house to live in. He, therefore, wrote to Lord Treasurer Danby offering to part with his Earldom on reasonable terms, perhaps to one of Danby's kinsmen; he could then use the proceeds to repurchase at least part of his estate which would give him enough to support his other, lesser title of Baron Ley.[13] Danby's response cannot have been positive as the title remained with Marlborough until he died.

A third criterion for creation or promotion was state service: in the army or navy, in high government or court office, or (less often) in local government. Defining high office is not easy: while there is no doubting that a lord treasurer or secretary of state or general or admiral held top office, others (not least those in the household) are harder to assess. To complicate matters, by the end of the period, many a new peer was, or had been, (say) a privy councillor, a commissioner of the treasury, a colonel in the army, a lord lieutenant and *custos rotulorum,* and a lord of the bedchamber: individually, perhaps, none of these amounted to a high office; collectively, they surely mark that peer out as an important office-holder. (The only local offices that I have taken as being significant in themselves are the presidencies of the Councils in the North and the Marches of Wales, which were abolished in 1641). One area of service which did not lead to rapid promotion was the law. Only one serving judge became a peer; solicitor and attorney-generals had to remain in the Commons; and the posts of lord keeper and even lord chancellor did not necessarily guarantee quick promotion.[14]

Two further types of criteria need to be considered. The first is royal favour pure and simple: it is difficult to find any other grounds for Charles II's creation of Charles Berkeley as Earl of Falmouth or William III's of Keppel as Earl of Albemarle. The other is politics. A peerage could be a reward for political services, or as a bait to win the support of a powerful individual. Peerages could be created with a view to strengthening the court or government side in the House of Lords, as when Charles I summoned the eldest sons of five (loyal) peers to the Lords in the Short Parliament in 1640 or Anne created 12 new peers (actually 10 new creations plus two eldest sons) at the beginning of 1712.[15] Peerages could also be the reward for loyalty in the civil war, or for services rendered in bringing about the Restoration in 1660 or the Revolution of 1688. Last but not least, with the growth of party divisions after 1679 - and still more after 1689 - a change of party fortunes in the Commons and the construction of a new ministry could also mean a small crop of peerages for the supporters of the new men at the top.

With so many variables involved, to ascribe a particular reason for a particular creation or promotion is bound to be somewhat arbitrary: sometimes several criteria are involved, to a greater or lesser degree. To complicate matters further, peerages may have been granted to one person in order to honour another: this was clearly true of the husbands of Charles II's daughters, but other examples can also be found. The titles of Thomas, Lord Darcy of Chiche, Viscount Colchester and Earl Rivers (granted between 1613 and 1626) were intended to pass to his son-in-law, Sir Thomas Savage, gentleman of the bedchamber. In much the same way, the Earldom of Feversham, granted to the 77-year-old Sir George Sondes in 1676, was intended to pass to his son-in-law Baron Duras (and indeed it did, the following year).[16] Nevertheless three general conclusions may be advanced.

(1)   The peerage grew substantially larger in the course of the 17th century. When James I came to the Throne there were about 60 peers. By 1640, that figure had almost exactly doubled and another surge of creations took the total to almost 150 by 1646. After a lull during which natural

wastage took its toll, there was another surge of creations taking the total back to between 150 and 160 late in Charles II's reign. Thereafter, it fluctuated slightly at just over the 160 mark, with a brief surge to 176 in 1715, thanks to the 12 new peers of 1712 and a clutch of creations and promotions on the accession of George I. It is clear, then, that the peerage almost trebled in size during our period.[17]

(2)   The higher peerage ranks became noticeably more thickly populated as the period went on. In 1603 there were no non-royal dukes. Buckingham (in 1623) became the first since the execution of Norfolk in 1572. Charles I created only one - his kinsman the Duke of Richmond, who was already Duke of Lennox in the Scottish peerage. Charles II revived two dukedoms (Norfolk and Somerset) and conferred hereditary ducal titles on six of his children and one mistress (Cleveland: Portsmouth's title was for life only). Apart from these, he created four new non-royal dukes: Albemarle, the architect of the Restoration, and three men whose contribution (or that of their families) to the royal cause had been enormous: Newcastle, Beaufort, and Ormonde. James II created only one Duke - his bastard son Berwick - and the real inflation of dukedoms began only after 1688: William III created seven and Anne eight. Thus the number of dukes increased from none in 1603 to 22 in 1709.[18] In much the same way, the proportion of earls to barons rose from about 1:2 in 1603 to slightly more than 1:1 at the end of our period; it had been higher; in 1628 there were about 65 earls to 50 barons.[19]

(3)   I would suggest that the period saw the development of a nobility based on government service, and particularly non-military service. Before the reign of Henry VIII, the Crown's administration had been run mainly by churchmen, who (while often members of noble families) could not themselves found noble dynasties. Those who entered the nobility did so mainly as a result of service in war or personal favour. In the 1530s and 1540s, Henry started to create a new nobility, recruited from civilian, lay administrators: families like the Wriothesleys and Russells, Pagets and Paulets. There were those who made their names through war as well, but all made their way through royal service and many profited from the plunder of the Church and the minority of Edward VI. Elizabeth interrupted this development: only one of her hardworking and devoted councillors - Burghley - was raised to the peerage during her reign: the rest had to await James's accession. Elizabeth's other creations owed more to the noble blood of the recipients than to any record of service: they were designed to replace or revive old titles, not to reward her own servants.[20] James I's first batch of creations read like a rollcall of Elizabeth's government and high command: Robert Cecil, Sydney, Knollys, Wotton, Danvers, Mountjoy - and throughout the Stuart period a significant proportion of creations and promotions consisted of men with a proven record of administrative or (less often) military or diplomatic service. With the rapid growth of the administration and armed forces after 1688, the trend became noticeably more marked.

This move towards a "service nobility" was, however, hampered or distorted by two factors. The first was the influence of the first Duke of Buckingham, whose greed, concern for his family, and increasing intolerance of criticism skewed the process of creation and promotion: no other individual came close to dominating the process of ennoblement in the way that Buckingham did. The second was the Civil War: between 1641 and 1646, Charles I's creations and promotions were mostly of men who served in the Royalist armies or contributed financially to the royal cause - and as that cause became desperate, those contributions did not have to be all that generous. Moreover, the bulk of Charles II's creations in 1660-1 and to a lesser extent thereafter - were either loyal Royalists or former Parliamentarians who had seen the light and helped to bring about the Restoration - most strikingly Monck, but also men such as Holles, Ashley Cooper, Annesley, and Crew.

Let us now consider chronologically the changing shape of the peerage under the Stuarts.[21] The first part of James I's reign - from 1603-15, before the rise of Buckingham - can perhaps best be seen as a restorative exercise. On one hand, James compensated for Elizabeth's stinginess, particularly to her own servants: as stated above, these found their reward under her successor. Of his 26 creations, at least nine held high offices and a further six had distinguished military records. On the other, he restored or confirmed eight titles: he reestablished the Earldom of Essex and restored several others (for example the Earldom of Southampton) forfeited after the Essex rebellion in 1601. Few of these creations failed to meet contemporary criteria. John, Lord Petre, was a Catholic, but was descended from Sir William Petre, mid-Tudor secretary of state, who had built up a massive landed fortune, worth about £13,000 a year in 1638.[22] The first Lord Spencer might be a sheepmaster, but was also said to be "the greatest moneyed man in England"; he was also just about unique in building up a really large landed fortune from efficient estate management, without the benefit of lucrative public office, fortunate marriages, or mineral deposits.[23] John Haryngton was raised to the peerage in recognition of the large estates built up by his family through a combination of office-holding and marriage. He entertained James on his way south on 1603 and was given charge of Princess Elizabeth - an expensive honour which severely depleted his estate. His elevation may also have owed something to the fact that (as James noted) he was descended from the Bruces.[24] Thomas Knyvett was created a baron in 1607, apparently as a reward for his role in thwarting the Gunpowder Plot.[25]

In general, then, James's early creations show restraint and respect for English preconceptions. There were two Catholics (the second being Arundell of Wardour, who had a distinguished military record), and only four creations of Scots, one of them indirect.[26] There was one case of purchase: William Cavendish paid Arabella Stuart for his Viscountcy, the granting of which she had received from the King.[27] Perhaps most striking of all, there were only seven promotions (and two of those were Robert Cecil, as he moved first to a viscount and then an earl: as he held three high offices - lord treasurer, secretary of state, and master of the wards - three honours in two years cannot in his case be seen as excessive).

The contrast between this period and the ascendancy of Buckingham, between 1615 and 1628, could not be more striking. In the second period, the number of creations was 57 (as against 26) and the number of promotions 52 (as against seven). In 1615, barons still outnumbered earls by about two to one; by 1628 there were more earls than barons. Many of the new peers, in fact, held important offices - at least 14 of the creations and 17 of the promotions (although these were often the same people). (It should be added that this period saw a very high turnover in the major offices of state - in complete contrast to the stability and continuity of Elizabeth's reign).[28] Only a handful had any sort of military credentials and only two - Lord Vere and Viscount Wimbledon - clearly owed their creation to their military prowess.

Far more significant as an influence on creation was some sort of connection with Buckingham. As he advanced through the ranks of the peerage, and established an ever more all-pervasive influence over James and Charles, so his family advanced with him. His brothers became Earl of Anglesey and Viscount Purbeck; his mother was made a countess (for life); one brother-in-law became Viscount Feilding and Earl of Denbigh; another became Viscount Mandeville and Earl of Manchester; the first Lord Ley, father of the unfortunate Earl of Marlborough mentioned earlier, married a half-sister of Buckingham, as did Lord Boteler; Lord Howard of Escrick married a niece, Lionel Cranfield, Earl of Middlesex, a cousin; Lord Dunsmore married the daughter of Buckingham's half sister.[29] In some of these cases, other factors - office-holding and purchase - were involved as well, but overall kinship with the Duke became a crucial factor in peerage creations.

Nor did his influence end there. At first, he drew all sorts - Papists and Puritans, supporters and critics of the court - into his patronage network; as criticism of his conduct grew, he increasingly concentrated his patronage on those he thought loyal to himself. Either way, his search for support influenced the grant of peerages. Thus in 1621, Edward Montagu was made a baron in an effort to win him over to the court; in 1624, Buckingham secured a promotion to viscount for a long-time critic, Lord Saye and Sele, who was temporarily at one with him over the need for war with Spain.[30] After his impeachment in 1626, the Duke was clearly determined to ensure that he did not lack supporters in the Lords. There were no less than 20 creations in 1627-8, few of men of obvious distinction: only Lord Keeper Coventry, Chancellor of the Exchequer Weston, and (perhaps) Comptroller of the Household Savile held senior offices. (Savile was also a privy councillor and vice-president of the Council of the North). Some, such as Lords Goring and Maynard (both gentlemen of the Privy Chamber), were long-time courtiers. Others had held only local office - for example, Lords Poulett and Mohun. A former critic of the Court, Sir Thomas Wentworth, was made a baron in 1628 with the aim of making him "the King's creature". He was promoted to viscount before the end of the year.[31]

If Buckingham damaged the prestige of the peerage by flooding it with his kinsmen and supporters, still more damaging was his sale of peerages. The full extent of this practice is hard to gauge. In a few cases, the transactions appear in official Exchequer accounts. More often they were clandestine or indirect: the peerage could be granted in return for the sale (or grant) of an estate to Buckingham or a royal favourite. Thus Lady Finch became a viscountess after agreeing to give up Copt Hall and a set of tapestries to the Duchess of Lennox. Sometimes the purchase money was used to pay the costs of an embassy abroad; often it went into the pocket of Buckingham, one of his family, or some other courtier. Altogether, at least 18 creations and eight promotions definitely or probably involved an element of purchase.[32]

The sale of honours could not but tarnish the image of the peerage, especially when seen in the context of a growing and justifiable belief that Buckingham's regime was "corrupt".[33] It does not necessarily follow that those who paid for peerages were unworthy of the honour. The ability to purchase a peerage was evidence of wealth. Most new peers, whether they purchased their titles, came from families which had accumulated wealth, often over several generations, from government service or the law: the Finches and Stanhopes, for example. John Holles was no friend to Buckingham and did not approve in principle of the sale of peerages; he nevertheless purchased first a barony and then the Earldom of Clare and in terms of wealth and government service clearly merited a peerage: he had a worthy military record and had been Comptroller of the Household to Prince Henry. As he remarked, if others less deserving than he were buying peerages, why shouldn't he?[34] Wealth, however, was not the only criterion for admission to the peerage. Blood and personal merit counted too. No less than four peers of merchant origins were created in the 1620s - four more than in the whole 18th century. Cranfield held high office, as Master of the Wards and then Lord Treasurer, but the other three did not. William Craven, who had inherited a massive fortune, was created a baron at the age of 19, in return for £7,000. (Ironically, he went on to a long and distinguished military career). Paul Bayning was created, in quick succesion, a baron and a viscount, apparently in return for a "loan" of £15,000 to the Crown, which does not seem to have been repaid. Finally, it seems possible that the creation of Sir Baptist Hicks, financial agent to the King, as Viscount Campden may have owed something to purchase, but the evidence is inconclusive.[35] To make matters worse, there is more than a hint that Bayning's payments were made under duress and there is a similar (and clearer) element of blackmail in the sale of a barony to the fabulously rich Cornish tin magnate, Richard Robartes, who had earlier been forced to "lend" the King £12,000 under the threat of prosecution for usury and now paid another £10,000 for his barony.[36]

The sale of peerages did not only dilute the blue blood of the peerage. Some were sold to Catholics such as Robert Dormer (keeper of the royal hawks and falcons), John Roper (whose office as Clerk of Enrolments of King's Bench was worth £3,500 a year) and Thomas Brudenell. Others went to dubious characters: Philip, Lord Stanhope of Shelford, had twice been indicted for sodomy and had recently been pardoned for a murder committed in his presence and by his command. Not all purchasers could be seen as unworthy: some even held high office, like Henry Montagu, who paid £20,000 for a viscountcy and the Lord Treasurership: unfortunately for him, he lost the latter within a year.[37] Montagu had for some years been Chief Justice of King's Bench (and had married Buckingham's sister), but it still needed money to procure him a peerage. In general, indeed, even at this time when the fountain of creations was gushing freely, government service alone was no guarantee of quick promotion. Only when Francis Bacon was promoted from Lord Keeper to Lord Chancellor was he raised to the peerage. The experience of Lord Ley and Lord Coventry was similar: the former was ennobled on becoming Lord Treasurer, the latter three years after becoming Lord Keeper. For lawyers, as always, promotion was slow.[38]

For a wide range of reasons - the manner of his peerage creations, the persons who were favoured, the general style of his government - Buckingham's impact on the image of the peerage was disastrous. I am not fully convinced by Lawrence Stone's argument that the inflation of honours was in itself damaging; the way the inflation came about must have been. Charles I was well aware of this. After Buckingham's assassination, the flood of peerages slowed to a trickle: the next 12 years saw only six creations and four promotions, mostly of men holding important offices. Only in 1641 did the flow of creations resume, as the King tried to rally support first against a highly critical Parliament and then to fight a civil war. The years 1641-6 saw 32 creations, three restorations and 10 promotions. Of these, five were of high office-holders and 23 went to men who either fought in the royal armies or contributed financially to the war effort. There seem to have been three cases of purchase, Lords Capel (possibly), Lucas, and Newport.[39] Four titles went to Catholics, four to Irishmen or Scots and one to a Dutchman, Lord Reede, who had tried, on behalf of the States General, to mediate between King and Parliament. In some cases, like that of Lord Leigh of Stoneleigh, assistance to the war effort seems to have been limited, but such cases were more the exception than the rule. If some of the new peers were lacking in terms of wealth or birth, their loyalty made up for it and the King rewarded them in one of the few ways he still could, with titles of nobility. In the exceptional circumstances of civil war, indeed, the peerage temporarily recovered much of its military character, but there were also other types of creation, like that of Humble Ward, the son of a goldsmith, who played no active part in the war and was created a baron in recognition of his wife's inheriting the title of Baroness Dudley.[40]

Between 1646 and 1660 there were only six peerage creations (one of them of a Dutchman). The other five were either of members of Charles II's court in exile or active Royalists, one of whom, Lord Langdale, was too impoverished to attend the Coronation in 1661.[41] The King's return brought a flurry of peerages: 16 creations, two restorations, and two promotions in 1660-1. This was not surprising: a new reign and a coronation always meant a sudden rush of new peers, while the circumstances of Charles's restoration meant that he felt obliged to reward Royalists and those Presbyterians who had helped to bring about his return. Of the 20 people just mentioned, at least 17 now held high office or had contributed to the Royalist cause or the Restoration: in some cases, all three. While there might be partisan grounds for complaining of the favour to former Parliamentarians - part of that indemnity to the King's enemies and oblivion to his friends of which Royalists complained - it would be hard to argue that Charles was motivated by anything other than a desire to reward service.

After 1661, the pace of creations slowed appreciably. The next 19 years saw 28 creations and 14 promotions, together with five creations for life (all women). According to Clarendon, Charles had decided by 1665 that the peerage was already too large and that in future he would do no more than make good natural wastage[42] and he seems largely to have adhered to this policy. The one notable exception was in his provision for his mistresses, their children, and the spouses of those children, who together accounted for 12 of the 42 creations and promotions in these years. Of the remaining 30, 12 went to holders of high office, two to leading military figures and three to important figures at court. Others went to two of Ormonde's sons, while the younger brother of the mentally disturbed Duke of Norfolk, and de facto head of the Howard clan, was created first a baron and then an earl. With the exception of the royal bastards, therefore, Charles's peerage creations were very much in line with conventional expectations. Promotion was, as always, slow for lawyers: Heneage Finch was made a baron a year after becoming Lord Keeper and was raised to the Earldom of Nottingham six years after promotion to Lord Chancellor.[43] Even the favours showered on his children were not indefensible by contemporary standards. Ormonde might complain (with justification) of the excessive expense which they involved, but no one could deny their royal blood and, as it turned out, several went on to serve the post-Revolution regime with distinction - and even became Whigs.[44]

Like his father, Charles II stepped up the pace of peerage creations in response to the threat of civil war. Although the Exclusion Crisis of 1679-81 did not lead to civil war, Charles was convinced that it had been a close thing. The years 1681-4 saw 11 creations and 14 promotions. Only two went to the King's own family and seven to the holders of high office. The bulk went to trusted individuals, mostly existing peers of proven loyalty and substantial territorial influence: this is especially true of the 10 promotions in 1682. At their head was the former Marquess of Worcester, the first Protestant in his family, who now became Duke of Beaufort and set out to use his vast influence in South Wales and the borders to crush Whiggery and Dissent, especially in the towns.[45] Other new creations - the Earls of Abingdon and Plymouth, Gainsborough and Holderness - were expected to perform a similar function in their own localities.

James II, in his short reign, was responsible for only seven creations and one promotion. These included Judge Jeffreys - for once a lawyer raised to the peerage before becoming Lord Chancellor - and John Churchill - as well as the King's bastard son, the Duke of Berwick (later a marshal of France - the Churchill blood may have counted for something here) and two husbands of royal bastard daughters (Derwentwater and Waldegrave). Five of the eight were Catholics. The next surge of creations came with William III's accession and coronation: six creations and 11 promotions in 1689-90 and a total of 20 creations and 22 promotions in the reign as a whole, with a particular bunching (eight promotions) with the installation of a Whig ministry in 1694. As already mentioned, these promotions included seven dukes. Of the 42 creations and promotions, at least 16 were of top office-holders and another five of leading figures in the army or navy. Six (at least) had played an important role in the Revolution of 1688; at least four can be ascribed primarily to politics. (Some individuals appear in more than one category). Three were Dutch, one Irish, and the nationality of another, Schomberg, is a matter for debate. In short, most of the peerages distributed by William were for service of some sort; relatively few reflected personal favour only. (Those to Keppel and Edward Villiers are exceptions). Only one, that to Lord Barnard of Barnard's Castle, had a whiff of corruption about it.[46]

Much the same can be said of Anne's reign. She created 27 peers and promoted 15. For much of the reign, she was more sparing than William: creations and promotions were bunched in 1706 (notably the commissioners who negotiated the Union with Scotland) and above all in 1711-12 (a total of 15 creations and three promotions, including the 12 Tory peers created to overturn the Whig majority in the Lords). Of the 42 creations and promotions, at least 22 were of holders of high office, plus four leading figures in the army and navy. Fourteen (at least) can be ascribed directly to political considerations. Four went to Scots, three of them already dukes in the Scottish peerage. Under Anne, cases of men raised primarily as a result of personal favour have almost disappeared: perhaps the only examples are Lord Masham (the husband of the Queen's confidante Abigail Hill) and more bizarrely, Lord Hervey, a Whig ennobled under a Tory ministry, for which the Duchess of Marlborough claimed the credit.[47] Even so, blood and broad acres counted for at least as much as merit. These alone explain the rise of the dim and malodorous Earl of Kent to first a marquessate and then a dukedom and, together with their political affiliations, help explain the dukedoms granted to Rutland and Montagu.[48] By contrast, the slowness of the rise to the peerage of Orford, Somers, and Charles Montagu (Lord Halifax), together with the slow promotion of Godolphin from baron (1684) to earl (1706) has to be put down to their relatively humble origins and/or estates. As always, the criteria for entry into the peerage were not uniform.

These last comments should warn against talking too glibly about the emergence of a service nobility. Nevertheless, the history of peerage creations and promotions over the period as a whole helps to explain how and why the peerage regained and maintained respect (and, perhaps, self-respect) after the excesses of Buckingham. More did not necessarily mean worse: quality was a more important consideration than quantity. The excesses of 1615-28 - and to a lesser extent 1641-6 - were an aberration which could be remedied by the more responsible policies followed by Charles II and his successors, helped by natural wastage. Moreover, the political world within which the peerage operated did not remain static, which leads me to my second theme, that of power.

Let me just reiterate my main contention: that in the early 15th century the roots of noble power were military and local or regional; by the 18th century, the nature of noble power in the localities had changed radically and noble power rested on offices in, and the patronage of, the national government.

Let us start by looking at the decline of the nobles' military power. To some extent, this can be put down to long periods of peace - between 1559 and the 1580s, between 1603 and 1625. The steady establishment of law and order was also clearly important: men could find protection in the law courts - they no longer needed a powerful noble to protect their interests - while noble violence which threatened the public peace was increasingly likely to be punished. The union of Crowns in 1603 accelerated the pacification of the Scottish border: although the borders remained bandit country, there was no longer the need for the large-scale military preparedness that had given the Neviles and the Percies their military power. At the same time, changing views of nobility substituted a civilian "governor" - wise, just, well-read, committed to the service of his "country" - for the older, military and chivalric ideal of the knight.

All of this, and much more, has been brilliantly analyzed by Stone.[49] One important point should be added: the extent to which the nobility's military skills were being rendered irrelevant by changes in tactics and technology. The preeminence of the nobility depended on the preeminence of cavalry; the nobles possessed the money to equip mounted knights and the requisite skills of horsemanship. The development of firearms changed all that. Artillery, fortifications, and siege warfare required new, more technical skills. Handguns redressed the balance between cavalry and infantry. Large bodies of infantry required training in the use of their firearms (so that they did not shoot each other); they also required standardized equipment - to have guns and ammunition of differing calibres was a recipe for chaos on the battlefield. Only the State (in England at least) could afford this quantity of equipment and could impose standardization. Increasingly, most firearms were located in the arms-stores of county or town militias, not the private arsenals of magnates, which tended to contain sporting guns and weapons that were more ornamental than useful. With the development of the militia in the second half of the 16th century, military service became a public rather than a private obligation and noblemen, as lords lieutenant, exercized military power as the servants of the Crown, not in their own right. This changed world was illustrated by the Essex rebellion in 1601: as the Earl and his fine swordsmen postured in the Strand, his emissaries were desperately trying to win the support of the City trained bands. Fine swords and fine swordsmanship were no substitute for firepower.[50]

Contemporaries were quick to complain of the decline in the military prowess of the nobility. Viscount Wimbledon wrote in 1627: "This kingdom hath been too long at peace. Our old commanders ...are worn out and few men are bred in their places, for the knowledge of war and almost the thought of war is extinguished."[51] Such jeremiads were exaggerated. In 17th century Europe, there was no shortage of wars, in which a younger son might learn the trade of soldier: by no means all the noble commanders in the civil wars were novices and those who were soon learned. Similarly, one should not place too much weight on William III's sour comment that "the humour and character of a peer of England do not agree very well with the discipline to which a colonel must be subject".[52] William certainly had a low opinion of the English nobility - he said all they could talk about was farming and horses - but he also had sound political reasons not to trust the army at the time he made this remark (1689). The fact was that English peers did continue to serve with distinction in the army, which increasingly offered an attractive career. In the 18th century, with the growth of the patronage system and of the purchase of commissions, the higher levels of the army and navy officer corps became increasingly monopolized by aristocrats. If the aristocracy's general ethos was no longer military, the ethos of the military high command was aristocratic.[53] Even William came to terms with this: by the end of his reign he was grooming an English peer, Marlborough, to carry on his role as commander-in-chief of the Grand Alliance against France.

An insight into public perceptions of the nobility's military prowess can be gained from successive editions of Chamberlayne's *Angliae Notitiae*. The first, in 1669, was scathing:

> If the English nobility, by a long continued peace, excessive luxury in diet, want of action &c were before the late wars born more feeble in body than their ancestors and by too fine and too full diet afterwards were rendered weaker in mind; and then during the late troubles by much licentiousness and want of fit education were so debauched that it was lately difficult to find the courage, wisdom, integrity, honour, sobriety and courtesy of the ancient nobility, yet is it not to be doubted that under a warlike, enterprising prince all those virtues of their forefathers may spring afresh.[54]

The passage remained unchanged in successive editions under Charles II and James II - clearly Chamberlayne did not regard them as warlike or enterprising. William III, however, was, and the 1694 edition concluded with the hope that "we shall soon see revived that brave martial spirit of those English heroes recorded in history...whose valiant exploits, and even their very names, more than once made France to tremble."[55] This passage was included in the remaining editions under William and was omitted under Anne: in her case, remarks about warlike princes were clearly inappropriate.

Chamberlayne's comments on the nobility - and those of his rival Guy Miege - were generally unflattering. In terms of arms, hospitality, and virtue, the current peers were described as markedly inferior to their predecessors. Miege hoped in 1691 that "a virtuous and generous prince will bring back the Golden Age", but in 1707 he declared; "that Golden Age is gone and when 'twill return 'tis not easy to guess".[56] Even if such claims of the demise of the nobles' military capabilities can be seen as exaggerated, there was still a great change in that they no longer posed a military threat to the State. Lord Russell argued in his trial in 1683 "how unlikely it was that any man could now raise a country; for so great an interest as was now requisite for that was now fallen with the greatness of the nobility and was no more known in England'"[57] The changed military role of the nobility was intimately bound up with the decline of their power over men in the localities. In the heyday of bastard feudalism, that power had had three main components. First, the household and retinue, including the sons of gentry who had come to be educated in noble ways. By the end of the 16th century, these households had shrunk to more cosy, domestic proportions; the great halls were divided up into family-size rooms. Large bodies of unproductive hangers-on were a luxury that few could afford. If the Duke of Beaufort had 200 persons in his "family" in the 1680s, this was very much an anachronism and a matter for comment.[58]

The second component consisted of the lord's tenantry. In the 15th century, many lords, especially in the North, saw their estates as first and foremost a source of men. They leased out their land in small farms and tended to keep tenancies in the same families for generations, thus building a bond of mutual loyalty between the families of lord and of tenant. With the 16th century price rise, many saw such estate management policies as a recipe for ruin. Profit became the prime concern. Small farms were agglomerated into larger, more profitable units and leased to the highest bidder. Landlords thus had fewer tenants and their relationship became a business rather than a personal one; disputes were settled not by an appeal to the lord's generosity but by litigation. England was moving, in Mervyn James's words, from a lineage to a civil society and with it the hold of lords over tenants was loosened. As John Selden explained, when landlords leased their land at below market rents, their tenants were willing to fight for them, "but now they will do nothing for them". Landlords retained their economic power and continued to exact a measure of deference, but the days had gone when the tenants of the Earl of Northumberland "knew no king but a Percy". In 1569, the Earl had to appeal to his tenants' Catholicism when rising in rebellion - and even then not many of them followed him. In 1642, at the outbreak of civil war, the Earl's tenants ignored his summons and some reportedly occupied Alnwick Castle.[59]

The third component of bastard feudal power had been the ability to construct networks of retainers among landowners and others who had no direct dependence on the lord: knights, gentry, abbots, officials. The retainer offered service - honorific, political, and legal more often than military; he received in return a fee (often modest), together with protection and support, in lawsuits and in seeking patronage, together with the arbitration of disputes. At times when the king could not or would not maintain order and justice, men had to find them where they could, and that meant seeking the protection of a lord with real local power. By the end of the 16th century, these bodies of retainers had not wholly disappeared, but they were smaller and rather more ornamental: they were particularly noticeable at funerals. In general, however, members of the gentry did not need the protection that the magnates had once offered; as for patronage, they did not need the nobility as intermediaries but went direct to the source, to the court. If they still showed deference to great lords, it was on a more limited scale: Beaufort's gentry neighbours pruned their hedges and trees to "humour his visitors" - not the same as fighting his battles or even wearing his livery.[60]

Now the decline of the nobility's regional power owed something to the Crown. Henry VIII dealt ruthlessly with possible rival claimants; Elizabeth carefully undermined the power of the Percies and the Neviles in the North.[61] Both had a somewhat ambivalent attitude towards retaining; they were wary of the threat it posed to public order, but appreciated its usefulness as a source of soldiers in wartime.[62] Elizabeth's reluctance to create and endow new peers in itself weakened the collective power of the nobility. Nevertheless, that weakening owed more to a complex of institutional, economic, military, and cultural changes largely independent of the royal will. They left the local influence of the nobility much attenuated. Landed wealth could still inspire respect and indeed fear; nobles were great landlords, employers, customers; they could exact but also merit deference by hospitality, charity, benevolent estate management and local leadership. With the growth of the House of Commons, especially under Elizabeth, many extended their electoral interests. As holders of offices - especially lord lieutenancies - they played an important role in local government, often exercising a general supervisory role. (However, the growing complexity and scale of local government meant that the key figures on a day-to-day level were now the gentry, especially as JPs). In general, indeed, the local power of the nobility now depended on influence, or management, rather than coercion. The first Duke of Newcastle recalled of Gilbert, 10th Earl of Shrewsbury, who died in 1616, that rich knights like Sir George Booth and Sir Vincent Corbett would wear the Earl's livery on St George's Day, "for thus they did oblige my lord to be their servant all the year after with his power, to serve them both in court and at Westminster Hall, to be their solicitor". On the other hand, if the Earl brought a command from the King, they would ensure that it was carried out.[63] Mutual favours - and mutual courtesy - helped to sustain aristocratic power, which could be reinforced by shared religious and political beliefs - or conversely disrupted by differences of principle. Yet at the same time as the old regional power of the peers was being destroyed, a new form of power was beginning to grow.

As we have seen, the 1530s and 1540s saw the beginning of a new nobility based on court and administrative service. That development was interrupted by Elizabeth's snobbish reluctance to create peers who did not already possess noble blood, but it resumed under James I. Given his somewhat reclusive style and lack of involvement in administration, those who exercised real power in his reign were those who were close to him: not just the more notorious favourites, Buckingham and Somerset, but more generally the gentlemen of the bedchamber. The volume of rewards accumulated by those in positions of favour was enormous: Buckingham received rewards worth maybe £500,000, five Scots (headed by the Earl of Carlisle) a total of £850,000.

Compared with this, the rewards of landownership could seem quite modest: the Earls of Worcester and Newcastle, the two richest peers in 1642, had landed incomes of about £23,000 a year; most peers whose incomes are known received much less than £10,000.[64] Buckingham's control over policy-making depended on his influence over, and access to, the King, rather than the offices he held. By contrast, the great officers of state exercised relatively little power (a situation not helped by the rapid turnover of officials). After Buckingham's death, the importance of the bedchamber declined and that of the regular officers of state revived somewhat, but the fiscal, religious, and other policies Charles pursued continued to provoke a great deal of opposition. In short, under James I and Charles I, a relatively small, favoured group of nobles wielded enormous power through their control of the central institutions of the court. They used that power to reward themselves and their clients, lavishly; but their monopoly of power, the way in which they used it, and the policies they pursued antagonized not only many of their fellow nobles but the bulk of the wider political nation as well. This was one of the main reasons why Charles I was so politically isolated in 1640.

The crisis of 1640-2 and the civil wars that followed went some way to reviving the influence of the peerage. Faced with the rebellion in Scotland and the apathy of his own subjects, Charles appealed to his nobility for support, calling a great council in the autumn of 1640: with his own political credibility badly dented, he wished them to deploy their considerable collective influence on his behalf. He summoned them to serve him in person, with an armed following. Many were ready to offer their advice - and, on certain conditions, their service - but that advice and those conditions were often far from palatable. (This was as true of some of the peers who had been at court in the 1630s - like Northumberland and Holland - as of those who had kept away). Many peers clearly saw themselves as brokers between a misguided king and an angry people, as stepping into the breach as the King's "natural counsellors" to undo the work of many years of evil counsel. This was a conception of the peerage which the King in considerable part shared: if the peers failed to prevent civil war, this was partly because some of their number asked too much (notably Strafford's head - "Stone dead hath no fellow", Essex declared), partly because Charles would not offer enough - more particularly, he would not appoint men to high office until they had earned it by serving him as he wished to be served. Reconciliation required a mutual trust which King and peers found beyond them. By 1642, in the 19 Propositions, Parliament was demanding formal curbs on the King's freedom to make decisions and appointments, which clearly reflected the distrust, born of bitter experience, of those who knew him best - the peers. It was the King's own noble councillors, past and present, who demanded a far more effective role in government for the Privy Council.[65]

Having said all that, I am unconvinced by recent attempts to reinterpret the civil war as a baronial revolt. The peers' attempts to act as brokers, or buffers, between king and people failed. The House of Lords' opposition to Strafford's attainder and the militia bill, and the presence there of the bishops and Popish lords, turned popular anger against the upper house. As popular involvement in politics erupted and the King fled his capital and began to prepare for war, attempts to resolve the crisis by means of high political readjustments, as proposed by the peers, became increasingly impractical and indeed irrelevant. Moreover, not too much should be read into the peers' military role in the war. Both sides relied heavily on peers to gather support in 1642 - nobody else had as much influence in the localities and indeed their ability to recruit was as important as their military competence in the war's early stages. Half of the colonels in Parliament's first field army were peers: the Commons felt impelled to demonstrate that they had no wish to challenge the existing social order.[66] Supreme military power was vested in the Earl of Essex, who assumed a quasi-regal style: his supporters talked of him as a new high constable of the kingdom. To some extent, this had the support of Parliament, which needed a quasi-royal leader to counter the appeal of the King and to justify their making war against him. Before seeing Essex as a latter-day Simon de Montfort, however, three points should be made. First, Parliament was in possession of the regular machinery of government; it was the King who was up in the North, trying (like a rebel baron) to use his and his supporters' power over men to cobble together an army. Second, the arguments used by Parliament to justify resisting the King increasingly centred on its deriving authority from the people, whom it represented - a concept in which the Lords had little or no part. Third, Essex's ambitions, limited strategy, and mediocre achievements alienated Parliament and indeed most of his fellow peers and he was removed from his command.[67]

Whatever the Civil War, and the revival of their military role, may have done for the power of the nobility, what followed did them no good at all. The majority had sided with the King. Many had their estates confiscated and, although most eventually got them back, houses had often been damaged, timber felled, and they found themselves saddled with heavy debts.[68] The rise of the New Model called into question the traditional assumption that military prowess went with gentle blood: the players had defeated the gentlemen, with a vengeance. Moreover, the army's triumph vested power in men who at best had no great respect for noble power and at worst were actively hostile to it. The rulers of England in the 1650s may have been a small, unrepresentative minority: they nevertheless held on to power with a tenacity which the more "gentlemanly" Royalists could not match.[69]

The Restoration brought a revival in noble fortunes and noble numbers. As we have seen, Charles II showed more restraint and responsibility in his peerage creations than his father and grandfather had done. Moreover, morally lax though his court may have been, it never attained the dizzy heights of profligacy and corruption of the heyday of Buckingham. Charles respected his nobility and ennobled his leading servants; high government office - rather than the court - became the main locus of power. The patronage resources of the Crown were now much reduced. The legislation of 1641 outlawed numerous fiscal devices and economic privileges, such as monopolies, which had been used for the purpose of patronage. Charles further restricted himself by establishing treasury control over government spending. He thus enjoyed full freedom to dispose only of funds outside treasury control (French subsidies, secret service money) and those outside England (particularly in Ireland). Meanwhile, the Lord Treasurer became the key figure in the granting of patronage. He might (like Danby) use his power for his own personal or political purposes; alternatively, treasurers (or treasury commissioners) might restrict grants in an effort to keep expenditure in check.

Deprived, for the most part, of extensive royal patronage, the peers were thrown back on their own resources. Despite the damage done to their fortunes during the Civil War, many thrived. Overseas trade and the money market offered lucrative, if risky, investments. With agricultural profits sluggish, peers took care to manage their estates in a rational and business-like fashion. High office remained profitable, if precarious. A small army and larger navy opened up new career opportunities. As always, new creations brought new wealth into the peerage. With a revival of wealth, went a revival of confidence. The peers, like the rest of the landed élite, sought to rebuild their authority and crush what they saw as the disaffected and insubordinate forces that had emerged in the 1640s and 1650s. Peers played a particularly conspicuous role in breaking the independence of corporate towns in the early 1680s.

The clearest illustration of the peers' continuing power came in 1688. Nobles raised armed men and secured the North for William.[70] James's flight on 10 December created a vacuum of authority of a kind that never occurred in 1642. Into that vacuum stepped a group of peers, meeting at London's Guildhall. They struggled to maintain order, in the face of a populace bent on vengeance against the Papists and panic fears that bands of bloodthirsty Irish Catholics were burning towns and slaughtering their inhabitants. Occasionally, Catholic peers (like Lord Dover) were the victims of this rage and fear. More often their Protestant brethren assumed a role of leadership and calmed the people. At King's Lynn, the corporation and militia looked to the Duke of Norfolk to protect the Protestant religion, liberty, and property. As the Earl of Ailesbury travelled through Kent, he used his rank and the declaration that he carried from the Guildhall lords, to reassure the people: panic turned to cheers and "acclamations of joy".[71]

The important role played by the nobility should not be seen as evidence that the Revolution of 1688 was an aristocratic coup. The Northern peers, together with rioting Londoners and Williamite propaganda, played a vital but auxiliary role, disrupting James's military preparations and undermining his and his soldiers' morale. The leading role, however, was played by William and his army, who alone had the military power to challenge James's forces. Peers acted swiftly to prevent serious disorder after James fled. They also exercised an influence, largely negative, on the Revolution settlement. Tory peers sought to deny William the title of King, but backed down when he threatened to go home and leave the English to sort out the ensuing confusion as best they could. As one Tory peer remarked: "We must not leave ourselves to the rabble."[72] Whatever the reservations of some peers about the way William came to the Throne, most bowed to the inevitable and indeed proved willing and eager to serve him.

The Revolution of 1688 changed the position of the peerage in unexpected ways. Under Charles II and James II, the royal revenue and the volume of patronage remained comparatively modest. The great wars of 1689-1713 brought a massive increase in taxation, the armed forces, and the sheer size of the State. Stone calculated that in James I's reign no more than 40 offices were regarded as worthy of a peer's dignity - and some of those were pretty marginal (or fell to Scots).[73] By 1714, the number was much larger, especially in the higher echelons of the (now permanent) armed forces and the much expanded revenue administration and diplomatic corps; there were still more when great offices were put into commission. Moreover, apart from great offices, there was a vastly enlarged pool of lesser patronage, through which peers could build up their own clienteles, extend their electoral interests, and provide for junior members of the family.[74]

After 1688, the Crown became financially dependent on Parliament for the first time. The Commons could force the monarch to abandon policies they disliked, by threatening to withhold supply. This enhanced the power of the peers in two ways. First, they used the patronage of the State - particularly after 1714 - to reinforce their own electoral influence and secure the election to the Commons of their sons, kinsmen, and clients. Thus the peers' influence over the Commons reached a peak under the first two Georges. Second, in their capacity as ministers, they used the threat of opposition in the Commons to persuade the monarch to follow their advice in matters of policy and appointments. They were not always successful: William (especially) maintained a considerable degree of independence and Anne never allowed her ministers the free rein they sought in the disposal of patronage. Nevertheless, by 1714, the nobility were well on the way to exercising supreme power, not by challenging the Crown's government, but by taking it over.[75] Whereas the 15th century nobility had been content with a rough and ready regional power, their 18th century counterparts controlled the national government: indeed, they controlled a state apparatus far more extensive, rich, and powerful than their medieval forebears could have dreamed of.[76] Whatever crises the late Tudor and Stuart nobility may have gone through, they had emerged triumphant by 1714.

Footnotes to this Chapter may be found on pages 196-9.

6: Adam Bruce
Lairds and blood feuds – the Scottish nobility to the Act of Union: 1707

LET US begin at the end, in 1707. On 1 May 1707, Anne, Queen of Scots, concluded a treaty of Union with Anne, Queen of England, on the advice of her commissioners and Parliaments in both kingdoms. The kingdoms of England and Scotland were dissolved, and the kingdom of Great Britain came into being with the Union Agreement as its skeletal, but fundamental, written Constitution[1].

So much for constitutional theory. In practice, the English Parliament continued much as it had done before the Union. It admitted 45 Scots MPs and 16 representative peers, elected by their brethren in Edinburgh. Scots constitutional and parliamentary tradition was overridden by the overweening English theory of the sovereignty of parliament. Within a couple of years, fundamental articles of the Act of Union had been legislated away, and in 1711 a motion in the House of Lords to dissolve the Union was narrowly defeated. More importantly for this paper, the Union had a devastating effect on Scots nobiliary law. The jurisdiction of the Court of Session, the supreme court of Scotland, was usurped by the Committee of Privileges. In peerage case after peerage case English law was applied, and Scots custom ignored. The election of the representative peers was carefully controlled by the Administration, and the 16 peers were seen as tools of the ministry. So much so that this rather ribald verse circulated at the end of the 18th century.

> Alike in loyalty, alike in worth,
> Behold the sixteen nobles of the North;
> Fast friends to Monarchy, yet sprung from those
> Who basely sold their monarch to his foes.
> Since which, atoning for their fathers' crime,
> Their sons, as basely, sell themselves to him.
> With ev'ry change prepared to change their note,
> With ev'ry Government prepared to vote,
> Save when, perhaps, on some important Bill,
> They know by second sight, the Royal Will.

But the Scots peerage were only part of the nobility of Scotland, whose most numerous were the feudal baronage, and the lairds. There were some 10,000 feudal barons and lairds in Scotland at the time of the Union. Sir Thomas Innes, the late Lord Lyon, estimated that over half the population of 18th century Scotland was directly related to a member of the nobility[2]. A more recent estimate puts the number of extant barony titles at 2,000[3].

What happened to this broad-based nobility? The years after the Union took their effect. The bonds of maintenance that had sustained the relationship between the peers and the barons broke up as the peers moved to London in search of preferment. The Heritable Jurisdictions Act of 1747 severely curtailed the local jurisdictions of barons sitting in their barony courts dispensing local justice for local needs. Scots' succession law that had allowed for such a broad-based familiar nobility were supplanted by the narrow rules of primogeniture, imposed by English judges who regarded Scots law as irrelevant.

In order to understand why the Scots nobility flourished in the years before 1707, it is important to grasp some tenets of Scots law. Scots nobiliary law possessed its own unique rules and practices which developed out of the fusion of Anglo-Saxon, Celtic, and Norman customary law in the 11th and 12th centuries. Equally important, many of these laws corresponded far more with practices on the Continent than they did with the rules of English law. For example, the strict rules of primogeniture applied to English peerages were never established in Scotland. The Scots rules of succession can be traced back to the Celtic custom of tanistry, where the head of a House would nominate his successor from within his family to ensure the best chances of survival for his lands and titles[4]. Although the ability of peers to nominate their successors was limited by the terms of their Letters Patent, the feudal barons and lairds still exercised this power regularly[5].

Scots law starts with the principle that titles of nobility are a form of heritable property. "A Scottish peerage...(is)...a species of heritable property which descends to heirs according to the canons, which in the law of Scotland, are appropriate to the descent of any kind of heritable property."[6] As such, a Scots peerage is subject to certain particular rules of transfer and succession. In English law, until the Peerage Reform Act of 1963, the vast majority of peerages were hereditary and, in the absence of instructions to the contrary, were held to descend *jure sanguinis* to the heirs-male of the body of the original grantee. Unfortunately, these unnecessarily strict rules of descent were applied to Scots peerage disputes by the House of Lords after the Act of Union. Although the Court of Session continued to adjudicate on peerage disputes after 1707, by the middle of the century the House of Lords appropriated its jurisdiction and began applying wholly alien rules and precedents. The Act of Union recognized and protected Scottish honours as matters of "Private Right" under the terms of Article 18, but this Article was ignored by the House of Lords which proceeded to set aside the rules of Scots law which protected those honours[7]. The House of Lords disregarded the ability of Scots peers to resign their titles, the recognition of Life Peerages, and the far broader and more equitable system of succession outlined above[8].

The presumption of descent to heirs-male of the body and the strict rules of primogeniture had severely limiting effects on the English peerage. In Scotland only a handful of titles descended to the heir-male of the body. Of the 366 peerages created in Scotland prior to 1707, 110 had special destinations, often to heirs of entail, 93 were descendable to females, 86 to heirs-male whatsoever, and only 14 were to heirs-male of the body of the grantee[9]. These figures corroborate the theory that Scots peerages were granted as a mark of honour on the whole family, and not just the individual who was granted the title. The looser succession laws thus allowed for a better chance of the honour surviving within the family[10].

Of the 110 Scottish peerage creations with special destinations, a significant number went to heirs of entail and provision. This form of destination was common in other continental jurisdictions, but had been declared obsolete in England with the Viscountcy of Purbeck case in 1675. A peer whose title descended to an heir of provision could nominate anybody as his successor without recourse to the Crown for a regrant of the peerage in that person's favour. The benefit of this form of descent was that the peer's estates could descend with his title, thus preserving the territorial nature of his peerage. In his judgment in the case of *Lady Ruthven of Freeland, Petitioner*, the Lord Lyon stated that, in granting destinations to heirs of provision, "the Crown left the magnate to run his own family as long as he could without trouble. Thoughtful genealogists overlook the similar law and practice in many other Kingdoms, and the real principle involved, adjustment of the dignity's descent to the most expedient branch for perpetuation of the peerage family in question."[11]

This ability to choose a successor can be seen in the peerage law of several other European states. In France in 1638 the Duchy of Aiguillon was bestowed on Marie de Vignerot, niece of Cardinal Richelieu, "pour enjouir par ladite dame, ses heretiers et successeurs, tant masles que femelles, tels qu'elle voudra choisir perpetuellement et à toujours."[12]

The abolition of this form of descent in England meant that post-Union the House of Lords refused to recognize petitioners who sought to establish their rights as heirs of provision. In 1735, the House rejected the petition of James Makgill to the Viscountcy of Oxenfoord (or Oxfuird), which had such a destination, in that by English law he had to be the heir-male of the body of the grantee, which he was not. The Lord Chancellor, Lord Talbot, held that the "point of (Scots) law seemed very difficult", and should not be applied[13]. Suffice it to say that the House of Lords overturned this decision in 1977, and granted the Viscountcy to James Makgill's descendant.

Scottish peers enjoy one final right which their English cousins do not. It is a right which governs the transfer of heritable property in Scots law, and one that has not been lost, despite the effects of the Union of 1707. A Scots peer, fearing the extinction of his peerage, or wishing to exclude one set of heirs, can resign his honours *ad favorem* into the hands of the Crown for a regrant in favour of another member of his family.[14] Before the Union the new grant was recorded in the Register of the Great Seal of Scotland, and was effective on registration. The peer cannot alter the terms of limitation of his peerage without this sanction by the Crown.[15]

No Scots peer has attempted to resign his title into the hands of the Crown since 1707, and this has led some to question the validity of the process. But, in an interesting legal opinion submitted to the 1963 Peerage Reform Committee, the then Lord Advocate argued that, "I can find nothing in the Act of Union, or in any later legislation, to suggest that it is not ... I am of the opinion that the pre-Union procedure has never been abrogated, and is still legally competent."

The pre-Union Scots Parliament was unicameral and consisted of three Estates; the Prelates, the Barons, and the Burgesses. Until the mid 17th century, the Scots Parliament was ambulatory. During the course of the 16th century, it began sitting regularly in Edinburgh, but even in the capital the accommodation was unsatisfactory.[16] In 1632, Charles I ordered the Town Council of Edinburgh to construct a new Parliament house to the south of St Giles' High Kirk. The plan for the new building became closely connected with royal innovations in church government, which involved transforming St Giles' into a cathedral, and became deeply unpopular. When the Estates assembled in their new hall for the first time in 1639 they recorded their gratitude by recording a "Protest" against royal absolutism.[17]

Privilege of Parliament in the English sense was late to develop in Scotland.[18] Even in the latter half of the 17th century, members of the Estates were imprisoned on royal command for speaking out in parliament.[19] In 1661, the Earl of Tweeddale was incarcerated for defending in parliament an accused in a treason trial, despite his defence of freedom of speech.[20] In 1702, Sir Alexander Bruce, later Earl of Kincardine, was expelled for stating that in his opinion the Presbyterian form of church government was inconsistent with the nature of monarchy, and a fresh warrant was issued for his constituency.[21]

The Estates were especial;y fastidious in matters of protocol and parliamentary custom. In particular, the Riding of Parliament which marked the start of each session was carefully orchestrated. Once the new Parliament Hall was built, the Riding would start at the Palace of Holyrood, and the members of the Estates would process up the Royal Mile to Parliament Square. In Sir Walter Scott's *The Heart of Midlothian*, Mrs Damahoy remarks to Mr Saddleton that, "Ye suld mind [remember] the riding o' the parliament in the gude auld time before the Union." It must have been a dramatic affair and a very vivid picture of the Riding remains.[22] The matter of dress and the order of ceremony was very important, and in 1606 the Privy Council laid down strict orders to regulate the proceedings. There were frequent disputes about precedence among both orders of nobility, and in 1600, an Act was passed "against quarrelling for priority of place or vote in Parliament".[23]

The principal Order of the nobility, the Estate of the Baronage, retained its pre-eminence in parliament up to 1707. The nobles who made up this Estate comprised the peers of Scotland in all five degrees. But in the Middle Ages this estate had been much wider. Up to the end of the 15th century the members of the baronage were those who held their land directly of the King, either in *liberam baroniam* as barons, or in *liberam comitatum* as earls.

The Earls

The earls in the Scots peerage are the descendants of the Celtic Mormaers, who held a personal office at the disposal of the King of Scots.[24] With the turn of the 12th century this office became hereditary, and held on feudal tenure. Until the 17th century, most earldoms were created by the erection of lands into a comital fief, held directly of the Crown. Thus the earldom created the earl, and whoever held the comital estates enjoyed all the privileges of an earl in the peerage of Scotland. In 1315, King Robert I created his brother Edward, Earl of Carrick by investing him in the lands of the earldom to hold them, "cum nomine, jure, et dignitate comitatis ..." An earldom could, therefore, be assigned to a third party. In the 16th century, James, Earl of Arran, conveyed his earldom to his cousin, James Stewart. The charter was confirmed by Parliament, and was held to be sufficient to confer on Stewart the dignity of an earl, and he sat in Parliament as such. The transaction was later reduced by the Court of Session, not because it was a *pactus illicitum*, but because the original earl was held to have been insane at the time of the conveyance.[25]

With the accession of James VI to the throne of England, the dignity of earl became a personal and honorific title; changing from corporeal to incorporeal heritable property. Creation by Patent took over from creation by Charter. In 1605 the Earls of Home, Perth, and Dunfermline were created using the new formula; "Noverritis igitur nos ... creasse, ordinasse, constituisse et erexisse ... comites de ..."

This alteration in the manner of creating peers reflected the change in nature of royal governance in 16th century Scotland. In the late Middle Ages the government of Scotland had been highly decentralized, with kings leaving much of the administration in the localities to the territorial magnates. Royal interference in local affairs amounted at most to playing one noble family off against another. This arrangement meant that the royal house was rarely challenged by a noble usurper. After defeat of such challenges, the monarch would create new noble dynasties to fill the vacuum in the lands of the vanquished rebel. Thus Robert I parcelled out the estates of the Balliols and the Comyns to his supporters, and James II created the Earls of Huntly, Errol, Argyll, Marischal, Morton, and Rothes to take the place of the disgraced Earls of Douglas and the Dukes of Albany. These newly elevated peers took time to establish their dominance in the localities, and their relative weakness protected the Crown from a Scottish War of the Roses. In time, the new earls built up a complex web of bonds and alliances with their neighbours and tenants, and it was these bonds which the crown sought to destroy when James VI reversed the policy of his forbears and moved to impose royal authority directly in the localities.

The Lords of Parliament

The creation of the first honorific earldoms was not wholly alien to Scots peerage law. Scotland had seen the creation of lords of parliament, in the English sense, in the 15th century. Until that time, the Estate of the Baronage had consisted solely of the earls and the feudal barons. It is thought that James I of Scots brought the idea of separate lords of parliament with him from England, but it is difficult to pin down an exact date for the first creation.

It appears that the first lords of parliament were created sometime in the 20 years up to 1445. With this new personal peerage, the new baronial dignity was annexed to the blood of the grantee, and did not run with the land, as a feudal barony did. The difficulty in pinning down the first creation is that both types of baron used the same formulation for their titles, and were part of the same parliamentary estate. While they were later to be distinguished as *Barones Majores* and *Barones Minores*, it is is difficult when confronted in the pre-1587 Rolls of Parliament with such a title as, *Dominus de X* to differentiate between a personal and a feudal title. The initial creations of personal barons were apparently made by nomination and investiture in Parliament. No writ was executed, nor were Letters Patent necessarily drawn up. As Lord Pitmedden, a Senator of the College of Justice wrote in 1677,

> "The nobility of Scotland were not created by patents as now, but the old way of creation was by some extrinsic solemnity or ryte, such as girding them with a belt in publick parliament, or other publick assembly, or by listing them in the publick rolls by the titles conferred upon them, or by deseigning them so in the publick charters and evidents of their lands."[26]

Interestingly the dignity of *Baro Major* appears at first to have been an innominate title as Baronet still is.[27] The grantee merely used his ordinary territorial designation, and if the case of the 1st Lord Saltoun can be taken as an example, frequently changed it. In the 15th century Lord Saltoun was referred to as Lord Saltoun of Abernethy, Lord Abernethy of Saltoun, and even Lord Abernethy in Rothiemay.[28]

Scots' authorities have always been touchy about the use or abuse of the *nomen dignitatis* , the nomenclature used to designate the peerage dignity. In 1959, Sir Patrick Spens, a cadet of the chiefly house of Spens of Lathallan, was elevated to the peerage by the *nomen dignitatis* of Spens *simpliciter*. James Spens of Lathallan, however, petitioned in the Lyon Court for Arms. The Lord Lyon held that he had no option but to declare that Lord Spens had been "regally designated" Chief of the Name and Arms of Spens, and assigned Arms to James Spens differenced from the chief of the family.

What usually happens is that when a cadet of a Scottish family is elevated to the peerage he is given an additional designation, usually territorial, to add to his surname. When the Lord Chancellor Lord Mackay of Clashfern, was elevated to the peerage, an article appeared in the *Scots Law Times* which stated that to describe him as "Lord Mackay" alone implied an infringement of the rights implicit in the chiefship of Lord Reay as chief of the Mackays. For the moment, of course, we can refer to him simply as Lord Chancellor.[29]

With Scottish personal lordships, it has been argued that the innominate dignity of the peerage could itself pass under any other *nomen dignitatis*. This explains the freedom of nomenclature enjoyed by Scots peers, with the reservation that is outlined above. This idea conflicts with the English principle that even a misspelled letter of a *nomen dignitatis* is irrevocably fixed by the Letters Patent. In some Scottish patents, the selection of a *nomen dignitatis* was even left for the grantee to insert at his pleasure.

The Masters

The Master is one of the features peculiar to the Scots peerage. The title is held by the heir apparent or heir presumptive of any Scottish peer, whether duke, marquess, earl, viscount, or lord of parliament, and it is not a courtesy title, but rather a substantive peerage dignity in itself.[30] The Masters sat in the Scots parliament, and after the Union were prevented, along with the Scots peers not elected by their brethren, from sitting in the House of Commons.[31] The title of Master appears in public records in the early 15th century as held by the eldest sons of earls; the Master of Fife and the Master of Atholl appear in the Rosslyn Chronicle in the 1430s.[32] One of the advantages of the existence of the master is that it points to the holder's father, or mother, being a member of the *Barones Majores* and can help to separate lords of parliament from feudal barons.

One of the features of the Act of Union and the southward drift of the Scots peerage, was the adoption of courtesy titles by the peers' children. The use of courtesy titles before 1707, and especially before 1603, was very rare in Scotland. Younger sons of peers carried no handle in front of their name; rather they were supposed to found their own house, and to add their own territorial designation to the end of their name. The situation is, however, different for a duke's, a marquess', and an earl's daughters. While in England, they bear the title "Lady" by courtesy, their Scottish sisters bear it as a matter of substantive law.

The Feudal Barons

The feudal barons were the bedrock on which the Scots nobility was built. Their existence was interwoven with the whole system of land tenure introduced into Scotland by David I. They held their lands directly of the

Crown, which had granted them their fief to hold *in liberam baroniam*. The baron's title ran with the land, and could, therefore, be conveyed along with the land itself, in an ordinary transaction of sale. In theory, a grant of land *in liberam baroniam* gave the vassal baron the duty of keeping the barony lands in order, dispensing justice within the barony, and holding a regular court. Not all grants of barony were awarded by the King of Scots; the Lord of the Isles had his own baronage, as befitted his status as a sovereign prince. A barony title gave the holder certain extra privileges over that of the holder of an ordinary feudal conveyance. The Scots property system is still based on a system of feudal tenure, and land is nominally held of the Crown, as ultimate Superior.[33]

The baron possessed certain regalian rights, of which only salmon fishings remain as having any real value. The most important rights that the baron exercised were the trying of offences in the Baron Court, and the use of the punishments of *furca et fossa*, or pit and gallows. The baron supplemented his rents and dues by fining tenants who were late in paying their rents and dues. The Baron Court was at the centre of a complex late medieval system of effective private dispute arbitration, which was curtailed in the 17th century with the violent intervention of royal justice.[34]

The feudal and parliamentary barons continued to sit in the Scots parliament until 1587, when the feudal barons were finally relieved of their obligation to attend, although they continued to make up the majority of the county representatives until the Reform Act of 1832. Despite their continued attendance in parliament, the relative power and influence of the feudal barons declined into the 18th century. The Heritable Jurisdictions Act of 1747 and the 1832 Reform Act effectively removed much of their legal and political authority. The use of the Baron Court declined with the strengthening of alternative Royal courts in the localities. Readers of Sir Walter Scott's novel *Waverley* may remember the Baron of Bradwardine whose Barony charter,

> "implied that he might imprison, try and execute his vassals and tenants at his pleasure. Like James I, however, the present possessor of this authority was more pleased in talking about prerogative than in exercising it."[35]

The Baron Court was, however, an integral part of the exercise of the rule of law in the localities in late medieval Scotland. It was the most effective arena for the settling of civil disputes between neighbours, who could not afford the time nor the expense of a trip to Edinburgh. The later Middle Ages in Scotland saw a dramatic growth in the number of written bonds between neighbouring landholders; often for mutual aid; but more often as contracts for potential dispute resolution.[36] Unlike England, where the written indenture of this period was usually for military service, overtly military bonds were rare in Scotland. Indeed, the state of armed readiness in the localities was little short of non-existent. In 1532, a wapinschaw, or weapon-showing, in the Burgh of Irvine, was attended by 29 lairds, and all their tenants. Only one man in the entire company turned up with weapons of any description.

The main reason for the growth of the personal bond - the bond of manrent - between laird and tenant, or between peer and baron, was that it assisted in reconciling feuding parties, and made for effective arbitration in the localities. In 1544, the Earls of Argyll and Angus drew up a bond that named arbiters who would deal with disputes between their kin, friends, and adherents. As Dr Jenny Wormald states, "(The higher nobility's) discipline over their followers could be effective, not in preventing bloodshed, but in preventing its escalation, often more quickly than any resort to the Royal courts could have done."[37]

The 16th century heralded a revolution in royal justice, in the civil and criminal courts. In 1532, James V received a Papal Charter to create a new Supreme Court in Edinburgh. The creation of the Court of Session, and the later establishment of the High Court of Justiciary in 1672, acted as a powerful counter to the virtual autonomy of the local baronial courts. Having established the Supreme Court in Edinburgh, the Crown moved in the 17th century to impose royal authority on the localities. JPs were appointed in each of the counties and royal justice was meted out. The crown's main concern was not in ensuring more equitable justice for all, but to divert the stream of income from fines and dues from the pockets of the nobility to its own. In the realm of criminal law, royal justice was concerned with punishment and retribution, and still is, while baronial justice had striven for reconciliation and compensation. Between 1705 and 1742 the Royal Justiciary Court in Argyll entertained 87 people on trial, of whom 86 were convicted; 14 were hanged, three branded, 10 nailed by the ears to the pillory, and the rest flogged or banished.[38]

The Seventeenth Century

The century between the Union of 1603 and that of 1707 was a traumatic one for the Scots nobility. It began well. When James VI and I moved to London he took a number of Scots courtiers with him. Indeed, he took so many that there was a predominance of Scots in the new British court. Many were rewarded with English lands and titles, and their sons served Charles I and II. The Scots courtiers controlled access to the king's presence. In 1625, seven of the 12 gentlemen of the bedchamber were Scots.[39] But by the reign of Queen Anne, only one out of 46 high offices of the Court was filled by a Scot.

The sons of the Scottish aristocracy sought other outlets for their desire for financial reward. Many entered the English House of Commons; so many that Lord Rochester called the Restoration Parliament, "a parliament of knaves and Scots."[40] Some Scottish noblemen found their fortune marrying English heiresses; the 1st Earl of Home carried off Lady Mary Sutton, only daughter of the Earl of Dudley. But the English were not so keen on reciprocal arrangements; as one commentator wrote, "to be chained in marriage to a Scotswoman were to be tied to a carkasse and cast into a stinking ditch".

The motivation for the move south of the nobility was provided by the widespread noble indebtedness that occurred in Scotland in the 17th century. Ten earls were known to be heavily in debt; the Earl of Lothian killed himself, and the Earl of Argyll fled to Spain under the pretence of converting to Catholicism. A number of the lords of parliament resigned their titles at the same time as selling their estates, a situation reflecting the Castilian law that if a nobleman fell into poverty he was reduced to the status of a commoner.[41]

The Crown's move to London saw royal patronage, pensions, and offices dry up in the early 17th century in Scotland. Combined with an economic slump, rapid inflation, and a fall in rental incomes, it pushed a number of the Scots nobility into revolt in 1637. Recognizing that the Crown was on weak ground, and with an eye to regaining the power they had lost in the localities, the nobility tried to regain the initiative. The National Covenant was their manifesto. Ostensibly a religious statement, it was, in essence, the declaration by the nobility of their role in the government of the kingdom. The "Nobleman's Covenant" was as much motivated by religious conviction as it was by political necessity.

The political vacuum created in Scotland in 1638 was filled by the nobility, who led on all fronts; political, religious, and military.[42] The peers and barons led locally raised regiments into battle in the two Bishops' wars, the Civil War, and the War of the Engagement. The Crown's inroads into the localities were rolled back, and noble hegemony over the localities, temporarily, restored.

The ascendancy of the peers on the national stage was mirrored by the increase in power and influence of the barons and lairds in the local arena. The civil and religious crises of the mid-century saw a revolution in the administration of the shires. By 1640, the lesser nobility had come to dominate civil government through the shire committees which dealt with law and order, and raised taxes, supplies, and munitions.[43] They also influenced hearts and minds, and stamped on deviancy through the kirk session.[44]

But with revolution came counter-revolution. By the 1650s in the Church and the Covenanting armies at least, the peers were seen as a liability rather than as an asset. Ministers who had entrusted the leadership of the Presbyterian crusade to the peers in the 1640s, sought to wrest it from them a decade later. Evidently, their zealotry was not convincing. With the

A

c

D

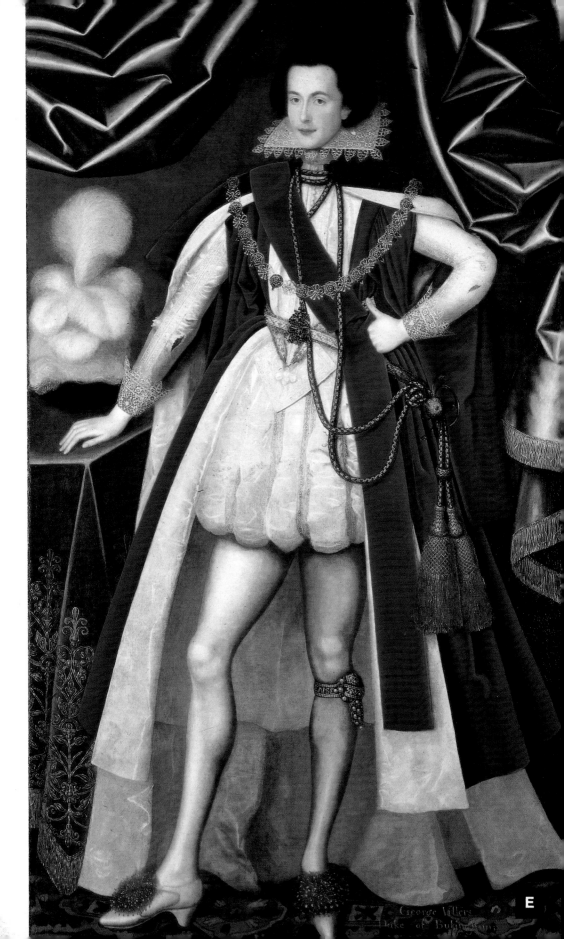

George Villiers
Duke of Buckingham

E

G

Sr Robert Walp
Earl of Orf

H

I

K

Restoration, any hopes of a noble ascendancy were dashed. Power and influence returned to London, and was doled out in small doses by faithful managers in Edinburgh.

The last revolution faced by the Scots nobility was over the Act of Union itself. The estate of the peerage voted by two to one for Union. In the face of a crisis over the succession to Queen Anne, economic collapse brought on by the Darien episode, and the threat of English sanctions, the Act was passed, and the Scots Parliament dissolved.

While the opponents of Union in 1707 may have used strong and emotional claims to defend the Imperial Crown of Scotland[45], the Union opened new doors to new opportunities in the burgeoning British Empire. Those nobles who held on into the 18th century took advantage of the agricultural and industrial revolutions which saw an unparalleled resurgence in the power and influence of the landed aristocracy, which was to carry them towards an Edwardian zenith and an Imperial sunset.[46]

Footnotes to this Chapter may be found on pages 199-201.

7: John Cannon

The nobility ascendant:
the Hanoverian settlement: 1714-1832

THERE ARE few things more irritating to the organizers of conferences than lecturers who abandon or subvert their own allotted subject in their opening remarks. But I would not wish lightly to give up a time-honoured tradition, and the short answer to the question – how did England escape revolution? – is that it didn't.

It had its revolutions in the 17th century – the Civil War, which resulted in the overthrow of the Monarchy, the abolition of the House of Lords and then disestablishment of the Church of England, and the Glorious Revolution of 1688 which sent James II into exile and substituted a curious, and unique, dual monarchy under William and Mary.

This had the great advantage that, by the 18th and 19th centuries, the English had grown respectable, could play down the radical implications of what had been done, and could lecture the French and the Austrians on the folly of revolutions. The English, who in 1649 had put their king on trial and cut his head off, were deeply shocked in 1793 when the French put their king on trial and cut his head off. The English said, quite fiercely, that *that* was quite different - which is what the English usually do say.

Now this ought to mean that we can all adjourn and surprise our hosts at Oriel by turning up for drinks two hours early. Alas, no such luck. Things are rarely that simple in history.

Why do I put such emphasis particularly on the Glorious Revolution? First, to appease Macaulay, who haunts me. I rarely forget that the great *History of England* was written only 20 miles north of my own University of Newcastle upon Tyne and that in Wallington Hall you can see the very desk on which it was composed. And Macaulay, you will remember, insisted that 1688 was, of all revolutions, the most beneficent: "It was because we had a preserving revolution in the seventeenth century we have not had a destroying one in the nineteenth."[1] If that does sound rather like an assertion that revolutions under Whig auspices are good and all other revolutions bad, it may not be far from what Macaulay had in mind.

Secondly, because the Glorious Revolution seems to me to be the foundation of the aristocratic supremacy, that Whig ascendancy, which characterized the 18th century. The hundred years after 1688 were the golden age of the English aristocracy.

Now, at this point, we find ourselves in a surprising amount of controversy because a number of historians, perhaps even the majority, have strenuously denied that the Glorious Revolution *was* of any real consequence. It was, they suggest, no more than a *coup d'état*, a mere aristocratic plot, which substituted a Dutch king for a Scottish king.[2]

You will remember that in 1988, when we were invited to celebrate the tricentenary of the Glorious Revolution, the newspapers, journals and colour supplements were full of articles begging us not to be taken in and assuring us that there was little to celebrate. The House of Commons had a somewhat half-hearted debate on the subject, during which Eric Heffer declared – I am afraid rather predictably – that 1688 was "neither glorious nor a revolution".[3] Some of the other contributions belonged to that quaint school of history which one can only categorize as Why-did-the-Norman-Conquest-not-introduce-a-national-health-service.

This revisionism – to use a fashionable if overworked word – came about in the usual way. First, a number of historians rediscovered what nobody else had forgotten – *viz.* that the Glorious Revolution was essentially the work of the aristocracy. There was scarcely a barricade, a tumbril or a *sans-culottes* within sight.

At that point, some of them lost interest. The most bizarre example remains Lucille Pinkham's book *William III and the Respectable Revolution*, which talked of its "failure to accomplish anything of lasting benefit". By "respectable" was meant establishment, limited, unexciting. The implication seemed to be, who would wish to hear about the doings of the nobility? The short answer is, anyone who is seriously interested in history since, whether one likes them or not – not a very relevant consideration – they wielded over many centuries very considerable power.

Subsequently, a rather strange coalition of left and right developed with the intention of downgrading the Glorious Revolution. One can understand the lack of enthusiasm of the Marxist left, who perceived that the events of 1688 did not do much for the workers or contribute directly to the triumph of the proletariat. In its cruder manifestations, Marxist history was so selective that many things seemed irrelevant to the grand design, and it waited for the crisis of capitalism as Beckett's tramps waited for Godot.

I am, incidentally, not sure that if one looked carefully at 1688, one could not argue that it did contribute, inadvertently, to the emergence of an industrial working class, by providing the stable political foundation on which financial and commercial development could take place. We might also note that the most recent writing on the subject denies that 1688 was no more than an aristocratic plot and argues that a considerable number of ordinary people played a crucial part in the rising.[4]

Commentators on the right are perhaps more difficult to understand.[5] They place great emphasis on the continuity of English history and argue that the constitutional limitations imposed upon the Crown by the settlement were not all that great. They insist, rightly, that the Monarchy continued to be at the heart of Hanoverian government.

There is clearly a limit to the amount of attention we can give here to what is a complex and protracted controversy. But a proper assessment of 1688 is so important to constructing a context for the role of the nobility in the 18th century that we must at least attempt some kind of reply. Had there been a tendency towards absolutist government before 1688? How important were the limitations then placed upon the Crown?

First of all, let us call in two monarchs. William III found the restrictions upon his power so irksome that, on several occasions, he seriously considered going back to Holland. You will remember how he was forced in 1699 by the House of Commons to dismiss his Dutch guards, despite an appeal that he would regard it as a personal kindness to be allowed to keep them. On that occasion, he had an abdication speech in draft. I cannot conceive of the King of Prussia in that period begging his Estates to be permitted to keep a personal bodyguard. Forty years later, George II contrasted the power he wielded as Elector of Hanover with the restrictions placed upon him in Britain and concluded that ministers were kings in this country.

Of course, one can argue that this moaning and groaning was little more than the posturings of political manoeuvre. But consider three limitations imposed by the 1688 settlement. Under the terms of the Triennial Act of 1694, which William had several times vetoed, Parliaments had to be summoned regularly. Would Charles I have regarded that limitation as of no great consequence? Would it have been seen as of little importance on the continent, where estates and diets were vanishing from the scene, decade by decade? Secondly the Bill of Rights declared that the monarch and his wife must not be Catholics – a limitation which is still in force. This meant that the monarch and his heir were the only people in the whole country whose religion was dictated to them. Would that have seemed of little concern to Louis XIV, who had just driven out the Huguenots on the principle that a monarch was empowered to decide the religion of his subjects? Thirdly, the army was brought under control by the clause forbidding a standing army in peacetime without parliamentary consent. Would James II have regarded that as perfectly acceptable? Would it have seemed very reasonable to the Habsburgs and the Hohenzollerns?

Before we accept the strange proposition that the Glorious Revolution accomplished very little, we should look at the testimony of some other historians. J R Western suggested that, between 1680 and 1688 England seemed to be moving inexorably towards absolutism.[6] J R Jones wrote that the establishment of absolutist government was "a much more practicable proposition after 1660" than it had been before.[7] W A Speck described absolutism as giving way after 1688 to limited monarchy.[8] Christopher Hill wrote that, after 1688, "any future ruler would at his peril defy those whom Parliament represented: no ruler did ... Henceforth, Parliament was a necessary and continuous part of the constitution."[9] One must be very Olympian to say, grandly, that none of this matters, or very confident of one's own perceptions to believe that all of these historians totally misunderstood the period on which they were working.

If we concede that the Revolution was primarily the work of the Russells, the Cavendishes, the Osbornes, the Bentincks, and the Keppels, it will come as no great surprise that they were the ones, above all, who profited by it. They gained ideologically, politically, and economically.

Ideologically, they could argue that the nobility had played, as classical theory insisted that it should, a balancing or moderating role between despotism and democracy, between the autocrats and the levellers. They could claim that in 1688, perhaps as never before or since, they had spoken for the nation, rescued the constitution, and saved the people from the perils of popery. They gained because the new parliamentary developments held out the prospect of a key role for the House of Lords, as a balance between King and Commons, inclining first one way, then the other, as circumstances dictated.

They gained politically because, with absolutism ruled out as a practical possibility and egalitarian democracy not even on the distant horizon, a governmental system based upon the landed aristocracy was the only viable one. Not until the great commercial and industrial changes of the 18th century had produced, in the middle and professional classes, an alternative basis for government, could their power be effectively challenged, and then the liberal regime which emerged in the 19th century was one with which the aristocracy could come to terms and which, for many years, permitted them a continuing role in government.

They gained economically because the practice of primogeniture, supported by the strict settlement or entail, which came increasingly into use in this period, led to the rise of the great estates, of Chatsworth and Woburn, Castle Howard, Belvoir, Longleat, and Alnwick. Their vast possessions gave the aristocracy access to political power, and their command of political power safeguarded their vast possessions.

Let me offer two small pieces of evidence by way of confirmation, though they are perhaps scarcely needed. Each illustrates the prosperity of those who placed their bets correctly in the Glorious Revolution handicap.

Until 1688, the title of duke was restricted, and confined jealously to members of the royal family or their particular favourites. Between 1572 and 1603 there were no dukes at all, and between Norfolk (1553) and Albemarle (1660), the only dukedom granted to a non-royal was that given to Buckingham by James I in 1623. But the increase after 1688 was dramatic, with no fewer than 23 dukedoms granted in the next 32 years.

Secondly, the practice of granting special remainders with peerages, which had been used very sparingly, became much more common. The laws of nature could not be defied, even by the Whigs, but they could be mitigated. The Russell family, which had provided a Whig martyr in Lord Russell, executed in 1683 for complicity in the Rye House plot, came into great favour with the change of monarch in 1688. The Earl of Bedford was granted a dukedom in 1694 and when the new duke's grandson married the daughter of a wealthy London merchant the following year, the duke was granted another barony, to go, by special remainder, to the granddaughter's offspring. In 1723, Sir Robert Walpole had no wish to leave the Commons, so a barony was granted to his son, with a special remainder to his father: in theory, the laws of natural inheritance were turned upside down. The Duke of Newcastle, doyen of the Whigs, had no children to inherit his title of Newcastle upon Tyne, and so was granted in 1756 a second dukedom, of Newcastle under Lyne, to go by special remainder to a nephew, and in 1762, for good measure, a further barony to go by special remainder to a cousin. The great dukedom of Northumberland, which became extinct in 1670, was rescued by a complex series of special remainders during the reigns of George II and George III.

John Kenyon once wrote that "who gained from the Revolution of 1688 has yet to be decided."[10] Caution may perhaps be carried too far, and while we wait for a categorical answer, some 300 years after the event, it may not seem precipitate to suggest that the nobility, unless they were Catholic, or very stupid, did not do too badly.

When I talked of the Hanoverian period as a "golden age" for the aristocracy, I was thinking of three aspects. First, even though medical science remained crude and death in childbirth still a real hazard for young women, life was, for the chosen few, a little easier. Houses were more comfortable, furniture more elegant, food more varied, entertainment more sophisticated, the gardens and parks more delightful with new specimens of flowers, trees, and shrubs. The income of many aristocrats permitted them to go in for rebuilding and for landscape gardening on a grand scale. The medieval clutter of farm buildings was removed to a distance, public footpaths and roads diverted, the lake dug, the copses planted, the orangery fitted out, the gates and lodges refurbished, the drive gravelled, and the whole enclosed by stone walls to obstruct the gaze of the vulgar. Public life was neither as bitter nor as hazardous as it had been in previous centuries, even if the heads of Jacobite peers on Temple Bar were a reminder of what miscalculation could bring. But in the 15th century, four successive barons of the Clifford family had died in battle: six out of seven holders of the Salisbury title met violent deaths between 1400 and 1538 the exception dying as a boy of 10. The Hanoverian world was a good deal safer for royal ministers and favourites. Wolsey had died in disgrace; Thomas Cromwell was executed weeks after being created Earl of Essex; Elizabeth's favourite, another Earl of Essex, was executed in 1601; Buckingham was stabbed to death; Strafford and Laud beheaded. By comparison, the worst that happened to the Duke of Newcastle when he lost favour in 1762 was that he went into opposition, while the Earl of Bute, on his retirement in 1763, was able to devote more time to his botanical interests.

Secondly, for most of the century, the position of the aristocracy as the natural rulers and the natural leaders of society was not seriously challenged. Even if the dark days of the Interregnum, with the Monarchy and House of Lords abolished, titles were still recognized. Though there were always complaints about the behaviour of particular peers, there was no sustained attack upon the peerage as an institution until the American Revolution, and more particularly the French Revolution. Even then, Tom Paine's fierce assertion in *The Rights of Man* that titles were "mere foppery" must have struck most of his fellow-countrymen as very eccentric.

Thirdly, the nobility, together with their allies in the gentry, held throughout the 18th century an almost complete monopoly of power. Their control of the armed forces, and of national and local government, meant that all the levers were firmly in their hands. The Commander-in-Chief was always a peer; the Lord Lieutenant of Ireland was a peer; of 18 Lord Chancellors at the head of the law, between 1688 and 1832, 16 were peers; of the lord lieutenants, who wielded power in the shires, only 14 out of more than 200 were neither peers nor peers' sons. They had a virtual monopoly of the Cabinet, save for the occasional man-of-business brought in, and of 26 first ministers between the accession of the House of Hanover and 1841, 20 were peers or sons of peers.[11]

Although once it is stated clearly that the 18th century was a period of aristocratic supremacy, it looks very much like a truism, it is curious that, until recently, the Hanoverian period was not seen in such terms. Observers like Disraeli, who described it as a Venetian oligarchy, seemed mildly eccentric. There are, no doubt, many reasons why this was so. In the time available, I would like to comment briefly on four.

The first is that 19th century historians were very much preoccupied with the development of the British constitution, and how it had evolved through liberalism into parliamentary democracy. This meant that much attention was paid to the slow decline of the Monarchy and the corresponding rise in the power and influence of the House of Commons. In retrospect, it is remarkable that when the *History of Parliament* was being planned, the decision was taken to disregard the House of Lords and to concentrate research exclusively upon the House of Commons. That produced a distinctly lopsided view of the politics of Hanoverian England. In addition, I think some historians were taken in by that splendid name, House of Commons, though in fact the Hanoverian house was anything but common. Sir Lewis Namier, the driving force behind the *History of Parliament*, wrote in 1928 that the intention was to write the biographies of "ordinary men" – an observation that looks rather strange in the light of passing years.[12] The Hanoverian House was the preserve of the landed interest with a strong infusion of noble influence.

The illusion that the Hanoverian system was more democratical than it really was is one that was sustained by other factors. By comparison with most continental regimes, it was parliamentary and liberal. There were elections, even if less frequently than in the past, and governments had to take note of public opinion. In many of the county constituencies and some of the boroughs, like Westminster, Preston, Bristol or Honiton, the franchise was wide and many citizens had the right to vote. In the many descriptions of the British constitution, attempting to equate it with classical modes of analysis, the House of Commons was always taken to be the popular part of the political spectrum. Blackstone seemed aware of a certain sleight-of-hand when he observed in the *Commentaries* that the House of Commons was "freely chosen by the people from among themselves, which makes it *a kind of democracy*." Yet the section of the people who were represented by it was narrow, haphazard, and, if anything, shrinking. Macaulay – if you will forgive a second appearance – denied in 1831 that the old system represented the property of the country: "It is government by certain detached portions and fragments of property ... preferred to the rest on no rational principle whatever."[13]

Secondly, in the 20th century, academic interest in the evolution of the constitution began to wane and was replaced by great attention to the nature of party and the development of a party system. One interest grew out of the other, since party discipline and party organization was a method of mobilizing public opinion and bringing it to bear upon the Monarchy and the House of Lords. Namier's efforts to eradicate the concept of party from the historiography of the 1760s muddied the waters for some time, and since he never produced the book which he promised on the rise of party, much remained after his death in 1960 to be done. The following decades saw great progress in our understanding of the role of party in 18th century politics, but, by definition, such an approach tended to divert attention from the aristocracy as such, and to emphasize factors which separated Whigs from Tories, rather than dwelling on the extent to which they shared common assumptions. The bitterness of party rhetoric often deceived people at the time and has taken its toll of historians since.

Let me, at this point, call as witness Samuel Johnson. As a young man in the later 1730s he was an ardent opponent of Sir Robert Walpole and hoped for great things at his overthrow, only to discover that the new ministers were very much like the old, that promises of reform were not kept, and that much of the attack had been insincere and rhetorical. He finished up by admitting what a fine fellow Walpole had been.[14] It is true that in his excitable moments, Johnson seemed to believe that, between Whig and Tory, there was a great gulf fixed. "The first Whig was the devil," he told Boswell, and he saw them as sour republicans, levellers, and king-killers. But in his sober moments, Johnson understood how much they had in common, and his mature opinion was carefully dictated to Boswell: "A wise Tory and a wise Whig, I believe, will agree. Their principles are the same, though their modes of thinking are different." They merely emphasized different aspects of government and tried to adjust the balance of the constitution in their own direction.[15]

The third factor which has militated against the view of Hanoverian society as under the domination of the landed aristocracy is the belief that such an emphasis runs counter to another trend in the period, which we have already mentioned – the growth in the importance of trade, finance, and commerce. This is indisputable and, to some historians, of greater significance than the existing structure. It is always difficult for historians to strike a fair balance between tradition and change in society, since changes do not conveniently develop at the same pace in different areas of life, nor at the same rate in different parts of the country. Views and behaviour which may be acceptable in London and Sheffield may not go down well in Lincolnshire and Dorset.

A number of distinguished historians stressed the dynamism of Hanoverian England – the commercial revolution, followed in turn by the financial revolution, and, if one dare say it, the Industrial Revolution.[16] They saw the period as the century of the middle classes, gaining greatly in strength, numbers, prosperity, and influence. Napoleon, after all, when engaged in his great struggle against England, did not denounce it as a nation of aristocrats but as a nation of shopkeepers.

The argument has been developed brilliantly in two outstanding books in recent years.[17] Each stresses the extent of change in Hanoverian England and the aristocracy, to which I have today devoted so much attention, is relegated to a comparatively minor role. Though these are books from which I have learned a great deal, I am not certain that the balance has been maintained. There was certainly more to aristocratic influence than a late chapter on "Macaroni Manners" would suggest,[18] while it seems excessive to suggest that the aristocracy was "increasingly made the tool of a dictatorial bourgeoisie."[19] I cannot myself perceive a dictatorial bourgeoisie, and I am not even sure that I clearly perceive a bourgeoisie, if, by that, is meant a powerful and united group, conscious of their common interests. But, most of all, such a formulation seems to me to pose far too sharp a clash between the in interests of trade and commerce and those of the land. That many writers feared such a clash would develop can hardly be denied. On the other hand, many landowners were only too anxious to exploit the mineral resources of their estates, to diversify their investment into shares and the great public companies, to develop harbours, and to promote better roads, canals, and, later, railways.[20] That the policies which suited them were not inimical to the interests of the middle classes seems proved by the growing prosperity of the latter.

Fourthly, it may be that the strength of the aristocracy has been underestimated by historians who looked to the House of Lords as the agent or source of power. But the position of the House of Lords in the 18th century turns out to be, like so many other things, a matter of disagreement and controversy. In theory it was, of course, the senior House, and their lordships liked to think that it was in practice. There are historians who agree with them – the editors of a recent volume on "dominant partner" in the constitution.[21] But at least one of their own contributors dissented.[22]

That the Lords remained the dominant house seems rather doubtful. The role in impeachment which it possessed was dramatic, but by the 18th century impeachment was more of an antique survival than part of the normal working of the constitution. The Commons had complete control over the power of taxation and though this was challenged by some lords at infrequent intervals, it was never seriously in jeopardy. In a period of incessant warfare when the search for increased revenue was one of the most pressing preoccupations of ministers, it gave the Commons a decisive advantage. We should also note that the leaders of the most enduring administrations sat in the House of Commons. Between them, Walpole, Pelham, North, and Pitt held the office of first minister for 61 out of 85 years between 1721 and 1806. Each was in the House of Commons during that time and each developed a special aptitude for dealing with financial questions.

In addition, we can point to a certain amount of contemporary testimony. When Lord Hervey was moved up to the Lords in 1734 to strengthen Walpole's debating there, his father, the Earl of Bristol, wrote to commiserate with him on going to "so insignificant a place".[23] When Walpole and Pulteney, transmogrified as Orford and Bath, met in the Lords in 1742, the former is said to have remarked that they were now two of the least significant men in the kingdom. William Pitt's loss of influence when he moved to the Lords in 1766 as Earl of Chatham is well known. George III, in an essay on the constitution for his tutor, Lord Bute, deplored the decline in importance the upper house, which he attributed to the decision in 1712 to create 12 peers to swamp the Whig majority and carry the peace of Utrecht.[24]

You may think that I have boxed myself into something of a corner. If the House of Lords was not, as I have argued, the dominant house, can the Hanoverian period be the golden age of the aristocracy?

The answer is the one I have already hinted at - that the nobility possessed very great influence over the House of Commons itself. First of all, peers controlled a considerable number of parliamentary boroughs, despite a resolution by the House of Commons that they were not to interfere in elections. In fact, their share increased markedly in the course of the century. The number of seats under aristocratic command (never susceptible to exact calculation) has been put at about 31 in 1702. By 1786 it had risen to something like 210 seats. Even allowing for the fact that the house had increased in size by 45 as a result of the Act of Union, and reiterating that the figures cannot be precise, the trend is indisputable. Of course, not all aristocratic nominees were the themselves aristocrats and many patrons allowed their members considerable freedom of action. But in a crisis, as in 1784, they could be sharply reminded where their duty lay. The Duke of Newcastle put the matter rather bluntly when he offered a seat in 1755 to Sir Cecil Bisshopp at Boroughbridge: "It is a seat in Parliament entirely my own ... but I am very cautious not to choose anyone but such as I can entirely depend upon in everything."[25] Secondly, there was always a considerable number of Irish peers and peers' sons sitting in the House of Commons. Indeed, the practice was strongly defended as a means of giving future peers a useful training and of ensuring that the interests of the two Houses did not fatally diverge. This proportion also rose. In 1708, there were 70: by 1796 it had risen to 120.[26]

In addition, dozens of members of the House of Commons were closely related to the nobility. William Aislabie and Sir Walter Bagot were archetypal country gentlemen: the first sat for Ripon for 60 years, the second represented Staffordshire and then Oxford University. Each was married to the daughter of a peer. William Cartwright and John Conyers, county members sitting for Northamptonshire and Essex, were grandsons of peers. The House of Commons elected in 1784, after the rout of the Fox-North coalition, contained 175 close relatives of peers, and a further 129 close relatives of baronets, amounting to nearly 55% of the total of 558 members.

Although disputes between the two Houses were not infrequent, they resembled family quarrels. Indeed, they provided a service to the nobility by disguising its basic unity and suggesting a degree of competition hardly borne out by the facts. In many cases, such disputes were party disagreements rather than confrontations between the two Houses as such.

Even had the peers possessed less influence over the House of Commons, it does not seem very likely that they would have been threatened by radical or egalitarian legislation. Such movement as there was seems mainly in the other direction – the introduction of property qualifications for MPs and JPs[27], decisions to limit the franchise in many boroughs, and legislation to exclude copyholders from the county electorate.[28] From the accession of the House of Hanover onwards, there was a decline in the number of persons casting votes at general elections. In 1715, the 20 contests in the counties of

England and Wales gave more than 70,000 men a chance to cast a vote: by 1747 there were only three contests, with fewer than 9,000 men voting. In the boroughs, the decline was less marked, but whereas some 73,000 votes were cast in 113 contests in 1722, by 1761 the number of contests had fallen to 42, producing some 34,000 votes. There is little evidence until towards the end of the century of any determined attempt to reverse the trend of aristocratic rule, either by bringing new boroughs into the representation or by a general extension of the franchise. Secret ballot, which would really have hit at the influence of the landed classes, was scarcely discussed.

We can see that the relative lack of prominence of the House of Lords in the 18th century, certainly by comparison with the melodrama of 1832 or 1910, was an indication of aristocratic strength rather than weakness. The Lords' powers were mainly defensive weapons, hardly called for in the absence of any assault. The most dramatic intervention of the House of Lords in 1783, when they threw out Fox's India Bill, was not, after all, a desperate attempt to hold back the tide of radical advance, but a reversion to their role of balancing the constitution in a struggle between Commons and Crown.

I hope I have offered some evidence to suggest why, despite great poverty and distress, and disorders like the Gordon riots, Britain was never close to revolution in this period. The army were safely under aristocratic control. Though the decision to institute a militia in 1757 alarmed some landowners on the grounds that it was imprudent to place arms in the hands of the people, great care was taken to ensure that militia officers were men of good standing.[29] I may perhaps have gone to the other extreme and offered a picture of so powerful a position that you will wonder how it could possibly have been challenged or overthrown. But no society is impervious to change and that very dynamism which helped to reconcile many people to aristocratic leadership, contributed, in the end, to undermining the old order.

Footnotes to this Chapter may be found on pages 201-2.

8: David Cannadine

The fall of the British nobility: 1789-1994

THE EIGHTEENTH century was a marvellous era to be an aristocrat; indeed, it probably witnessed the apogee of privileged patrician existence in this country. Compared with the Stuart century, life was more stable and more secure. In 1688, the English landed classes had brought about a revolution which simultaneously preserved property and liberty. As the group who enjoyed more property and more liberty than any other, they naturally benefitted most, safeguarding themselves, their estates, and their descendants from the renewed threat of royal absolutism that had been presented by James II. From the time of William and Mary until the first two decades of the reign of George III, the aristocracy and gentry of England lived lives of assured ease, ample comfort, and unchallenged prestige, as such great houses as Chatsworth, Blenheim, Woburn, and Houghton remind us.

But from the late 18th century, the shades of the prison house began to close in on the seemingly limitless vistas and unassailable privileges of the country house. The French Revolution proclaimed a new ideology, of "Liberty, Equality, and Fraternity", which was totally opposed to the exclusive and hierarchical nature of nobility. The Industrial Revolution made possible the creation of new forms of non-landed wealth, which in time would challenge even the richest aristocrats. The growth of population, and the massive expansion of towns and cities, meant that numbers and individuals would soon count more than lineage and property. In the long run, equality, industry, and democracy were bound to overwhelm the traditional titled and territorial élite, as they have done in every modernizing country in the century of the common man - and of the common woman.

Nevertheless, like King Charles II or Rasputin, the English aristocracy has been an unconscionable time a-dying. Two hundred years after the storming of the Bastille, it has certainly declined, and in some instances undeniably fallen. But the hereditary nobility, the owners of great houses, are with us still. Not, as in the 18th century, as the governing élite of the country. Nor even as the undisputed wealth and social élite. Rather, they continue to exist as a low profile and in some ways marginal group, whose survival depends increasingly on their discretion rather than their distinction. How, then, do we explain the remarkable transformation in their fortunes, their functions and their circumstances that has taken place during the last 200 years or so?

During the century from the 1780s, aristocratic life was never as anxiety-free as it had been in the hundred years after the Glorious Revolution. But for most of the time, it was less challenged than the most pessimistic patricians were inclined to suppose. Of course, the Industrial Revolution meant that new forms of wealth were being accumulated in greater amounts than ever before - by industrialists such as Arkwright, Wedgwood, and Cubitt, by bankers such as Baring and Rothschild, and by many entrepreneurs working successfully, but on a smaller scale. The massive expansion in manufacturing and commerce - cotton, iron, and railways in particular - inevitably meant that landed wealth was neither so privileged nor so supreme as it had been in earlier times, when the economy had been overwhelmingly agrarian: the country house was being challenged by the counting house; the steam engine was superseding the horse.

Moreover, there was a definite shift in the balance of political power, which reflected - however belatedly and inadequately - these changes in the distribution of wealth. The passing of the Great Reform Act in 1832 did not usher in democracy: despite the doubling of the franchise, only a tiny fraction of the population actually had the vote. But the fact that Parliament had been influenced by public opinion; that the House of Lords had been successfully coerced into passing the measure; and that the number of rotten boroughs had been drastically reduced - all this portended the end of an aristocratic polity, something which the successful campaign against the Corn Laws 14 years later, and the passing of the Second Reform Act in 1867, seemed to confirm. Gradually, reluctantly, but inexorably, oligarchy was giving way to what would eventually become democracy.

All this meant a change in the values of society, away from those of a leisured aristocracy, towards those of a labouring bourgeoisie. The cult of work was one of the great creations of the Industrial Revolution, and it was shared by the men who ran the factories, and the thousands who toiled in them. The great heroes of mid-Victorian England were the self-made entrepreneurs and businessmen, immortalized in Samuel Smiles's best selling volume, *Self-Help*. By comparison, leisured aristocrats, who were never forced to soil their hands, seemed to many to be irrelevant, effete, unjustifiable, and anachronistic parasites. The ideology of "Liberty, Equality, and Fraternity" had not carried all before it in England: but it certainly gave rise to a climate of opinion in which the aristocracy had to justify itself more convincingly than ever before. Rank certainly had its privileges: but what were its duties?

Nevertheless, the picture, though not as roseate as in the halcyon days of the 18th century, was far from being all dark. To begin with, many landowners came to exceedingly profitable terms with the Industrial Revolution. Nor should this be any surprise, since, especially in its early phases, the Industrial Revolution was largely to do with getting minerals from under the land, with building houses on top of the land, with constructing canals and railways across the land, and with building docks and harbours on the edge of the land. As a result, many landowners, whose estates were advantageously located, enjoyed massively augmented incomes, from mineral royalties, from ground rents, from shares in canal and railway companies, and from harbour dues. Indeed, by the 1820s, magnates such as the Dukes of Bedford, Norfolk,

Devonshire, and Portland, and Lords Dudley, Westminster, Derby, Durham, and Fitzwilliam were enjoying incomes in excess of £100,000 a year.

At the same time, agriculture remained in an extremely prosperous state for most of the period. During the Napoleonic Wars, prices - and thus rents - reached unprecedented heights, and after the postwar slump and the crisis over the Corn Laws, British farming again boomed during the period from 1846 to the mid-1870s. Even those landowners who did not enjoy huge incomes from other sources were thus still more than comfortably off, jogging along on £10,000 a year or so. Indeed, taking the landowning class as a whole, it remained unquestionably the wealth élite. Between them, the aristocracy and gentry owned most of the land of the British Isles. And the richest landowners remained the wealthiest people in the land. Even during the mid-Victorian period, the new fortunes accumulated by businessmen and entrepreneurs rarely rivalled those of old, titled money.

At the same time, many landowners managed to hold on to more political power than they dared to expect in the dark days of 1789, 1832, or 1846. Despite the two extensions of the franchise, the social background of those returned to the House of Commons remained essentially what it had been before: the overwhelming majority were drawn from the landed gentry or from relatives of the peerage. In the same way, the House of Lords was still dominated by the territorial aristocracy and, in all matters except money bills, retained the right to veto legislation sent up from the House of Commons. Not surprisingly, British Cabinets throughout this period were dominated by peers and country gentlemen, who were often related to each other. Almost every prime minister from the Younger Pitt to Gladstone was the owner of a landed estate, while the majority were closely related to the peerage, or peers themselves, like Lords Grey, Melbourne, Aberdeen, Derby, and Palmerston.

Control at the centre inevitably implied control in the localities, and this, too, the landed élite continued to exert, long into the reign of Queen Victoria. Despite the Great Reform Act, many small borough constituencies survived, often under the influence of a single family, such as Woodstock, which was effectively owned by the Dukes of Marlborough. In many county constituencies, representation was often controlled by a handful of landowners, who regularly divided the representation between a Tory country gentleman and the son of a Whig duke. The administration of the counties was as aristocratic as was their representation. There was no elected body: instead, the justice and the government of the county was administered by JPs, usually a self-perpetuating body of landowners, often - and revealingly - described as the "rural House of Lords". Nor should we forget the professions: the Church, the law, the civil service, and the armed forces were dominated, in terms of ethos and personnel, by younger sons drawn from the landed classes.

Since the titled and territorial classes survived as the wealth and the power élite of the country, it almost automatically followed that they survived as the status élite as well. Their prestige - as owners of great estates, and as the great governing families of the nation - endured unchallenged. The honours system remained virtually their monopoly: despite the Industrial Revolution, scarcely any great entrepreneur was recruited to the ranks of the peerage, and the House of Lords was still an almost exclusively landed body. Notwithstanding the French Revolution, class, hierarchy and inequality were essential - and widely accepted - props to Victorian society. From the time of the Napoleonic Wars onwards, the aristocracy had brilliantly reinvented itself as a responsible, hard-working élite, disinterestedly governing the country on the behalf of everybody - a claim, and a function, which were widely recognized and widely accepted.

One final change in the circumstances of our national notability needs recording for the century from the 1780s, and that is the melding of the separate aristocracies in England, Ireland, Scotland, and Wales into a truly supranational, British élite. There are many reasons for this. In part, it was a glut of marriage alliances which put together the great transnational territorial agglomerations held by families such as the Butes, the Sutherlands, the Fitzwilliams, and the Londonderrys. In part, it was because the unprecedented prosperity of the period 1780-1815 meant that the hitherto impoverished landowners of Scotland and Ireland increasingly felt themselves on terms of equality with their English cousins. In part, it was because the Act of Union with Ireland (1801) tied the Irish nobility directly into the British House of Lords. And in part, it was because notables from Scotland and Ireland increasingly saw that their future lay in serving the British State and the British Empire, classically in the case of Arthur Wellesley, scion of an Anglo-Irish family, and later Duke of Wellington, a soldier of fortune in India, victor of Waterloo, and British Prime Minister.

As the last quarter of the 19th century opened, therefore, the aristocracy and gentry of the British Isles continued unchallenged in their traditional preeminence. Adaptation and modification there certainly had been; some changes had been distinctly unwelcome: but the earth had not moved. As in the 18th century, they still formed the wealth élite and the territorial élite of the country. Despite all the disruptive changes associated with the Industrial Revolution, great superpowers like the Sutherlands, the Devonshires, and the Buccleuchs remained the richest men in the kingdom, measuring their territorial empires in hundreds of thousands of acres, and counting their annual incomes in hundreds of thousands of pounds. Indeed, one quarter of the land of England and Wales was owned by 710 individuals, and four fifths of the whole of the British Isles was held by a mere 7,000 landed families. It was, as Benjamin Disraeli once remarked, a time when the world was for the few - and especially for the very few who owned most of it.

Despite two Reform Acts, the aristocracy still took it for granted that they should rule the nation as a right: that was, after all, the justification for the continued existence of a leisured class. Until the early 1880s, the majority of MPs were still landowners or their relatives; peerages were only given out to those who owned substantial estates; and all cabinets, whether Liberal or Tory, were dominated by patricians. Dynasties like the Derbys, the Devonshires, the Bedfords, and the Salisburys continued to regard themselves as being the great governing families of the realm. Not surprisingly, a British "milord" had no rival, either among other social groups in Britain, or among the continental nobilities; and the untitled landed gentry still enjoyed immense prestige. Naturally, the men and women who made up Britain's traditional aristocratic and landowning élite possessed a strong sense of corporate identity. They knew they were the lords of the earth, the makers of history, the stars of the firmament. In short, they were strongly conscious of themselves as being God's elect.

Today, there are still many traces of this largely-vanished world of aristocratic supremacy and confidence. Some landowners, like the Dukes of Westminster and of Buccleuch, remain astonishingly rich. Scarcely 10 years ago, the Foreign Secretary was an authentic grandee: Lord Carrington. The Governor of the Bank of England was until recently a country gentleman and Lord Lieutenant of Kent: Robin (now Lord) Leigh-Pemberton. And popular interest in the peerage is still such that the disappearance of Lord Lucan some years ago was front page news, not just in Britain, but throughout the English-speaking world. But these are the lingering residues of a once preeminent patrician world which has long since gone the way of the dodo. Even before 1914, it was already in conspicuous retreat, and since the Second World War, this once unchallenged aristocracy has gradually but inexorably retreated to the margins of British politics, British society, and British life. As such, their decline and fall ranks as one of the greatest changes to have occurred in modern British history. How, during the last 100 years or so, has it come about?

A significant part of the answer lies in the democratic triumph of the "masses" over the "classes", something which was portended by the passing of the first two Reform Acts, but which only came about much later. In Ireland, there was a widespread rejection of "landlordism" in the early 1880s by increasingly militant nationalists: tenants refused to pay their rents, landowners were subjected to widespread intimidation, and as a result, the patrician ascendancy was never the same again. In Scotland and Wales, there were similar agitations, modelled on Ireland and, in the context of the time, decidedly alarming. Throughout the United Kingdom, the passing of the Third Reform Act in 1884-5 greatly extended the franchise, and brought the representational structure more into line with the changed social and economic realities of the last 100 years. Politics became more concerned with class issues: not for nothing did Lord Salisbury write an essay entitled "Disintegration".

One politician who made hostility to the aristocracy an essential prop to his platform was Joseph Chamberlain, a radical Birmingham industrialist, who in the 1870s and early 1880s had likened the nobility to the lilies of the field, "who toil not, neither do they spin". A generation later, a "damned Welsh attorney" named David Lloyd George preached class war in more violent and more memorable words. "Aristocracy", he remarked on one occasion, "is like cheese: the older it gets, the higher it becomes." In another speech, he likened the House of Lords to "five hundred men, chosen randomly from among the ranks of the unemployed". By his demagoguery, his passion, and his gift for memorable phrases, Lloyd George did more than any other man to undermine and discredit what had survived of the patrician mystique. The passing of the Parliament Act in 1911, which ended the Lords' powers of veto, was the single most symbolic event in the decline and fall of the British aristocracy.

By 1914, the old élite thus found itself increasingly embattled: aristocracy and democracy did not comfortably coexist. Then came the First World War. Initially, it was greeted with rapturous enthusiasm by young notables like Julian Grenfell. Here was the supreme chance for aristocracy to justify its existence: by temperament and by training, they formed the warrior class, leading their men into battle. But this time, they paid a mortally high price. The deaths in action of Julian and Billy Grenfell, of Hugo and Ivo Charteris, are well known. But many a noble family suffered at least as severely. Of the great Lord Salisbury's 10 grandsons, five were killed in action; and in Chester Cathedral, there is a monument to the Grey-Egerton family, 13 of whose members died on active service. Beyond doubt, this terrible patrician holocaust undermined their confidence in themselves, and greatly weakened their desire to rule. The passing of the Fourth Reform Act, in 1918, which brought with it universal male suffrage, did much to undermine their capacity to rule as well.

From the late 1870s onwards, many landowners also found that their wealth was becoming less Himalayan and less secure than it had seemed in their mid-Victorian heyday. The late 19th century witnessed the first agricultural depression, as prices plummetted with the influx of grain from North America and lamb and beef from the antipodes and Argentina. As a result, farmers' profits were hit, and rentals fell by as much as one third. Many landowners, encumbered by debts, found themselves in increasingly straitened circumstances, and agriculture continued in this depressed condition until the Second World War and beyond. In addition, massive new plutocratic fortunes now began to rival all but the very greatest aristocratic accumulations: Cowdray, Lever, Guinness, and Northcliffe in this country; Mellon, Astor, Rockefeller, and Morgan in the United States. At the same time, successive governments began to tax landowners as never before. Death Duties were first introduced in 1894, initially at an extremly low rate. But they were inexorably increased, until by the 1930s they stood at 60 per cent on the largest estates.

The result of these developments was that land became a less attractive or secure means of holding wealth, and many owners disposed of some or all of their historic estates. In Ireland, a succession of Land Acts enabled the landowners to sell out on reasonably advantageous terms between 1885 and 1914, so that by the time Southern Ireland became independent, the old estate system had virtually disappeared. In Wales, Scotland, and England, there were massive sales in the years immediately before and after the First World War, a "revolution in landholding" which had not been seen on such a scale since the Norman Conquest or the Dissolution of the Monasteries. At the same time, many of the greatest magnates' London palaces - Grosvenor House, Devonshire House, Lansdowne House - were sold off to the new rich, or were demolished. From the mid 1880s onwards, the disposal of great works of art became a familiar phenomenon, beginning with the Duke of Marlborough, and culminating in the Duke of Westminster's sale of the The Blue Boy to Samuel Huntington of America.

Inevitably, these developments weakened the aristocracy's local position as the élite which had for centuries represented and ruled the countries of the British Isles. The much larger and independent electorate which was created by the Third and Fourth Reform Acts, combined with patrician impoverishment and territorial decline, meant that fewer landowners were standing for Parliament, and fewer still were getting elected. With only one or two exceptions, the politics of Barset were largely at an end. By the First World War, the majority of county seats were no longer represented by members of the old guard. At the same time, the establishment of county councils in 1888 finally brought democracy to the shires and spelt the death-knell of the "rural House of Lords". As local government became more democratic, and then more bureaucratic and professionalized, the old style of amateur, patrician administration seemed increasingly outmoded, inappropriate and anachronistic.

In Ireland, the nationalist agitation of the 1880s swept away most landed Members of Parliament, and by the time the Tories reformed local government there in 1898, the old patrician ascendancy had effectively ceased to count in the public life of the majority of the country where Catholics were numerically preponderant. Only in the Protestant enclave of Ulster did the traditional landowning class survive. But even there, the grandees and gentry preserved what remained of their power in the countryside only on the sufferance of the big bourgeoisie of Belfast, who were by this time effectively in charge of the Province's affairs. During the tense and troubled years before 1914, James Craig mattered much more than the Duke of Abercorn or the Marquess of Londonderry. In the aftermath of civil war and partition, the patricians hung on in the north as minority partners among the governing élite. But in the newly-independent south, they effectively disappeared altogether.

As the notables gradually surrendered their role as the governors and representatives of the localities, it inevitably followed that they were ceasing to be the governors and representatives of the country as a whole. Within 50 years, the landowners' dominance of the House of Commons was abruptly eclipsed: at the general election of 1885, a Lower House was returned for the first time in which the relatives of peers and members of the gentry were in a minority. And by the 1930s, scarcely 10 per cent of the Commons could claim authentically patrician lineage. A similar transformation took place in the Upper House. From the 1880s onwards, peerages were increasingly given out to the non-landed rich, to civil servants and soldiers, and to MPs from business and professional backgrounds. Instead of being an exclusive bastion of territorial nobility, the Lords had become a body to which people from many different walks of life might plausibly aspire.

In the Cabinet, the aristocratic contribution also declined markedly. The late 19th century governments of Lord Salisbury were "the last administrations in the western world to possess all of the attributes of aristocracy in working order", and were so patrician in their membership that they were known as the "Hotel Cecil". But by the time the Liberals took office in 1905, landowners had ceased to be in the majority, and with the brief exception of Bonar Law's Cabinet of 1922-3, this remained the case thereafter. Prime ministers, too, were no longer drawn from the traditional titled and territorial élite. Salisbury and Gladstone were authentically landed, and so were Rosebery and Balfour. But Campbell-Bannerman was at best a marginal case, and neither Asquith nor Lloyd George came from the "upper ten". The Labour leader, Ramsay MacDonald, was born lowly and illegitimate. The three Tory prime ministers of the interwar years - Bonar Law, Stanley Baldwin, and Neville Chamberlain - were all businessmen by background.

Among the traditional patrician professions, it was essentially the same story. The introduction of "open competition" into the Civil Service meant that recruitment by merit gradually superseded recruitment by connection. Only in the Royal Court did - and does - the old system of patronage survive. The law became more professionalized, and the Church became less attractive to younger sons - partly because the value of the livings had declined as a result of the agricultural depression, and partly because it was a less fulfilling job in an increasingly urbanized and secular world. The abolition of purchase in 1870 had the same effect on the army that the introduction of "open competition" had on the Civil Service. As war became more messy and technologically sophisticated, it ceased to be an appealing occupation for a gentleman. Among the great professions, only the foreign service retained its aristocratic tone into the interwar years. But in the aftermath of the First World War and Lloyd George, the Foreign Office did not enjoy the prestige it once had, while "old diplomacy" seemed an increasingly outmoded profession.

As the old élite declined in these varied, interrelated, and self-reinforcing ways, there were protests by some of its more high-minded (or resentful) members that the standards of public life were slipping. From the 1880s, knighthoods and peerages were given out in far greater numbers than ever before, and to people of much more varied social origins. As its name implies, the Order of Merit, established by King Edward VII, was for excellence regardless of ancestry. The Order of the British Empire, set up in 1917, was deliberately designed to be democratic, rather than exclusive, in its multilayered membership. In the years before 1914, the Liberals and the Conservatives began to reward generous benefactors to party funds with peerages, which gave rise to justified, but unverifiable, allegations of corruption. During the premiership of Lloyd George, from 1916 to 1922, titles were openly hawked about London clubs, and were bought and sold for cash according to a recognized tariff. Thereafter, the honours system was cleaned up a little; but the old status structure of patrician exclusiveness and disinterested decency had been irrevocably undermined.

Equally threatened, and equally vulnerable, was the general social pattern of aristocratic and genteel living. In London high society, the exclusively patrician monopoly was broken, and the new super rich, like Sir Julius Wernher and Sir Ernest Cassel flaunted their parvenu wealth with opulent vulgarity, often supported by King Edward VII. By the interwar years, after the sale and demolition of their great town palaces, the aristocracy had all but abandoned large-scale entertaining, and what was left of society was lead by socially-ambitious American adventurers like Henry Channon, Emerald Cunard - and Mrs Wallis Simpson. In the shires and the countryside, the picture was essentially the same: instead of being a patrician preserve, it was increasingly a plutocratic playground. Impoverished landowners sold or let their houses: the new rich bought or rented them. In different ways, the motor car, the shot gun, and barbed wire dealt mortal blows to the traditional style of country living, and the massive land sales after the First World War effectively destroyed the territorial basis of the old county community.

As the old guard withdrew from the London season and from county society, they spent more time than ever before overseas, as what remained of the leisure class became increasingly the pleasure class. Some holidayed on the Riviera, bought villas in the Mediterranean, wintered in Egypt (hence Lord Carnarvon's involvement with the discovery of the tomb of Tutankhamun), sailed their yachts, or took to the air. Some went big-game hunting, in the United States, in India, or East Africa. Some were obliged to leave home because of financial embarrassment or sexual misdemeanour, like Lord Arthur Somerset in the aftermath of the Cleveland Street scandal, and Lord Beauchamp because of his alleged homosexuality. Some, like Wilfrid Scawen Blunt, or Aubrey Herbert, took refuge from the travails of modern life by going on knight-errantly quests to the Middle East. For whatever reason, these notables were in motion as they had never been before - a restless, rootless, fragmenting élite.

How did these increasingly beleaguered patricians respond to this unmistakable evidence of their own decline, and that of their class? Some decided that the only solution was to earn their livings, and became in the process labouring aristocrats - itself rather a contradiction in terms.

The Hon C S Rolls sold high-class cars to high-class people. Lord Rayleigh went into the milk business. Lord Montagu of Beaulieu founded and edited *Car Illustrated*. Some wrote mildly salacious memoirs, in the hope of keeping their creditors at bay, like the Countess of Warwick or the Earl of Rosslyn. Some turned to fiction, like Osbert Sitwell, Nancy Mitford, and Vita Sackville-West. Some sought American heiresses, like George Curzon, the Duke of Manchester, Lord Randolph Churchill, and the Duke of Marlborough. Some became completely and pathetically déclassé, like Moreton Frewen (better known as "Mortal Ruin"), and Lord Castlerosse, who ended up as a gossip columnist in Lord Beaverbrook's pay.

Among more adventurous (and more needy) notables, the City beckoned alluringly, as a possible way of restoring the family fortunes. But it was often a risky undertaking. Some naïve and greedy aristocrats allowed their names to be used as "guinea pig" directors, by unscrupulous company promoters. In *The Gondoliers*, first produced in 1889, W S Gilbert satirized such unhappy figures in his creation of the Duke of Plaza-Toro - ostensibly a Spanish grandee, but in fact an impoverished English nobleman, who floats himself as a public company. A decade later, the Marquess of Dufferin and Ava, after a lifetime spent in ambassadorial and proconsular postings, retired and became chairman of a company run by the shady financier Whittaker Wright. It collapsed soon after, and so did Dufferin's health, finances, and reputation. But other notables were more successful (or more lucky) in their business dealings, like Viscount Churchill, who was chairman of the Great Western Railway, and Lord Herbert Scott, a son of the Duke of Buccleuch, who was an appropriately aristocratic chairman of Rolls-Royce.

Even more adventurous were those "gentleman emigrants" who settled in far off places. During the 1880s, it became quite the fashion for young bloods like Lord Lonsdale and Lord Aylesford to go cattle ranching in Texas: they normally returned home poorer, and little the wiser. A decade later, some of the more disreputable scions of the aristocracy attached themselves to Cecil Rhodes. They invested in his British South Africa Company (some also became directors), they took large concessions of land in Rhodesia, and they were even involved in the Jameson Raid itself. But it was Kenya which saw the most sustained attempt to transplant British country house life to the Empire during the interwar years. Some were serious figures, like Lord Francis Scott, another son of the Duke of Buccleuch, who were determined to do their best to build up the country. But many were déclassé misfits, like Lord Erroll or Sir Delves Broughton, whose notorious misdoings and misdemeanours in "Happy Valley" have been so vividly described by James Fox in *White Mischief*.

Meanwhile, there were other patricians who devoted themselves, unavailingly, to trying to defend their increasingly beleaguered position back home in Britain. Some, like Lord Bledisloe and Algernon Turnor, tried to persuade successive governments to take a greater interest in agriculture: but to no avail. Some, like Lords Salisbury and Selborne, tried to win back the House of Lords veto, which had been lost in the Parliament Act of 1911: again to no avail. Some, like Lords Dunraven and Lord Midleton, tried to prevent the partition of Ireland, and to preserve a role in the south for the old landed élite: once more, to no avail. And some, like the Salisbury clan, increasingly diverted their energies away from running the affairs of the country to running the affairs of the Church of England. But this was merely a tacit admission of how peripheral the aristocracy had become to the mainstream of British life.

But there were also more direct, and more extreme political responses, as angry grandees, fearful gentry, and disappointed former landowners flouted the rules of genteel political life, in the vain hope that by such desperate, uncharacteristic actions, they might restore the world they rightly feared they were losing. The pioneer patrician apostates were the Whig grandees, who in the mid 1880s abandoned their historic and progressive traditions, withdrew their support from Gladstone's policy of Irish Home Rule, turned their backs on the Liberal Party, slowly allied themselves with the Conservatives, and eventually disappeared into oblivion. A generation later, in enraged response to Lloyd George, the Tory Die Hards, led by Lord Willoughby de Broke, espoused a more violent, antidemocratic credo, which skirted the very bounds of treason. They vainly sought to defy the Liberal attempts to emasculate the House of Lords at the time of the Parliament Act crisis, and they even contemplated armed insurrection to prevent Irish Home Rule and to support the Ulster loyalists.

During the interwar years, a later generation of disillusioned, disenchanted, and disoriented notables moved not only to the extreme right, but also to the far left. Patricians like Sir Charles Trevelyan, the Buxton brothers, Lord Parmoor, and Bertrand Russell joined the Labour Party, not so much because they rejected the values of their genteel upbringing, but in the vain hope that it might prove a more effective vehicle for safeguarding paternalistic decency than the declining Liberals or the plutocratic Tories. Most were disappointed in this hope, and their political careers fizzled out. At the other end of the spectrum, even more aristocrats flirted with extreme forms of antidemocratic authoritarianism. Sir Oswald Mosley was himself the son of a broad-acred baronet, and his British Union of Fascists was (among other things) an attempt to run Britain as if it was a landed estate. For the same reason, the Fascist dictatorships of Germany, Italy, and Hungary had their share of aristocratic admirers, including Lord Londonderry, the Duke of Bedford, and Unity Mitford.

But while some aristocrats vainly and violently lamented their loss of power and prestige, there were others who were enjoying a period of renewed - indeed unprecedented - social celebrity. From the 1880s, many of them behaved like minor royalty in British cities, serving as lord mayor or as chancellor of the local university (like the Dukes of Norfolk in Sheffield, and the Earls of Derby in Liverpool), and bringing colour and glamour into drab urban lives. Others established a new identity as nonpolitical, disinterested public servants, chairing royal commissions and government inquiries, and holding a variety of formal positions in the worlds of education, the media, and the arts. One such figure was the Earl of Crawford and Balcarres, who was, among other things, Chancellor of Manchester University, a trustee of the British Museum and of the National Gallery, and chairman of a royal commission to inquire into the BBC. He enjoyed it all, and was rather good at it, but admitted it was not the same as being involved in politics.

Alternatively, there were proconsular opportunities abroad, where well-paid imperial governorships offered prestige, income, leisured living, and honorific rewards. From the 1880s to the Second World War, the governor generalships of Canada, South Africa, Australia, and New Zealand were almost invariably occupied by men drawn from the traditional titled élite, and the same was also true of Viceroys of India. There was another, lower level of patrician preferment: state governorships in Australia, and the Indian provinces. For those who played the game of proconsular snakes and ladders with skill and luck, there was the prospect of a lifetime's employment, as in the case of Lord Willingdon, who in the course of his career held two Indian state governorships, then became Governor General of Canada, and eventually Viceroy of India. As A J P Taylor once remarked, "going out and governing New South Wales" became, for many notables, an abiding consolation.

By the time the Second World War broke out in 1939, the condition of the British aristocracy was very different from what it had been only half a century before. Of course, they had not disappeared altogether. But as almost any interwar memoirs, or any interwar novels make plain, they were well aware - and rightly aware - that they they were no longer God's elect. The lords of the earth had become strangers in their own land. The makers of history had become the victims of history. The stars of the firmament no longer shone with unrivalled brilliance. Indeed, it was only the vicissitudes of 1940 that brought to power a man widely regarded as a marginalized and anachronistic diehard, a class warrior who was hostile to democracy, a wayward and unstable adventurer, an Anglo-American "half-breed", the sometime heir to one dukedom who in later life was offered another, the last aristocrat authentically to rule these islands: Winston Churchill himself.

Beyond any doubt, the Second World War was in some ways the aristocracy's "finest hour", as well as Winston Churchill's. Patricians like Montgomery, Alexander, and Alan Brooke were among his foremost lieutenants. Despite the terrible losses of the First World War, many young notables rushed to join the colours once more. But in the long run, this great conflict accelerated, more than it arrested, the aristocracy's decline. In part, this was because they suffered the greatest deprivations: loss of income, loss of servants, loss of houses, and loss of life. But even more importantly, the Second World War was almost universally seen, not as a battle to defend the old, established order, but as a crusade to build a new and better world, a Welfare State society in which traditional aristocratic privilege was neither wanted nor admired. The general election of 1945 only seemed to confirm these gloomy forebodings.

Economically, the combination of continued austerity and increased taxes meant that once again estates tumbled into the market in the years after 1945, and that country houses, town palaces, works of art, and nonagricultural assets were destroyed or disbursed at an unprecedented rate. Some owners gave up and emigrated; many were forced to turn to the stately homes business; the majority were obliged to go out and work for their living. The subsequent recovery of agriculture, the rise in land values, and the influence of the "Getty factor" on art prices means that some families, like the Westminsters, the Buccleuchs, and Devonshires, are still very wealthy today. But the majority of land is no longer held in traditional estates, many bearers of once-great names are now indistinguishable in their lives and their occupations from members of the business and professional classes, while some patricians are completely separated from the lands their forbears once owned, and are themselves very poor indeed.

Politically, the postwar picture has been even more bleak. The Labour government of 1945 was the most radical and the least landed ministry in British parliamentary history; the Tory administrations of 1951 to 1964 were more patrician in façade than substance, and inept and transient prime ministers like Eden and Home only discredited still further the idea of the landed élite as the ruling élite. At the margins of power - in Rhodesia and in Kenya, in Northern Ireland, and in the deepest of the shires - the landowners lingered on. But even there, by the mid-1970s, their position was being fundamentally eroded. In the world of Wilson and Callaghan, Heath and Foot, public life in Britain was less aristocratic even than in the days of Attlee. In the rampantly petty bourgeois 1980s, Margaret Thatcher saw off Carrington, Pym, and Whitelaw. And Mr Major not only seeks to make Britain a "classless society": he has entrusted the one remaining Cabinet patrician, the Hon William Waldegrave, with overseeing the implementation of the "Citizen's Charter".

In social terms, too, the grandees and gentry who remain are far less conspicuous than once they were. The honours system is now completely divorced from its old territorial and patrician base. The introduction of life peerages by Harold Macmillan struck at the very root of traditional, hereditary aristocracy, and has fundamentally changed the character of the House of Lords, while even the Order of the Garter is today full of people of distinctly un-aristocratic background: Wilson, Callaghan and Heath. Today, no political party, not even the Conservatives, defends the idea of a predominantly hereditary second chamber. At the same time, the great ornamental positions in the Empire have vanished in the aftermath of decolonization, and similar positions in Britain itself are now more likely to be held by people from very different social backgrounds. The disappearance of the great

London palaces, of so many of the grandest country houses, and of the once numerous servant class, means that the labour-intensive theatricality of country house life has virtually come to an end. In today's unsympathetic climate, a low profile existence seems more prudent, and more necessary, than continued conspicuous consumption.

Only in one sphere has what remains of the aristocracy sought to assert itself, and to acquire a new, public role in the years since the Second World War, and that is as the self-styled "guardians of the national heritage". Today's surviving patricians are not so much the owners of private possessions, so the argument runs, as the custodians of culture on behalf of everyone. Compared with many of their philistine forebears, they have raised their cultural consciousness and thrown open their houses to the public. It is an ingenious - and thus far exceptionally successful - example of aristocratic reinvention, mingling altruism and self-interest in a recognizable way. In fact, most country house owners regard the stately homes business as an unavoidable necessity that must be endured if they are to preserve what remains of their much diminished inheritance. By making their art treasures accessible, they themselves hope to survive. How far they can or will, only time will tell.

There is, then, no definitive end to this account of two hundred years of aristocratic history: only another interim conclusion - and that is this. Whatever the qualifications that have to be made - and there are many - the fact remains that Britain's once-proud patricians are no longer God's elect in the ways that they were a little more than 100 years ago. To some, this is cause for regret; for others, it merits celebration. Either way, the decline and fall - and survival - of the British aristocracy is an extraordinary story, peopled by outsized characters as diverse as humanity itself, caught up in circumstances sometimes tragic, sometimes comic, which they could neither adequately control nor fully comprehend, in one guise playing melodrama, in another acting out farce. Perhaps that is what Oscar Wilde meant when he once observed that the peerage was the best thing in fiction that the English (*sic*) ever did.

A further reading list for this Chapter may be found on pages 202-3.

9: J Enoch Powell

Will the Lords Survive?

IN AN unwritten constitution, such as ours has been at any rate until the European Communities Act 1972 and its successive amendments, the powers and authority of an institution such as the House of Lords derive from prescription - that is, from from the fact that in the course of time it has come to be constituted as it is and to exercise the powers and authority that it does. Prescription is the word for this which Edmund Burke bequeathed to us.

Whether the effect of prescription is destroyed or diminished by changes in the composition of an institution is not a question capable of being answered in general terms. Obviously, a change may be so trivial that it would be unreasonable to regard it as having destroyed one institution and replaced it with another. For example, the statute of 1958 which authorized the Crown to create peerages for the duration of one lifetime and women peers to sit in the House of Lords has not been treated as having abrogated the prescriptive powers of that institution: the House has, by general tacit agreement, been treated as if it continued to be one and the same institution. Of course, the same would not necessarily apply if, by the effluxion of time and the continued exercise by the Crown of the powers conferred on it in 1958, the House of Lords were to be *seen* as having ceased to be the same prescriptive institution and consequently as possessing the same prescriptive powers.

This case in point draws attention to a peculiarity of our unwritten constitution - a term which, perhaps, I was guilty of an oversight in failing to define when I used it first. I define, then, an unwritten constitution as follows. All societies, except during brief and necessarily transient periods of violence and oppression, are governed in the way they are because those who compose them consent, or sufficiently consent, to be so. The proposition is not restricted to those societies which our American cousins would deign to recognize as "democratic": tyrannies endure and emperors bear rule because sufficient consent exists, however odious they are and to whatever causes the consent is attributable. If you object: that is an argument in a circle. I retort: What of it? An argument in a circle is an excellent argument.

When I, therefore, say that in our unwritten constitution - prior, be it always understood, to the European Communities Act of 1972 and despite any treaty or other document to which that Act purported to give effect - the law is only made by and with the consent, duly signified, of "the lords spiritual and temporal in Parliament assembled"; I mean that the people of the United Kingdom sufficiently consent to regard legislative provision thus made to be binding upon them. If you ask me why, I can only reply: "Because they are the sort of people who have come to behave in that way." They have, however, another relevant peculiarity. They are disposed to believe that anything can be made law by Parliament. It used to be said that Parliament can do anything except make a woman into a man; but nowadays even that assertion would be less confidently voiced. Toleration has, moreover, been extended by the people of the United Kingdom to their Parliament when it made a law - this was something which it did in 1972 - depriving itself of the power to make law. Whether it could do that thing was debated at the time; but the public effectively settled that debate by consenting to the consequences. It follows that Parliament can by law destroy or modify any of the effects of prescription, including powers which are exercised by prescription, as those of the House of Lords are.

It can, therefore, be assumed that the same Parliament which has enjoyed toleration and public consent when it transferred to institutions outside this realm powers hitherto exclusively possessed by itself and, in particular, by the House of Commons would encounter similar tolerance if it proceeded, as precedent indicates that it can, to alter radically what remains of law-making authority in the United Kingdom - as for example by abolishing the House of Lords, or altering it radically, or depriving it of its present indispensability to legislation. In a nation with an unwritten constitution, which has consented to Parliament changing that constitution fundamentally, prescription, even though it is the basis of the existing institutions, can afford no protection to them.

I have thus arrived at a conclusion sufficiently bleak to have qualified me for membership of the Labour Party's advisory panel on policy in the days when Neil Kinnock was "making all things new". Because, however, something *can* happen, it does not follow that it *will* happen: many things that could have happened have not happened. I turn, therefore, to consider reasons why the thing, which I have just demonstrated could happen, may nevertheless not do so.

In the first place, a change in public sentiment is not impossible. I do not mean that the British people could become reenamoured of prescription. That I do not expect, because one of their peculiarities is a lack of interest in the principles upon which they consent - so far as they do consent - to be governed. What I mean is that there may be a revulsion of feeling against the hitherto tolerated dismantling of the legislative power of Parliament.

Such a revulsion is not unrealistic, when one considers that the legislative function of Parliament is, under our electoral system, the sole link between the sovereign people and the manner in which they are governed; and it is not inconceivable that they could acquire a dislike of that link being destroyed. In constitutional terms, there is nothing to prevent that revulsion being given effect by means of the repeal or restrictive amendment - the latter much more probably - of the European Communities Act 1972. In this respect, that Act is on the same footing as the Road Traffic Acts. No expressions of opinion, intention, or sentiment on the part of the executive, and no engagements to external bodies into which the executive may have entered, bind or limit the prescriptive omnipotence of Parliament. The "grim two-handed engine at the door stands ready to smite once and smite no more". If this sequence of events, which I have been speculatively exploring, were to occur, the Parliament whose prescriptive legislative authority would be restored by it would be a Parliament which legislates "by and with the advice and consent" not of one house but of two. It is not easy, when appealing to prescription, to dismember it at the same time.

Do not imagine, please, that the thoughts of others - and of others in high places - have not sometimes wandered down the same path which I have been tracing, or that they have not arrived by it at the edge of the same precipice. It was, after all, in 1992, an administration flushed with election victory which saw itself obliged to whip out of the Sovereign's mouth words before she could utter them about Europe which it euphemistically feared "might be misunderstood" and replace them by phrases which were more "Parliament-friendly". Now when politicians begin to wonder if they may not have to backtrack, they start to appraise with fresh interest the conveniences which might be reaped from such a manoeuvre. It is, therefore, perhaps not a waste of time to list some of the amenities offered by a prescriptive legislature whose members sit, or are warmed by the hope of sitting, in the seats of power.

Nothing is more handy for those engaged in political management, otherwise known as the art of governing, than a goodly reservoir of patronage, a pocketful of baubles by the distribution of which the wheels of government may be greased. Thanks to the English virtue of snobbery, we enjoy in this country the blessings, unknown across the Atlantic, of inexpensive patronage. Of that patronage there is no source more convenient or plentiful than is afforded by a prescriptive upper house of the legislature. When knighthoods for long, laborious, and obedient service in the lower house have been devalued in one of the main political parties and are eschewed on principle in the other, the attraction which a peerage offers of honourable retirement or honorific dismissal is precious indeed. Wherever else the abolition of hereditary privilege is favoured, there is one quarter which can be relied upon to defend it. That is the whips' offices, upon whom falls, in government and in opposition equally, the duty of securing attendance and organizing support whenever the respective leaderships stand in need of it. For a prescriptive second chamber of Parliament, patronage is a recommendation not to be despised or overlooked.

A second legislative chamber has other charms. Governments in being and governments in waiting have an invincible propensity to overload themselves with commitments to legislate, and to legislate upon novel and complex subjects. From this propensity flow two pressing requirements. One is an unslakable thirst for legislative time. Take no notice of contemporary noises

- they emanate from all newly elected Parliaments - which call for government business to be timetabled so as to economize the available time. That is a stampede which comes to a speedy halt as soon as the newly arrived innocents discover that armed with a timetable (including a limited working day), government always gets its way, or else never gets its way - neither of which outcomes is manifestly acceptable. Parliamentary debate, by definition and necessity, is open-ended debate. There is, therefore, no easy device for extracting more legislative time from the pint pot of a parliamentary session; and in this predicament there presents itself to those who govern or aspire to government the delightful relief of being able to initiate and process legislation in an alternative chamber to the House of Commons, a chamber, moreover, which the deteriorating physical condition of its members and the absence of party rancour produced by the extinction of political ambition predisposes to eschew pertinacious and wearying opposition. As Joseph Chamberlain used to say about the alleged "Conservative working man", if a specimen can be found of a nobleman avid for all-night debate, he ought to be captured, stuffed, and preserved in a glass case.

Pressure to legislate produces further inconveniences for governments. In their haste and eagerness they are liable, whether legislating against killer dogs or upon other like subjects which currently cause excitement, to lay before the House of Commons proposals which presently turn out to be nonsensical or impracticable. If there has ever existed a minister who enjoyed admitting that he had introduced an absurd or unworkable Bill, I am sorry to say that I fail to recall him. This being so, a second legislative chamber enables the blemishes, if possible, to be removed with the minimum of publicity and embarrassment

The second legislative chamber might even come in handy for defeating government legislation. I tread here upon distasteful, but unavoidable ground. What an absolutely dreadful thought, that governments might sometimes wish to devour their own offspring! It is cannibalism to be mentioned only in hushed tones; but it exists. How come? Governments, particularly governments of a radical or reforming tendency, can come into office committed to legislation which either they do not really want, or which they presently discover to be undesirable. What to do? Thank heaven if there stands ready a murderer whom they can disavow, or over whom they have no visible means of control; and what could fit that specification better than an independent legislative chamber?

Since the days of the old Liberal Party we have been accustomed to hear much about the House of Lords being the poodle of Conservative administrations, so much that we have overlooked the more interesting fact that the House of Lords is the patent incinerator of radical governments. To serve this purpose, however, it must be possible to heap upon it all the familiar terms of abuse; nonelected, undemocratic, obsolete. A Don't-blame-us-for-what-it-does-we-are-going-to-reform-it-only-we-have-not-got-time-just-at-the-moment legislative chamber is just the job. The horrid secret is that the vested interest in an allegedly indefensible chamber is the vested interest of the Labour Party, whom alone it enables Cronos-like to destroy its own unwelcome offspring. If anybody has wondered how the House of Lords survived so many radical administrations which came and went and came and went, let him wonder no more.

I slipped in a rather important word just then, while nobody was looking. The word was "indefensible". That part of the constitution which is prescriptive, as are the composition and powers of the House of Lords, is of necessity "indefensible" in the sense that they are not able to be deduced from any accepted *a priori* principles. In an age such as that in which we live, the elective principle is accepted *a priori* under the catch-all, cure-all heading of "democracy". As a matter of fact, the House of Commons is no more defensible by reference to any definable democratic principle than the House of Lords. By what process of reasoning other than from prescription is the right to make binding law enjoyed, subject to certain procedural rules being followed, by a simple majority among 651 persons whom a simple majority of electors aged 18 or over resident in the respective constituencies elects to "represent" them? A respectable proportion of those electors, if their opinion were canvassed, would, we know, unhesitatingly reply: "It is not fair, it is not democratic". But, rejoin you and I, it is prescriptive.

Nevertheless, the description of the House of Lords as indefensible rests upon an implied contrast with the House of Commons as an "elected" and, therefore, presumably "representative" chamber. That is the lion which lies crouched at the portals of the House of Lords. "Let us", say the would-be reformers, "replace it by some other house equally defensible with the House of Commons." A moment's reflection discloses the yawning gulf at the feet of those who so propose. If the elected representative chamber, representative because its members are elected, is defensible, the proposed defensible other chamber must be equally representative, which is to say, equally elected. Unless a less representative chamber, that is a less credibly elected chamber, is to replace the present House of Lords, the consequence is manifest: the decisions of the new upper house will be as valid - they could, if the job were done well, even be *more* valid - than those of the House of Commons. What we should have constructed is a situation of permanent deadlock, no longer resolvable at a pinch by the supposed lesser defensibility of the House of Lords. A House of Commons which legislates to replace the House of Lords with a defensible institution fashions a rod for its own back: two assemblies, equally defensible. "Be off with you," the public would say to the House of Commons; "what right have you to prevail over an equally defensible house which you yourselves created? Their decisions are as good as yours any day!"

It would be a grisly predicament. In vain would the House of Commons have exerted its prescriptive control over finance to enforce the superiority of its own decisions over those of the other House of Parliament. The House of

Commons would stand confronted by the spectre which it dreads most - the spectre of an institution able to overrule it. No tinkering about with fancy alternative forms of election or staggered dates of elections will help: the sorcerer's apprentice always ends up facing the unanswerable question: "Why did you create a less validly elected chamber? And how can you, unless upon your own admission it is less validly constituted, presume to defy it?"

You and I are not the first people to have trodden this dialectical track. We have come to the spot where would-be reformers of the House of Lords have always arrived. The labyrinth is one in which Michael Foot and I entrapped and eventually butchered in 1969 the only attempt at reform which ever got far enough to risk inhabiting the shape of a parliamentary Bill. The same fate awaits all future essays, unless, of course, those seeking election to the prescriptive House of Commons are bold enough to tell the electors to their face that henceforward they must like a one-chamber Parliament or lump it if they don't. I may, of course, be wrong; but I fancy the British electors would prefer Jacques Delors and his Brussels bureaucrats.

10: Sir Colin Cole

Introduction of peers into the House of Lords

THE SUBJECT on which I have chosen to address you concerning the House of Lords is the ceremony which takes place whenever a newly created Peer of the Realm (or one advanced in degree, a rarity today) is introduced into the Upper House. This happens after a new peer's title has been settled, and Garter King of Arms has much to do with both processes in his advance to the dignity of peerage . I hope that is not the reason for the misunderstanding with which some members of the public view these matters. If there is any such misunderstanding among you of my audience this morning, I trust to dispel it before long. The sources on which I draw for what I am about to describe include not only my own experience in office as Garter King of Arms from 1978 to 1992, but also the rather more reliable Standing Orders of the House of Lords and the material published by the Journal and Information Office of the House.

The ceremony of Introduction is summarized in a short passage in *Jacob's New Law Dictionary* (1792) thus:

> "When a Lord is newly created he is introduced into the House of Peers by two Lords of the same Form in their robes, Garter King of Arms going before, and his Lordship is to present his Writ of Summons etc. to the Lord Chancellor: which being read, he is conducted to his place."

This ceremony, upon which I will expand, dates from 1621 when King James I required that there be some simplification of an older ceremony which is traceable to two even more ancient rituals, investiture of a peer by the King on first creation and the placing of a peer newly created, or on succession to his dignity, in his seat in Parliament by Garter (the latter office was instituted by Henry V in 1415 and it is possible to calculate that Garter's responsibilities for the precedence and placing of peers developed in the 15th century and were fully in being in the early 1500s). The putting of a nobleman in his correct seat was held to be the perfection of his dignity.

Let me touch now upon the details of the ceremony which has so long a historical record and is now enshrined in being part of the Standing Orders of their Lordships' House. At the appointed time (ie after the House has sat) with the Lord Chancellor (he is ex o*fficio* Speaker of the House of Lords) on the Woolsack and Prayers having been said, Black Rod, an officer of the Order of the Garter whose antecedents go back to 1360 or thereabouts, and who, as a permanent official on duty in the Lords, has "to keep the doors" and maintain order in the precincts, comes to the robing room. There, Garter and the new peer, with his supporting peers of the same degree, are waiting, in processional order, single file, the junior peer (in date of creation) acting as supporter or sponsor leading, the senior peer bringing up the rear, the new peer between his supporters. Black Rod, carrying his Rod of Office over his right shoulder, moves off, followed by Garter wearing his tabard of the Royal Arms and holding in the right hand his sceptre headed by the Royal Crown and insignia of the Order of the Garter, and in his left hand a scroll of vellum with the Great Seal attached representing the new peer's Patent of creation, it being impractical for the actual Patent to be carried. The Patent, however, is in the House and the new peer has to sign a receipt for it before he is permitted to take it away and retain it. The three peers, each wearing their parliamentary robes, carry cocked hats held vertically against the left breast; sometimes the new peer finds it convenient holding his hat in the left hand to have his Writ of Summons secured between his thumb and the inside of the hat, so that he can produce it at the right moment, with a suitable flourish, rather than fumble for it under his robes. The Writ is a vital document in the peer-making process. Without it, the peer may not come into the House nor take his seat. It is by direction of the Lord Chancellor that a Writ of Summons issues from the office of the Clerk of the Crown in Chancery and it is the responsibility of the new peer to bring his Writ with him, to offer it to the Lord Chancellor - although I can recall the odd occasion when this has not been done, with resulting complications that I will not describe.

The procession, with Black Rod notionally clearing the way, and with the cry "Hats off strangers", passes through the Peers Lobby into the Chamber. There, each in turn halts at the Bar of the House and gives a head bow in the general direction of the Throne, but in fact honouring the Cloth of Estate which marks the position which would be occupied by The Queen if present. Black Rod, Garter, and the three peers resume the procession along the temporal side of the House - ideally it would be in continual flow, with no great time taken for the bows - and approaches two further points of bowing, at the Reading Clerk's table and at the corner of the Judges' Woolsacks (ie where the judges attending the State Opening of Parliament sit). Black Rod, on reaching the Lord Chancellor on the Woolsack stands at the right of the Lord Chancellor while Garter goes to the left and faces the new peer as he proceeds to the Lord Chancellor. (The Lord Chancellor is sitting in court dress, gown, full bottomed wig, and tricorne hat - which he keeps on for most of the ceremony, doffing it but three times to acknowledge salutations from the three peers at the Barons' Bench when at a later stage of the ceremony they have been conducted there by Garter). At the same time as the new peer on one knee (whether right or left is of no moment) hands his Writ to the Lord Chancellor, Garter proffers the Patent of Creation and both documents having thus been presented to the Lord Chancellor are returned by him, the Reading Clerk receiving them. The new peer rises, turns about, and processes back to the table, stopping just beyond the Despatch Box where, Garter and Black Rod standing behind the clerks at the table, he places his hat on the table (this is not done by women peers who wear their tricorne hats with a golden cockade on the left side throughout the ceremony). The Reading Clerk reads out the Patent and the Writ and administers the Oath of Allegiance to the peer who may swear to it or (for conscience) make a solemn affirmation. He then signs the Test Roll in his peerage name. The Oath runs as follows "I, Thomas, Baron Brookes of Bockington, do swear by Almighty God that I will be faithful and swear true Allegiance to Her Majesty Queen Elizabeth, Her Heirs and Successors, according to law. So help me God". Remembering to retrieve his hat from the table and placing it on his left breast as before, the peer, with his sponsors, the senior now leading, follow the example of Garter and Black Rod who, as they cross the Chamber towards the spiritual side then back again towards the temporal side, turn and bow one after the other to the Cloth of Estate.

Although there has been a rehearsal of the whole ceremony earlier in the afternoon under Garter's direction, it is remarkable sometimes how the "team" of three peers manages to produce an eccentric variation on what previously they had performed with élan, harmony, and dignity and the next part of the ceremony on occasion provides an example of this. It must be acknowledged that the "hat drill" through which Garter takes the peer with his supporters is not something in which unison is always achieved. To perform this part of the ceremony, Garter leaves Black Rod on the floor of the House facing the end of the Earls' Bench, while he leads the three peers up the steps leading to the Barons' Bench ensuring that as each moves into position his robes do not impede him in what is rather a narrow space. The peers line up with the senior as a kind of "right marker" and Garter faces them from the other side of the Bench along which they are standing. They follow his whispered words of request that they sit, put on their hats, rise, and taking off their hats, make a sweeping bow from the waist, three times, these salutations being to the Lord Chancellor who, remaining seated on the Woolsack, acknowledges each by taking off his hat. Garter then requests the peers to follow him, their hats being held against their left breasts as before, the procession moving down the temporal side of the House, each member giving a head bow at the table and at the corner of the Judges' Woolsack, in the direction of the Cloth of Estate. The new peer, standing, is shaken by the hand from the Woolsack by the Lord Chancellor and the procession resumes its movement, again in single file, out into the Prince's Chamber while everyone in the House signifies his and her acknowledgment of the new peer's presence by calling out Hear! Hear! Having disrobed, the peer, escorted by one or both of his sponsors, goes back into the Chamber to take his seat on the Government or Opposition side, or on the cross benches. It is not expected of him that he should make a maiden speech on the same day as his introduction, which stands by itself as a means whereby a newcomer is identified by his new name and title as a member of the Upper House, and once identified correctly, as the rituals ensure, is accorded due recognition by his fellows in time-honoured fashion.

Peerage Titles

As you will recall from the beginning of this address, the settling of the title of a peer is an important precursor of his or her Introduction into the House of Lords. From his responsibility for placing a peer in his seat in Parliament, there was attributed to Garter King of Arms a knowledge of the existing nobility such as to enable him not only to advise the Crown on a peer's precedence among his fellow peers, but also to determine by what style, title, and name it would be appropriate to designate a peer on his creation and in what name to summon him to give counsel to the Monarch in Parliament. Since the 1958 Act providing for the creation of life peerages in persons additional to Law Lords (Lords of Appeal in Ordinary) there has been a great upsurge in the number of such peerages created for the life of the holder; and each new peer, male and female, has been bidden in the terms of Writ of Summons which each has received "that considering the difficulty of the said affairs and dangers impending waiving all excuses you be personally present at Our aforesaid Parliament with us and with the Prelates Nobles and Peers of Our said Kingdom to treat and give your counsel upon the affairs aforesaid..." It is implicit in this ancient formula (dating from the 14th century) that those going to Parliament be known when they arrive there and that each be recognized by his or her *Nomen Dignitatis*, the name of the dignity which each enjoys, and that the dignity itself should have a territorial designation.

Thus Garter, in working out with the newly nominated peer his peerage title suitable for one below the rank of Earl, has to have regard to two elements, the *Nomen Dignitatis*, the title actually used, and the Territorial Designation, which indicates a place in the United Kingdom with which the peer and hence his Barony has a reasonably close association. Confusion sometimes arises because it is not appreciated that a place name or a family surname chosen for the *Nomen Dignitatis* has to be, of itself, distinctive, and unless it is, another, a territorial, name has to be incorporated with it. An example is provided by the case of Archbishop Ramsey. His family name of Ramsey was not eligible to become his peerage name because one Lord Ramsay (son of the Earl of Dalhousie) had a like sounding courtesy title: hence the *Nomen Dignitatis* for the Archbishop which was settled upon was "Ramsey of Canterbury" to which there had to be added the territorial designation of the peerage, so that the full style and title submitted for royal approval became: "Baron Ramsey of Canterbury, in the County of Kent".

There are other rules and conventions which apply when this intimate business of choosing a peerage title is gone into between Garter and the person nominated to be created a peer and to ensure that an appropriate name for the title is arrived at, pleasing to the person concerned as well as being within the regulations approved by the sovereign, Garter has a certain discretion in the submissions he makes, but naturally relies on established precedent and does not if he can help it break new ground. While the rules require that a place name, if it is to form part of the *Nomen Dignitatis*, must be that of a place in the United Kingdom, exceptions have been made when, for example, the recipient in war has won a remarkable victory. In this connection, one thinks at once of Lord Montgomery who was created "Viscount Montgomery of Alamein" in 1946. In the exceptional case of Sue Ryder, Baroness Ryder of Warsaw, by reason of her high reputation in

Poland the Government of the United Kingdom sought and obtained the agreement of the Polish Government to the inclusion of Warsaw in her *Nomen Dignitatis*. The territorial designation as well, on rare occasions, has included the name of a place outside the United Kingdom as well as one in it. The title of Baroness Gardner of Parkes, of Southgate in Greater London, and of Parkes in the State of New South Wales and Commonwealth of Australia, provides an example. Another rule is that the choice of a title must not be provocative of undue merriment, but I think it would be better if I did not give you an example of this. Your own imaginations will tell you what to avoid in such a context - some places have most peculiar names.

Another rule, generally applied with some firmness, is that a place the name selected for the *Nomen Dignitatis* must be neither too great nor too small. That of a large parish would be about right for a baron, but the name of a county would relate more to an Earldom, while a street name, unless also an area of some dignity, like Whitehall, pertains not at all to a peer's title. The name has to be of an existing place, hence the Ordnance Survey is resorted to if there is any doubt. The general object of the rules and practice is to safeguard the Crown so that it is not embarrassed by the creation of a peerage with a *Nomen Dignitatis* or territorial designation that might engender criticism, lend itself to ridicule, be prone to controversy, or militate against the Crown as the fount of honour.

Ignorance and any risk of error must be avoided; hence while titles incorporating Scottish names are governed by the same regulations as titles of English provenance, in cases where the individual nominated to become a peer asks for his title or territorial designation to consist of a Scottish name, Garter and Lyon King of Arms in Scotland consult each other to ensure that correct Scottish practice is observed. Nevertheless, it is a peerage of the United Kingdom, not of England nor of Scotland, that the Crown creates, and the same regulations apply in the creative process whether the peerage is one for life or is an hereditary peerage.

There is much more of this grand subject, as I consider it to be, which I am sure it would interest you to hear, but in conclusion let me repeat that I like to think that it is in extension of his ancient role of placing a peer in his proper place in Parliament that today, in the case of each new peer, it falls to Garter to communicate to the Prime Minister's office the peerage title which the Garter submits as one that meets all the circumstances of the case and is in accordance with the rules - which rules and regulations were amended and consolidated in 1965 and were then on the submission of Harold Wilson (now Lord Wilson of Rievaulx) formally approved by Her Majesty The Queen, the fount of honour.

11: The Lord Sudeley

A working peer

I HAVE been asked to talk about a working peer, which is really to describe what the House of Lords does on a day to day basis. Apart from the fund of my own experience, especially in Church affairs, to which I will refer, I will also be drawing on a variety of printed sources, including the books by the late Lord Massereene, Lord Longford, and especially Donald Shell, which I much recommend.

To look first at the composition of the House of Lords, Lord Longford gave the total number of peers as 1,196, made up of 800 hereditary peers, 381 life peers, 26 bishops, and 31 law lords. Among these totals, Lord Longford found more women than in the Commons: 67 women in the House of Lords compared with 40 in the House of Commons. Principal sources of supply for life peers are men of business, trades unionists, academics from universities, civil servants, and most of all ex-MPs from the House of Commons. About one third of MPs elevated to the peerage have been in the Cabinet, and most of the remainder have at some time held ministerial office. From the total number of peers, regular attenders are made up by about 150 life peers and 100 hereditary peers.

Before the passage of the Life Peerages Act in 1958, the House would often sit from Tuesday to Thursday, with business not starting before 4.00pm and possibly ending by 7.00pm. This has been transformed by the Life Peerages Act. Average attendance, which used to be about 100, is now well over 300; and the House of Lords usually sits from Mondays to Fridays, with business often continuing until well after dinner.

On party allegiances, Lord Longford computed that, when he wrote, there were 417 Conservatives, 245 Labour peers, 42 Liberals and 43 Social Democrats. Nevertheless, the Government had been defeated more than 100 times since 1979. This was not least due to the cross benchers who ensured that the Conservatives, though the largest party, did not command an absolute majority.

Among attenders, let us glance now in particular at the Front Bench, the lawyers, and the bishops. At the beginning of this century, the Prime Minister and up to half the Cabinet were in the Lords. Now, however, with the greatly expanded scope of Government business, the number of ministers has much increased, most of them sitting in the House of Commons, leaving too few peers on the Front Bench in the House of Lords to cover the whole range of business. Lords in Waiting can expect to act as spokesmen for at least three departments, and in no sense as originators of policy. They have to keep closely to the brief provided for them. The House of Lords does, however, still retain at least two Cabinet ministers. The Lord Chancellor acts as Front Bench spokesman chiefly on legal aspects of Government legislation, but also on other matters. The Leader of the House, with his overall responsibility for Government legislation, may also have assigned to him specific ministerial duties; frequently he has responsibility for the Civil Service.

About one tenth of the House of Lords are lawyers. Legal learning is chiefly represented by the Lord Chancellor and his predecessors, and the Law Lords. Where Law Lords have been asked by the Government to chair commissions or committees of inquiry, they are expected to participate in debates on these subjects. Examples are Lord Donovan's commission on trades unions in the 1960s, and Lord Scarman's inquiry into city unrest in 1981.

Bishops are prominent on matters of conscience such as divorce, homosexuality, abortion, and capital punishment. Legislation on these issues of conscience is usually introduced by private members and passed on a free vote, though a good deal of Government legislation also deals with ethical and social questions, for example, the Government Bill to remove restrictions on Sunday trading.

My final remarks on the composition of the House concern how backbenchers are organized among themselves. Backbenchers of all parties, including the cross benchers, have their private meetings on Thursday to discuss the forthcoming business of the House. The Conservatives' weekly Whip notice is prepared on the same day giving the divisions which are to be expected with appropriate underlining. The ground for the Thursday meetings of Conservative and Labour peers is prepared beforehand. The Conservative peers, who meet on Thursdays as members of the Association of Conservative Peers (ACP), have the ground prepared for them by the Executive of the ACP. The ground for the Thursday meetings of the Labour peers is prepared by their coordinating committee which includes attendance of the Leader, Deputy Leader, and Chief Whip, and meets fortnightly. Their party whips and principal Opposition spokesmen also consult together immediately before the Thursday meetings. Organization among the Liberal and SDP peers is looser. In the Liberal Party, the line between front and back benches has been somewhat blurred. In 1987, for instance, apart from the Leader, Deputy Leader, and two Whips, no fewer than 25 peers were named as party spokesmen, and not all spoke from the Front Bench. After occupying the rear Opposition benches behind the Labour peers, the SDP peers have now joined the Liberal peers. After their separate Thursday meetings, the Whips of both parties always meet. Among the cross-bench peers it might be said that despite their Thursday meetings they have no organization at all. They have no leader and, indeed, could not have one since they share no common views.

To come now to the activity of the House, let me look at the manner, customs, and conventions by which the business of the House is conducted before proceeding to an examination of what it actually does. While points of difference are extremely well argued in the House of Lords, the "temperature" is very low. With regard to the keeping of order in the House, a member of the old Roman aristocracy asked me whether the Lord Chancellor has to be a man of exceptional physical strength. In fact, the Lord Chancellor's duties as speaker are confined to putting questions on motions of order submitted to the House. The House keeps its own order, and is occasionally guided on points of order or procedural difficulties by the Leader of the House. For example, during Oral Question Time, it is the Leader of the House who tries to move proceedings on if they become protracted, and he will usually do so by suggesting that the Lords move to the next business. In the absence of the Lord Chancellor, there are Deputy Speakers on the Woolsack; and when the House goes into committee, the Chairman of Committees takes the chair at the table to conduct proceedings. Where the Lord Chancellor takes part in the committee stage of a Bill, he sits on the Government Front Bench without his wig and gown. The Chairman of Committees is appointed after informal consultations on a motion by the Leader of the House, and on his appointment withdraws entirely from politics.

There is no limit to the number of peers taking part in a debate. The order of speakers is arranged in the Whip Office. Heavyweight speakers are put first, which makes it more difficult for other peers to follow, since the number of points to be made in a debate may be limited. Other peers have to think out a line not already covered by the heavyweight speakers. In the House, it is much preferred if later on in a debate a peer says merely that a particular point he had in mind has already been made, than that he should try to make it all over again. A peer may interrupt a speaker, but only briefly, and if he is not on the list of speakers he can intervene at the end before the minister replies. It was the custom of the House to permit very brief notes and, indeed, to encourage peers to speak extemporarily. Today copious notes are allowed with the result that speeches can be dreary and lacking in spontaneity. I regret this trend. In the past, any peer who read his speech was called to order. With speeches so thoroughly prepared, peers refer less to one another, and there is less of a debate. It is an accepted courtesy that peers taking part in a debate remain till the end to hear the winding up speech by the Minister. In winding up, the Minister has to read his brief, especially if the subject is technical. In his winding up, the Minister refers to many of the points made by peers in the debate. If a peer expects an answer on some technical point, he is wise to inform the Minister beforehand so that the Minister can consult his Department.

Unlike the Commons, there is no official register of the pecuniary interests of members of the House, but it is a long standing custom that peers should declare such an interest if it affects the subject of the debate.

Since 1985, the proceedings of the House of Lords have been televised, so that four million viewers can see what happens compared with 200 to 900 people in the public gallery. During the first few weeks of television, the proceedings of the House were distorted by some peers who rather enjoyed a "starring" role. During Question Time, they erred in the direction of stating their point of view rather than seeking information from the Government, and debates were unduly prolonged. But the House quickly settled down. There was some controversy about televizing the proceedings of the House. My own view is that it has done the House much good by showing the public what it actually does, and its proceedings have risen considerably in public regard.

Our time in the House is allocated between business introduced by Government and business introduced by backbenchers. Roughly between a quarter and a half of the business of the House is introduced by backbenchers or cross-bench peers, most of it before Easter. Thereafter, there tends to be a bottleneck of Government legislation from the Commons, since legislation has to be complete in all its parliamentary stages in both Houses within a single session (roughly 12 months). The target at which backbench peers must aim when introducing their motions and questions in the House is the answerability of the Government, obliging it to realize the implications of policy which may not previously have been thought of. Examples of individual peers who have worried away successfully at the Government are Lady Burton of Coventry on civil aviation, Lord Houghton of Sowerby on animal welfare, Lord Melchett on environmental and planning issues, and Lady Masham on the disabled. More pertinacity than is apparent from the published proceedings of the House may be required to follow points through. In his book on the House of Lords, Donald Shell cites the example of a peer who got a poor response from the Government to his debate, wrote to the Minister for a better reply, and after a long delay received a further poor answer. It was only after saying that he would put down further questions in the House that he got a much more satisfactory letter from the Secretary of State.

Every day of business in the House begins with four Oral Questions, which are a very useful way of exerting pressure and drawing information from the Government. The peer putting down his Oral Question is wise to phrase something bland and innocuous to which it may not be too difficult to anticipate the reply, prepared by the Civil Service, the Minister will read out. The seriousness with which the Question is taken may be measured by the length of the reply. The art of an Oral Question lies in the awkward Supplementary Question. Other peers may also rise to their feet to bowl Supplementary Questions. All questions have to be cast in an interrogative form; if as often happens the peer begins to state his own point of view, other peers cry Order. You can state your own view, but in the context of: "Has the Government considered...?" In this way, you may get an answer, which can be quoted back at some later date, or the Minister may have to go away and think about it. Unlike the Commons, where much of the debate centres on scoring minor or amusing points, questions in the Lords force an answer immediately, or consideration for a later answer from the Government - surely a more effective way.

Oral Questions last for half an hour. An hour or so later, the business of the House may be interrupted by a ministerial statement on a matter of public importance. These statements are, as far as possible, synchronized to be given in both Houses at the same time. Front Bench responses follow, and backbenchers may ask questions. Exchanges can be quite lengthy.

Wednesdays are usually set aside as a half holiday in the House of Lords for debates of general significance, introduced by either of the main parties. Wednesdays may also be used for two short debates introduced by backbenchers. Motions for short debates tend to be worded in such a way as to indicate the particular concern of the peers who put them down. These are more specific than unlimited time debates, and give the opportunity to raise subjects which their party leaders would not choose. In the same way, peers can introduce Bills as a vehicle for a specific subject of debate. This is what I did to uphold the Prayer Book on three occasions, in 1978, 1981, and 1984, against the heavy opposition of the Government which argued against me on constitutional grounds that all legislation on Church matters should emanate from the Synod of the Church of England instead of being initiated in Parliament. Parliament must approve or reject Synodical Measures, but it cannot amend them. In 1981, I cleared my Bill in a division on Second Reading. This did not, nor was it intended to, change the law, but it did demonstrate the feelings of a majority of the House in respect of the Prayer Book issue, which the Church authorities wished to change from the 1662 version to the Alternative Services Prayer Book, by common literary consent not a patch on the earlier work.

Private Bills from the House of Lords have a low rate of success in the House of Commons. The Government can stifle a measure by not allowing enough time for it. In the House of Commons, Lord Cranborne MP cleared my Prayer Book Bill only under the Ten Minute Rule rather than Second Reading, but with the satisfactory result of showing what a majority of MPs, like the peers, felt about the issue. The effect of this limited success has caused Parliament to view legislation coming from the Synod with more care.

The main part of the business of the House on all days except Wednesdays tends to be concerned with Second Reading Debates on Bills from the Commons and amending them. Since the Parliament Act of 1911, the power of the House of Lords to reject legislation from the Commons indefinitely was reduced to two years; since 1949, that power has been further reduced to one year. In practice, the House of Lords does not reject Bills from the House of Commons on Second Reading. Instead, peers hostile to a Bill resort to one of two procedures to force a division without risk of loss of the Bill: a Resolution after the Bill has been given its formal Second Reading, and a Reasoned Amendment specifying what aspects of the Bill are deprecated.

When in Opposition, the Conservative Party has used neither of these devices. When in power, the Conservative Party has secured the defeat of their quite frequent use by the Labour Opposition.

When, however, we come to the amendment of individual clauses to Bills, the power remaining to the House of Lords, despite the 1911 Act, becomes much more apparent. Amendments may be divided into different categories. There are technical amendments which improve a Bill by making its impact more precise. There are probing amendments which are never intended to be carried into effect, since their purpose is just to elicit information from the Government. Then there are substantive amendments to concede important points without altering the basic purpose of the Bill. The bulk of such amendments, where they are successful, may indeed be sponsored by the Government, but often in response to pressure exerted on the Government by backbenchers in both Houses, either in the form of criticism, or actual defeat during earlier stages of the Bill's passage. Such pressure is often brought to bear on the Government by interest groups outside Parliament altogether who approach parliamentarians to be their spokesmen. Finally, there are wrecking amendments which do not change the basic nature of the Bill, but which take the guts out of it so that it may have to be abandoned altogether. Usually, due to the ascendancy of the House of Commons as an elected chamber, the Lords will not flex its muscles to the extent of putting down wrecking amendments, although it can come into its own here where neither main party has a clear overall majority, as during the Callaghan administration in the late 1970s.

Whipping in the House of Lords is a lighter affair than in the Commons. Party loyalty in the Commons is fostered by aspirations among MPs to office, membership of certain Select Committees, and other advantages. In the House of Lords, it is much more that the argument wins. In his book on the House of Lords, Lord Longford says that my old Conservative Whip, Lord Denham, told him: "I have always myself held the view that amendments to a Bill won by argument on the floor of the House as against those won by a vote in the division lobby are of a ratio of something like 10 to 1."

Amendments are not selected and any peer can put one down. Sometimes this helps towards abuse of the privileges of the House at committee stage by filibustering. I remember how, during the passage of the Industrial Relations Bill in the 1970s, Labour peers would spin out time and filibuster by putting down amendments to give tedious recitations of their life stories. It was most unfortunate then that, unlike the House of Commons, the House of Lords had no guillotine.

After Committee, a Bill goes through the two further stages of Report and Third Reading. At Report stage, the Bill is not considered again clause by clause, consideration being given only to the new amendments put down. And Third Reading is usually brief. Sometimes, the Opposition may put down a motion deprecating the Bill, especially if the Government has resisted its amendments at every stage.

Of course, the two Houses may not always agree. If MPs reject any amendments made by the peers, the Bill is returned to the Lords with the Commons' disagreements to the amendments attached to the Bill; and a fuller explanation of the disagreement is to be found in the Commons' Hansard. Usually at this stage, the peers acquiesce; though during the period of the hung Parliament in the 1970s it was a little different. The Government was then defeated in more than 80% of divisions in the House of Lords, and on two or three carefully chosen occasions the Opposition did dig in its heels.

The day of business in the House of Lords may not end with all the business I have outlined. It can conclude with Unstarred Questions, the purpose of which is to elicit information from the Government about why they have not taken a certain course of action, or prod them into taking it. Such Unstarred Questions may be particularly useful in raising matters, as it were, on the side, not within the mainstream of political concern. In 1973, I asked such a Question on the export of historical manuscripts, one of the quiet glories of Britain. In 1980, I asked an Unstarred Question on cathedral finance, to draw attention to the anomaly that VAT is charged on restoration of churches and cathedrals, while new building construction is exempt. Very useful though Unstarred Questions on such side issues are, their disadvantage is the lateness of the hour at which they come up in the House, when there is only a thin attendance.

Apart from participating in the day's business, peers can put down Questions for Written Answer and the reply is printed at the back of the daily Hansard. Questions for Written Answer are often to be preferred, since the reply the Government gives tends to be more thorough than answers to Oral Questions.

We should also consider what might be termed the miscellaneous business of the House. The House of Lords is the Supreme Court of Appeal for the whole of the United Kingdom in civil cases, and for all of the United Kingdom, except Scotland, in criminal cases. Most of the work is done by the Lords of Appeal in Ordinary (Law Lords), though the Lord Chancellor and lords who have held judicial office may also sit on the Appellate Committee. About 70 cases a year are heard. Judgments are given at specially convened sittings; and when Parliament is not sitting the appeals themselves may also be heard in the Chamber.

The 1911 Parliament Act, which prevented the House of Lords from blocking Bills from the Commons for more than two years, did not affect delegated legislation, that is to say Statutory Instruments and orders made by ministers under subordinate powers contained in existing legislation. The quantity of such legislation has greatly increased since the beginning of the century. Statutory Instruments are of three kinds. There are *general instruments* which do not have to be laid before Parliament at all, though sometimes they are. There are *negative instruments*, so called because once laid before Parliament they come into being automatically unless either House carries a motion (technically known as a prayer) calling for their annulment. There are *affirmative instruments*, so called because they need the positive approval of both Houses. While debates in the House of Lords on affirmative instruments are brief, the Minister does have to give an explanation of what the instrument is about, and peers can probe them for clarification. The power of the House of Lords to reject delegated legislation is used very sparingly. Rather than reject an Order formally, the House may sometimes put down a reasoned amendment.

As already noted, legislation on Church matters comes before Parliament from the Synod in the form of a Measure. Ever since the Enabling Act of 1919 set up the Church Assembly, now the Synod, as the governing body of the Church of England, there has been a custom in the Constitution that legislation on Church matters cannot be initiated in Parliament.

Perhaps the most important function of the Lords is its work in small committees fine-tuning legislation. Some of this committee work concerns Private Bills which enable individuals, groups, and bodies to do something which the law of the land as enacted in public legislation may not allow, but in certain individual circumstances might be desirable. Personal Bills deal with the rights of a specific individual; they deal with estates, private naturalization claims, and individuals to become married in circumstances which the present law does not allow. Other private bills are known as hybrid, since apart from affecting specific private interests in a way different from other interests of the same kind, they alter the general law of the land. Personal Bills are always introduced in the House of Lords. The number of other Private Bills allocated for introduction to each House is nearly equal. Those largely financial in character tend to be allocated to the Commons, while the House of Lords takes most local authority legislation. About 30 Private Bills come before the House of Lords every year.

The procedure for Private Bills in the House of Lords is as follows. Personal Bills have to be approved for introduction by a Personal Bills Committee. The promoters of other Private Bills can only introduce them after their petition has been granted by Clerks of the Parliaments appointed as Examiners, whose task is to ensure that all interested parties know about the Bill. Second Reading is moved by the Lord Chairman of Committees, though if opposition to the Bill is likely, the promoters of the Bill must find some other peer to introduce it so that the Lord Chairman can preserve his neutrality. The aim of Second Reading is to ensure that the House feels the Bill may properly proceed to committee. Sometimes, the House will give an instruction to the committee requiring it to give emphasis to some factor in the Bill. Unopposed Private Bills are committed to an Unopposed Bill

Committee which consists of the Lord Chairman of Committees and any other peer who sees fit to attend. Opponents to a Bill may lodge a petition against it, in which case the Bill is referred to a Select Committee of five peers chosen to represent the balance of political parties in the House. The promoters and seconders of the Bill are usually represented by Learned Counsel. At the conclusion of the proceedings, the promoter's Counsel and the public withdraw while the Select Committee reaches a decision. Only about half a dozen Private Bills are opposed in this fashion in every session. After passing through one House, both Unopposed and Opposed Private Bills must go through the other; and unlike Public Bills they may be carried from one session to the next.

Under the Treaty of Rome in 1957, all states belonging to the European Union are subject to legislation introduced by the Community, and since 1979 there have been direct elections to the European Parliament. There is nothing, however, to prevent national parliaments from scrutinizing and influencing Community proposals. Indeed, such a role was specifically agreed upon in a Declaration by Heads of State at the conference on political union at Maastricht in December 1991. The European Communities Committee in the House of Lords fills this role very well. Its terms of reference are to report on proposals which raise important questions of policy and principle; in addition it can consider other questions to which it feels the attention of the House should be drawn. The Committee therefore reports on policy as much as legislative proposals. Because of the great number of proposals and other documents coming from Europe, the Chairman of the Committee, helped by explanatory memoranda from Government departments, makes an initial sift, setting aside about a quarter which he deems to be worthy of consideration. Full sifting is beyond the capacity of any individual or indeed the full committee, and is, therefore, handed over to subcommittees, all orientated towards different subjects. The subcommittees do most of the work. The reports of subcommittees are built up partly from written evidence collected from various sources, in particular any bodies affected by European proposals to whom the Clerk of the Committee has written; partly from oral evidence if it is called for; and partly from evidence provided by officials in Government departments. It is only on important occasions that ministers are called on to give evidence. The Government responds to reports in writing before any debate takes place. Where debates are recommended, they can take place without delay.

Like the European Communities Committee, the Science and Technology Committee works through subcommittees. Most of its reports are debated to draw a preliminary reply from the Government. Further published reports from the Government are preferred after the debate.

Since 1970, the House of Lords has had *ad hoc* Select Committees on public bills, almost always private members' legislation. Those committees investigating broad aspects of Government policy, such as unemployment, overseas trade, or entry into the European Monetary System, cannot be expected to have any immediate effect. On the other hand, narrower investigations into such particular issues as the complex and outdated law on charities can be expected to have much more tangible effect in bringing about legislative change.

Other committees to which I should briefly refer are the Committee on Statutory Instruments, the Ecclesiastical Committee, and the Committee of Privileges. The Committee on Instruments is a joint committee of both Houses. It is apolitical since it is concerned with the technical propriety of Instruments rather than any implications of their policy. The Ecclesiastical Committee has 15 members from each House, appointed by the Lord Chancellor and the Speaker, though in the House of Lords it is customary for the Lord Chancellor to consult the Whips. The Committee can declare forthcoming legislation from the Synod not to be expedient. Peers and MPs belonging to the parliamentary group, Church in Danger, have recently shown much interest in the Ecclesiastical Committee. The Committee of Privileges decides on peerage cases. At the Manorial Society's conference in 1985 on the history of my Tracy family, Dr J H Baker, a leading authority on judicial biography, spoke of how the Committee of Privileges decided against Irish claimants to the Tracy peerage. In 1968, they sat to hear the petition presented by Irish peers to resurrect the election of 28 of their number as representatives of the peers of Ireland. Adam Bruce deals with the Scottish Peerage to the Act of Union in 1707. Thereafter the peers of Scotland elected some of their number to sit in the British House of Lords; from the Act of Union with Ireland in 1801, Irish peers had the same privilege until the creation of the Irish Free State in 1923. Since 1958, all Scottish peers can take their seats in the Lords.

In 1867, the great Victorian constitutional theorist, Walter Bagehot, wrote that "the danger of the House of Lords is that it is not safe against inward decay. Its danger is not in assassination but atrophy; not abolition but decline." The picture I have given of the House of Lords today is not, I think, of the moribund institution Bagehot thought it would become, or possibly how it would have seemed when I came of age and could first sit there more than 30 years ago in 1960. If not an actual power, it is a considerable influence on general and special subjects. It is able to take long views for which the House of Commons is not famous. Nor does the Commons have the time to go through the detail of its own proposed legislation. Much of the refining takes place in the House of Lords. That none of us in the Lords is elected and most of us sit there by accident of birth, we may seem to foreigners to be a privileged anachronism. Old we are and, like the Commons, we enjoy the privilege of subsidized catering. But as Lord Mackay says at the beginning of this book, an institution that has survived almost a millenium must have something going for it.

A list of further reading to this Chapter may be found on page 205-6.

12: Keith W Wallis

Classless society?

IN DISCUSSING the class structure in England, compared with other countries, particularly America where I grew up, I might do no better than start with my own block of flats in Chelsea.

In theory there are in this block a head porter, an assistant head porter, four other day porters, and a night porter (who is sometimes relieved by one of the cleaners), but the head porter has died and not yet been officially replaced. While he was still with us, I called him Mr Cocker, he called me Mr Wallis. The assistant, now acting, head porter I call Frank; he calls me Mr Wallis. The next two in rank among the porters also have the privilege of calling me Mr Wallis. The lower porters wear a sort of footman's livery, or at least what was footman's livery half a century ago. (At Hatfield today, they wear what looks like some kind of beach pyjama). Because of their lowly position, they are not allowed to call me Mr Wallis. To them, I am simply, "Sir".

Besides their various behind-the-scenes duties, like seeing to the heating, the hot water, the endless struggles to keep the lifts working, to making sure that no one enters or leaves the building without being thoroughly vetted, and a few odd chores like delivering parcels, the duties of the porters chiefly concern waiting on the residents and their guests while they pass through the front-hall. If the weather is so cool that the front door must be kept closed, a porter stands right by it all day long and far into the night to see that no resident will be put to the disagreeable chore of having to push it open for himself. When a resident is seen approaching from the street, a porter will dart to the lifts to make sure that one is available, or at least rapidly approaching, so that the resident will not have to put up with a ghastly wait of anything up to 15 seconds before he can climb aboard. If a resident arrives bearing parcels, these are deftly but firmly whisked from his hands so that he will not have to carry them all the way to the lift by himself. There is never any question of the resident or guest being expected to offer tips in return.

At a glance, all of this might seem to indicate a strict class system gone quite mad in its insistence upon minutiae. Only the most abject or needy, one would think, could bear to take a job that is largely a matter of acknowledging that almost anyone who passes by, resident or guest, is one's superior who must be flattered by the most humiliating services. But things are not really what they might seem at first glance.

With the likely exception of the most junior porter, Ken, I think that all the porters in my flats are very near, or past, retirement age, who have taken the job as something not too demanding which will supply them with a certain amount of extra money while they make the transition to full retirement, though the transition seems in most cases to take quite a few years.

Frank, the acting head porter, is a Hungarian, having come to England, I think, at the time of the 1956 rising. How he occupied himself before he went into the portering trade I am not at all clear, but if the careers of most of his colleagues may be taken as a guide, he was in some sort of trade connected with decorating or DIY for he has an immense array of tools and can very quickly repair any sort of domestic breakdown in any of the flats. He drives his substantial motor car back to Hungary for a holiday at least once a year, stopping off for a day or two at various resorts *en route*.

Ted, second in command, has, apart from being English, a background not dissimilar to Frank's. He has sons who are in the business of making curtains, repairing electrical faults, and the like. I think it likely that, passing 60, he decided to retire a bit early so that the sons could take over the business.

Apart from looking like a semi-retired butler, Ron, No 3, acts very much like one and recalls to mind my earliest days as a country house visitor, when, hardly out of my teens, I looked upon butlers as among the most lofty of God's creations. On occasions, he sports a House of Lords necktie, which I think means that he served some noble household. It would be hard to think of Ron as oppressed by anyone.

Of the two lowest porters - the ones who dare not call me Mr Wallis - Jack, the elder, is ex-army. He now lives not far from Chelsea, for he can get back and forth in well under half an hour, and with a garden large enough to take up most of his spare time. He has recently resigned from the Royal Horticultural Society on the grounds that the subscription has quintupled since he first joined many years ago, and that the Flower Show is no longer a place where one can wander about at will and look at whatever you want for just as long as you want. Now – at least according to Jack – one is hustled along in a scrum of squawking people, more interested in catching a glimpse of any celebrity who might have wandered in than in gardening. Jack can certainly not be classed with the *lumpen proletariat*.

Of the most junior porter, Ken, the only one who clearly is not beyond retirement age, I know little, but to judge by the extreme trendiness of his garb when off duty, I find it hard to believe that he regards himself as in any way oppressed.

But if the porters do not feel oppressed and desperate to hold their jobs, why all this bowing and scraping, the holding open of doors for the most junior residents, the dash to carry their smallest parcels? I suspect that it may simply be a matter of wanting to do their jobs as well as they can possibly be done. I think that this is made easier by the fact that they seem genuinely to like most of the residents, but this is very far from their regarding the residents as some sort of superior beings before whom they must at all times appear humble and submissive.

I doubt that there are many other parts of the world where such an attitude among porters and their ilk would prevail. A recent incident will illustrate my meaning.

I was descending in the lift one morning when it stopped at the fifth floor to take aboard another passenger. The new arrival was a young man, clearly an American, who clutched a smart Samsonite briefcase in one hand and glanced repeatedly at his wrist-watch to indicate how important was his time, in short, almost a caricature of yuppiedom. On arrival at the ground floor, he hurled himself from the lift without offering precedence to his elder and better and darted towards the front door. Just before he reached it he swerved to the left in order to shake the duty porter warmly by the hand. The duty porter – it happened to be Ted – grinned at me over the shoulder of the energetic hand-shaker. When we were alone, he explained the yuppie's rather curious behaviour: "Do you know why he always insists on shaking my hand? It's to show that he thinks I am just as good as he is", and we both laughed at the suggestion that this jumped-up yuppie might possibly think himself superior to the intelligent and hard-working Ted, with most of a successful lifetime behind him.

This trifling incident is a pleasantly precise indication of why the British class system is so very different from that of almost every other country on earth, including those of the erstwhile Communist bloc. Those who were well-established in the United States before the Civil War and had imported the English social system almost intact I class with the Britons, and there are probably similar groups elsewhere in the white Commonwealth.

The fundamental way in which Britons differ from the rest of the world in their view of "class" is that few Britons can really take seriously the idea that one person can be fundamentally "better" than another in any deeply important way. When they hear tales of New York cab drivers or Neapolitan waiters asking crossly: "What's the matter? You think you're better than me?" they can hardly think that the question is meant seriously - unless, of course, they have spent some time in New York City or Naples. For historical reasons – and everyone's psychology is deeply rooted in the history of their race – the question of who is "better" than whom is almost meaningless in Britain. Yet it is deeply important in most other countries, and forms the basis of their class system.

I am not for a moment suggesting that no Briton has ever looked down on most of his or her fellows as not being as good as they. Miss Austen had no doubt met quite a lot of Lady Catharine de Burghs in her time, and even I have met not a few. I merely argue that such people are, on the whole, exceptional. Take a non-fiction contemporary of dear Lady Catharine's, the Duchess of Buckingham, whom historians will insist on calling "that crazy old Duchess of Buckingham", although she did have sense enough to unload that huge and ill-proportioned lump of masonry at the end of the Mall, Buckingham Palace, onto the Royal Family. One day someone, perhaps in rather malicious mood, took the Duchess off to a Quaker meeting. Her Grace emerged scandalized. "That extraordinary person," she exclaimed in disbelief, "claims that I am no better than those ragged wretches who beg for bread at my park gates." One would have thought that such an outlook was altogether typical of the upper classes in the 18th century. The odd thing is that Society at the time considered the whole thing to be an absolute hoot. The correspondence of the period is full of jokes at Her Grace's expense for having such an absurd outlook. Not a few of Horace Walpole's correspondents saw him exercise his wit on the extraordinary foolishness of the Duchess. Her view was far from typical of her contemporaries in the upper reaches of Society.

Yet everywhere else on earth, apart from England and the American colonies, the Duchess's remark would have seemed wise and sensible, and the Quaker preacher would almost certainly have ended in jail. Once again, as so often, and usually to her credit, Britain was the odd man out.

Since what we now know as civilization first developed in the Near East five or six millenia ago, the word has implied the existence of states, and states have always had, until the last century, two principal purposes: to wage war and to raise taxes to pay for soldiers and for their military equipment. This applied not only to the ancient empires, but, with particular savagery to the "cradle of democracy" at what we look back on as its most glorious days, the subsequent "world empires", the Greek one of Alexander and the Roman one of the Caesars, and to all the succession states of eastern and western Europe and to the rest of the world almost to within the memory of some still living. There is, so far as I am aware, only one notable exception, England.

No doubt Harold Bluetooth, Eric Bloodaxe, and the other Founding Fathers of parliamentary democracy did not foresee in any detail the splendid results that their energetic activities in the 10th and 11th centuries would have. Their plundering of monasteries and the wealthier estates of the Saxon nobility, carrying off anything of value, including the able-bodied and the attractive, into slavery and slaughtering the rest, put the English nobility, whose role in life was to defend their country, into a difficult position. It was not just that the Vikings were better fighters – though on the whole they were as the result of new methods of war that they had devised – but that it was so difficult to bring them to battle. Whenever a Saxon appeared while the Northmen were raiding, they would simply climb back aboard their ships and sail a bit further up the coast where they could finish with their plundering and be off again long before any defending forces could arrive. A pitched battle like the Battle of Maldon was largely an accident.

The only practical way of getting rid of the raiders was to buy them off with ample amounts of Danegeld. Fortunately, not only was England rich enough to have quite a lot of gold readily available, but the kings of Wessex were masters of a quite efficient system of administration based on written records – the Domesday commissioners would have been quite incapable of finishing their task so quickly without written evidence from which to work – and this made it possible to raise large amounts of gold by taxation in a relatively just and efficient manner. Naturally, most of the gold was held by either monasteries or by noblemen, so these necessarily bore the brunt of taxation. While no one likes being taxed very much, it was certainly better than the alternative of seeing all one's property and loved ones consumed by scarlet flame. There were even a few Saxon noblemen – Eadric Streona springs to mind – who made rather a good thing out of the imposition of Danegeld, buying up land at very low prices when monasteries were compelled to sell to pay their taxes.

So matters went for several generations until a Danish king, Cnut, replaced the Saxon on the Throne of England. Knowing that if he sat too near the water's edge when the tide was coming in he would get his feet wet was only the second brightest of Cnut's ideas. The brightest was to notice that the nobility of England had fallen into the habit of quite readily paying taxes, and to decide that this was such a good thing that it should be continued. So, while changing its name to *heregeld* or war-tax, Cnut continued to collect geld annually throughout his reign. When the Saxons, in the person of Edward the Confessor, returned to the Throne, there seemed to be no good reason why kings should not continue to enjoy an annual geld, at least until the Confessor's father-in-law, who happened to be the greatest landowner in England, and therefore the greatest tax-payer, made him stop. The Conqueror, happily, had no in-law problems, so when he had seized the English Throne in 1066 he at once began to take the geld annually, though at a considerably higher rate than his Saxon and Danish predecessors. So did his sons. For some reason which is not very clear, Henry II stopped collecting geld about halfway through his reign.

The standard view until a very few years ago was that so many people had been given exemptions from paying the geld, that the tax was no longer very productive. This view has recently been challenged in a series of articles by various hands. It is certainly striking that no king of England since the Conquest until the death of Henry II had any very serious financial problems, but immediately afterwards they became severe and perennial, and other forms of taxation which could be counted on to bring in large sums had to be devised. And when the new taxes were devised in the the decades around 1200 – the aids and subsidies of the later Middle Ages – it apparently occurred to no one that the nobility had any serious claim to be exempt from them. So all through the Middle Ages and since, noblemen have had to pay their taxes just like everyone else, only usually rather more.

Matters were handled very differently on the continent. The nobility there had never paid taxes and deeply believed that their sole duty towards the State was to defend it in time of war, usually collecting for so doing large sums which the State had previously collected from the non-noble. No continental government was ever strong enough to compel its nobility to pay taxes, apart from one or two of the Spanish kingdoms in very special circumstances. The position of the monarchy was typical: to tax non-nobles who happened to be the tenants of noblemen – and a very large number of Frenchmen outside the towns were – it had to strike a bargain with the nobles that they might keep for their own use a large portion – usually half – of whatever taxes royal officers were able to collect from those who were nominally their tenants.

So matters continued until the end of the Old Regime in France and almost everywhere else on the continent until well into the 19th century. Naturally, the right to escape direct taxation was one which the continental nobilities prized very highly and one which they were determined under no circumstances should be lost to them. Very careful rules were worked out to determine just who was noble and who was not. Early on they were able to have it accepted that all the sons of a nobleman were noble themselves – very different from the practice in England – and so on until the end of time. Thus the nobilities in continental kingdoms grew to a considerable size. Lest anybody be tempted to confuse them with those just beneath them in the social scale, they developed a style of living very different from everybody else, *la vie nobiliaire*. It was very important that at no time they ever be found engaging in any useful work, particularly any that was paid. War and government were the only occupations open to them. Even looking after their own estates too carefully was a bit risky to their social prestige. As a result, their estates soon ceased to produce much useful income – the fact that any time a peasant was able to amass a little bit of wealth he had it quickly taken from him by the taxman to be divided between the king and his lord speeded the process – and noblemen came to rely almost entirely on the State for their livelihood, in France at any rate.

The only place that a French nobleman could really feel confident that no one might mistake him for his social inferior was at the court of his king, hence Versailles. The greatest disaster that could befall any nobleman in the great days of the *ancien regime* was to find himself so out of royal favour as to be asked to leave Versailles and retire to his estates. Whenever this happened, the poor victim, doomed to life in the countryside, generally became very quickly much too fat or much too thin and soon died. In the country, he had to lead a solitary life, for there was no one about with whom he could mix without the risk of loosing caste. I do not mean his peasants. The rusticated nobleman never saw them except at a great distance. He had plenty of underlings to deal with them, to beat them if they tried to claim that severe illness was grounds enough for not working very hard in their lord's fields, or if their children seemed too plump and happy, or if they fell asleep and so failed to keep quiet at night the frogs whose croaking was apt to disturb the slumbers of Madame la Comtesse. What the countrified nobleman must be particularly on the watch for was the approaches of neighbours who were only a little beneath him socially: successful government and civil servants, war heroes on the make, rich merchants, and others who had prospered in trade and industry. They were the real threats to his position, and at each level going down, men and their wives must be careful to avoid and scorn those on the level just beneath them, people who were "not as good as they", lest they be sucked down.

I left the English nobleman somewhere about the beginning of the 13th century when he had accepted, no doubt with some regret, that he must go on paying taxes as he had been for some two centuries, just like everyone else. This meant that he objected equally whenever new taxes were imposed, just like the rest of his countrymen. He quickly realized that a good portion of any money that came to him from the State came from his own taxes, so, unlike his continental brethren, he ceased to look to the court for his livelihood and decided that he had to find some means of supporting himself. In certain periods, the late 14th and early 15th centuries, for example, war might bring in a good income, just as it did for continental noblemen, but most of the time he paid far more in taxes to pay for war than he could ever hope to make from plunder, ransoms, and the other profits of war. He thus saw that he must look to his own resources if he were to survive and flourish, and almost the only practical resource he had was land. He must learn to farm it profitably. To do this, two things were necessary: he must have available sufficient labour to work the land; and the countryside must be kept in sufficient order so that farming might prosper. Through the 13th century, the rapid rise in population meant that there was seldom any serious shortage of labour to till the land. There were always enough younger sons of serfs anxious for work as day labourers to replace those serfs and others who absconded to the towns. But this changed quickly with the coming of the Black Death in 1348 which brought a sharp fall in population. Suddenly, there was a severe shortage of farm labour. Those who survived could demand a greater return for their labour, or much less forced labour, or a combination of both. Edward III brought in a series of wage-control measures, but to little avail. It soon became clear that the landowner must make working his land sufficiently attractive to his villeins so that they would continue to stay and work and not slip away to find a more generous landowner a few miles down the road, or into the greater promise, but also greater risks, of town life.

The problem of keeping order in the medieval English countryside was much more serious than in France or most of the continent. In France, a considerable effort was made by royal and baronial agents to see that the peasantry were kept unarmed, for armed peasants would seriously have complicated their task of helping themselves to whatever of the peasant's property they thought they might make some use of. In England, on the other hand, from at least the time of Henry II's Assize of Arms and doubtless for long before, the government wanted, nay, insisted under penalty of law, that the peasants be well-armed. From the late 12th century on, well-trained and well-armed peasants were an important part of English armies. When English peasants armed with simple long bows arrived on the field of Crécy or of Agincourt, their presence was noted with great scorn by the well-armed, iron-clad knights of the French aristocracy.

Well-armed peasants might have their uses on foreign battlefields, but they presented, at least potentially, serious problems at home. While a few of the larger towns had rudimentary police, there was nothing in the countryside in the way of forces of law and order except for a few village constables, who were generally chosen from among those who were too old and decrepit to do any useful work. In Saxon days, there had been sworn tithings in which every able-bodied man in the land made himself responsible for the good behaviour of all the others in his tithing, but this admirable arrangement hardly survived the Norman Conquest. Thereafter, the keeping of law and order was entirely in the hands of country gentry, individually commissioned by central government as justices of the peace.

In the decades just after the Conquest, most landowners probably had a few armed men in their household for protection and to fulfil their feudal duties. By the 13th century, these had largely disappeared except in time of crisis. Thereafter, to keep order, the gentry had to rely largely on the respect they could win from their tenantry and their humbler neighbours.

First of all, a landowner had to build a reputation as a good landlord. If he tried to put up his rents and the services due him too far above the level which his tenants considered just; if he was overstrict in punishing offences against the game laws; if he seduced their wives and daughters and won notoriety as a drunken layabout; above all if the judgments he handed down as a JP were clearly unjust and self-serving, then there was bound to be trouble. Rioting was so common in the countryside, and grew ever more so until well into the 19th century, that it came to be looked upon as a nuisance; but it was also seen as a healthy and useful way of letting the humblest make clear his opinion about how he was governed. Whereas in France, the landowners were terrified of their tenantry and kept as far from them as possible, the English gentry felt compelled to hobnob with theirs, to play cricket with their sons, and tease their daughters, to listen to their problems and to try to help if at all possible. If a landowner gained a reputation for not being able to get on with his tenants and there were endless quarrels and riots on his lands, his fellow gentry would tend to shun him – he would be "cut by the county" – for they dared not risk their own tenantry becoming unsettled through contagion. Incredible as it seemed to the continentals, the English gentry from the 13th century to the 19th ruled the countryside, on the whole wisely and well, with almost no armed force to back it up.

In the years just after the American Revolution, Britain had lost the American colonies and it was clear to all – on the continent – that England must soon cease to exist as a nation of any importance. It was, however, recognized that English agriculture was quite good – it could hardly be any worse than continental agriculture – and a bright young Frenchman named Dumont thought that it would be a good idea to cross over to England to study English agricultural methods before it was too late. So he wrote to Lord Harcourt, who was famous for being in touch with all the latest agricultural techniques, proposing himself for a visit. Harcourt wrote back to say that he would be delighted, and so Dumont duly arrived. His Lordship was rather flattered by the Frenchman's interest and promised to take him for "a nice long tramp across the fields" in the morning. Dumont could hardly believe his ears. He knew that all the English were extremely eccentric, but this talk about tramping over muddy fields seemed to verge on insanity. Everyone knew that the way to learn about up-to-date agricultural methods was by intelligent conversation with the knowledgeable in book-lined studies.

But the next morning out they went, Harcourt pointing out matters of interest as they passed, Dumont desperately trying to dodge puddles and cow-pats while trying to insert the odd interested question. To one of these Harcourt was puzzled to give an answer. But they were in luck. "That's old Tom's cottage just there. He's bound to know the answer.". To Dumont's horror, his host then set off briskly to call on one of the minor tenants. Whether Dumont accompanied him we shall never know. The various shocked letters that he wrote to friends after he got home broke off the narrative here to express his tremendous outrage at the behaviour of an English nobleman who did not even know how to keep the peasantry in its place. If the English gentry did not very quickly reform their ways, their country was bound to be torn by savage revolution within their lifetime. The year was 1787.

While I think that there is a large measure of truth in the rather rosy picture I have painted of social relations in the English countryside in the days when agriculture was still profitable, much of this outlook continues today. But in the last couple of centuries, country-dwellers have formed an increasingly small minority of Englishmen. Apart from the countryside, from the early days of the Industrial Revolution quite a lot of class attitudes developed. The difficulty was in large part because so many of England's iron ore and coal mines lay in the north of the country or in wildest Wales. The remarkably uniform culture that had spread out from the Home Counties over much of England by the time of the Napoleonic Wars had not yet penetrated there. So to south-eastern ears, many of those who had prospered the most from the Industrial Revolution spoke a weird and unattractive dialect and had the most extraordinary and unpleasant manners. Not only the landed gentry but their social inferiors in the south-east looked on these newly-rich northerners almost as a race apart with whom they preferred not to mix.

Today this outlook has not changed all that much. The divide between the industrial classes, whether chairman of the board, shop steward, or trainee boiler maker from almost everyone else in England is greater than that which separates the moderately well-born and well-off from their servants, tradesmen, and artisans in the rest of the country. This has come to seem so natural a state of affairs that one is apt to forget that it is on the whole quite unusual. It is very much not the case in the United States for clear historical reasons.

When, on the ratification of the Treaty of Paris in 1783, Americans suddenly awoke to the realization that they were now on their own, one particular problem seemed more pressing and dangerous than any other: in the former 13 colonies, there was very little industrial activity because the Mother Country had carefully arranged for Britain to supply almost all America's industrial needs. Alexander Hamilton's famous *Report on Manufactures* of 1790 warned of the seriousness of the situation and called for drastic measures to encourage manufacturing in the United States. Ever since then, the industrialist has been looked up to by the rest of American society in a way that his British counterpart can only envy. On the other hand, from the early days of the Republic, those in the commercial and service industries were often cast as villains. Banks were thought insufficiently anxious to supply the funds for necessary new investment. Railroads were accused of charging far too much for transporting the raw materials and the products that were essential to manufacturing industry. Many people overseas think of Wall Street as something that most Americans look up to, but even before 1929, to say nothing of the shenanigans of the 1980s, stockbrokers and corporation lawyers were deeply distrusted. I well remember the family row which blew up when one of my brothers announced that he was going to be a stockbroker. Fortunately, he failed in that enterprise almost immediately and became instead an ordinary jobbing printer in Reno, Nevada. The family were greatly relieved. Not only had he decided to take up a respectable trade, but, with his tiresome habit of being divorced every year or so, Reno was an ideal place for him to live.

I think that many people in Britain were shocked and surprised at some of the things that went on in the City in the 1980s. Americans were not in the least taken aback by the even worse things that were going on in Wall Street. It was just what one would expect of people who allowed themselves to get mixed up in the sordid world of high finance.

This distaste for industry – which, I suppose, is at bottom a class thing – still persists in Britain today. Peers of the realm of ancient title fall over themselves to become directors of City firms. The remuneration must be very good indeed for such noblemen to consider an offer from an industrial corporation. Tory ex-Cabinet ministers flock to the City. When Jim Prior went to General Electric, people just took it as further evidence that he was not, as his ex-boss would have put it, "one of us".

I fear that this distaste for industry on the part of so many Britons, particularly among the prosperous and articulate, may be the real "British disease". While Britain began the Industrial Revolution, partly because of the happy accident that so many of her deposits of iron ore were near her supplies of coal, it was at least equally important that, through her success in overseas trade, she had accumulated sufficient capital so that there were funds readily available to exploit this accident, to build all the thousands of new factories and also the roads and canals that were essential to service them. Long after Germany and the United States, with France not all that far behind, had built lots of splendid new factories for themselves, Britain was able to keep ahead economically because of her far greater financial and commercial expertise and the rich investments she had in so many parts of the developing world. But now that most of the world's developed countries have caught up with Britain in commercial and financial know-how, Britain seems to be lagging further and further behind industrially. Much of this must surely be due to the reluctance of many young Britons, those with the best brains and the highest energies, to prefer careers almost anywhere else than in industry. Thanks to Margaret Thatcher, the days are now behind us when we could blame most industrial problems on the bovine stupidity of the British worker in allowing himself to be pulled out on strike at every possible opportunity. Now Britons must turn their attention to dealing with the real problem.

This distaste that so many Britons feel towards industry and industrialists must have something to do with the enthusiasm that so many of the latter feel for ever closer ties with Europe at a time when so many of their countrymen are wary, to say the least, of goings-on in Strasbourg and Brussels. On the continent, the old aristocracy had thoroughly discredited itself by the end of the 18th century by its oppressions, selfishness, and general inefficiency. At the beginning of the 19th century, the combined might of most of Europe was soundly thrashed by a small off-shore kingdom which would not even allow itself to keep a standing army in peacetime. The best minds on the continent addressed themselves to determine how such an extraordinary thing could possibly have happened. Surely, it could not have been because of the superiority of British virtue or courage, for these clearly did not exist. Even British government, so tediously praised by liberals, should not have been able to surpass the superb administrative efficiency of Napoleonic Europe. No, there could be but one reason why Britain had conquered. It must have been because of her blind good luck in being the first nation to have had an industrial revolution.

The greatest powers on the continent, therefore, turned their energies towards having their own industrial revolutions as quickly as possible. Everywhere the industrial tycoon became the hero of the nation. States spared no effort in seeing that he had everything he could need for industrial supremacy. This meant, of course, that agriculture had to be to some extent neglected, so that, rather surprisingly to most Britons, British agriculture today is in general a good deal superior to that on the Continent, and why Britain is contributing so much more the Common Agricultural Policy than she can ever hope to get back from Brussels. British captains of industry, when they go to the continent, find themselves treated with far more respect than they can ever hope to enjoy at home, admired as the only people who really know how the world works, an opinion which they warmly share. Hence their enthusiasm for making Britain as continental as possible.

Before turning to the United States, I should state that it is 30 years since I spent anytime there. Nor am I a sufficiently regular viewer of American television, that faithful recorder of life as it really is, to have been able to get at all caught up. I am also convinced that anything as complicated as class, whether social, economic, or political, can only be usefully treated by way of comparisons between various systems. As I know far more about Britain than any other country that was the obvious comparison. It is particularly useful in that in the United States of my day there were in fact two class systems, one inherited from Britain, the other, as a result of the great immigrations of the decades around 1900, from the poorer countries of Europe, where the continental class system was at its most pronounced.

When I was a child, it was understood by everyone I knew that there were three standards by which "real Americans" might be distinguished from "other people":
1: They must come from English or Ulster (known in America as Scotch-Irish) stock – real Scots were a little doubtful – or, in New York state, Dutch. Every American president or vice-president until Kennedy and Goldwater met this criterion, with the single exception of Judah P Benjamin, the vice-president of the Confederate States, and also, so far as I can remember, every candidate for president or vice-president.
2: Their immigrant ancestors must have been gentry, or at least of gentry stock.
3: All their American ancestors must have arrived in America before the War between the States (1861-5).

This last, at least in the eyes of those who did not meet these criteria, was probably the most important. There used to be a curious organization – for all I know it may still exist – called the Daughters of the American Revolution. By the time the Second World War came along, they had already become something of a joke through their incredible snobbery. One heard about them chiefly in the "Society" columns of the less particular sort of newspaper. "Real Americans" zealously avoided being mentioned in these rather odd columns, except for weddings and funerals, when it was understood that allowing themselves to be mentioned there was entirely for purposes of spreading useful information to other "real Americans". There was only one qualification for becoming a member of the Daughters: to have had one direct ancestor who had fought on the colonial side in the American Revolution. As I was born in England of a British father, I must confess that only half of my direct ancestors had fought on the "patriot" side, but my half brother was the only person I can recall having met before the age of about 15 *all* of whose ancestors, alive, active, and male at the appropriate time had not fought in that conflict. For to have been a proper American before Hitler's War implied that all of one's ancestors had been in America since at least the 18th century.

Naturally, they were a rather small and interbred group. Many Britons, I notice, are somewhat puzzled when, after each new president is elected, there appear newspaper stories pointing out his family relationship to at least a dozen of his predecessors, but it is a simple fact that almost every United States president before Kennedy – Andrew Jackson is the only exception I can think of – had not a few previous presidents among his cousins, several times removed.

A good many people look upon the Social Registers of major eastern and mid-western American cities as something of a joke, and with regard to New York City it certainly is. But it was – I speak as some one 30 years out of date – a guide to distant family connections. When I arrived at my first boarding school, feeling very lost and alone, my day was brightened by finding waiting for me half a dozen letters from people who lived not very far from the school and promised that if I had any problems or wanted to be taken out for a meal, I need only get in touch. My grandmother had merely consulted the Social Register for Philadelphia – my school was on the outskirts – to find the addresses of people whom she almost certainly never actually met, but who would recognize her name at the bottom of the letter.

There is one aspect of the lives of all these distant cousins which may at first seem a little surprising, but by my theories can be traced back to their family origins in England (or Ulster). While a good number of them were very rich, they went to no little trouble to pretend not to be. Whenever some aunt or cousin died and the size of the estate was published there was always general surprise in the family at how large it was., "Fancy, dear Aunt Lucy having all that money!" For they all did live quite simply, though comfortably. My grandmother's house, which was fairly typical of the houses of all her sisters and cousins and second cousins, had only four bedrooms, two of them very small, and two servants' rooms; none of the rooms downstairs was at all grand. I think that we once did manage to get 20 people sitting down to dinner together, but it was quite a crush. The only indoor servants were the cook and a housemaid, and they were quite adequate to look after a house of that size. There were also a chauffeur and two gardeners. In those days, decent people grew almost all their own greengroceries, just as they drew water from their own wells, so the kitchen garden had to be a good size.

Most of these quite modest family houses were built at about the same time, shortly after the Civil War, as the vast palaces of Newport and other smart residential areas in the East were going up, built by Vanderbilts, Belmonts, Morgans, and their like. These sometimes had literally hundreds of rooms.

One of the Belmont boys wrote home from Harvard to ask if he could bring back his entire class to celebrate his 21st birthday. His mother said that she only had room for half his class as she already had quite a large houseparty for that weekend.

These gaudy and ostentatious people had many of the qualifications of the older families, but they lacked an important one: they had been quite poor early in the 19th century and only became rich at about the time of the Civil War. Thus they were driven by an insatiable craving to show off to everyone just how rich and important they had become. They had become rich not in industry but in some form of service industry. Before the war, Cornelius Vanderbilt had earned a scanty living from a few garbage scows on New York City's rivers. It was by greatly expanding this fleet and pulling off all sorts of subsidiary "deals" that he became one of America's richest men. Others, like the Harrimans, made their money in railroads, and won an ill reputation for the ruthlessly high rates they charged small towns in the developing West where they provided almost the only form of transport and sustenance. Others, like the Morgans, made vast sums in wheeling-and-dealing on such a scale and in such dubious enterprises as would not be seen again until the 1980s. In the early 20th century, it all got so out of hand that there was nationwide clamour, led, not quite unselfishly, by the industrialists, for the government to step in and forbid the most glaring outrages – imagine industrialists today shouting for government intervention to control business – and Theodore Roosevelt became a national hero by "trust-busting" ruthlessly.

It is families like these whom, I suspect, many Britons have in mind as typical of the American upper classes, despite the scorn thrown on them by the novels of Henry James and Edith Wharton. (Mrs Wharton became so disgusted with what New York City was becoming that she left it forever and spent the rest of her life in Paris.) Certainly, these families got far more publicity than those who had been richer longer, particularly when they married one of their overrich daughters to some English nobleman. For this reason it is, or was, thought quite shameful for an American woman of old family to marry an Englishman. There was a terrible fuss when my mother announced that she was going to marry an Englishman, even though he was but a colonel. There was great alarm that everyone would think that she was just another Jenny Jerome or Consuelo Vanderbilt, one of those terrible people who married for sheer snobbery. When my mother got to England, she discovered that it was just what the English did think. Everywhere she went, the first question was always about the size of her dowry.

My chief theme has been how very different the English upper classes are from almost everywhere else on earth except for that class, for the first 150 years of the Republic very dominant, which were largely descended from the English gentry and inherited its ways and outlook. The English went their own way because in England the aristocracy had no privileges – except for the right of a few hundred to sit in the House of Lords – to set them off from everyone else, most importantly, the right of not paying taxes. They therefore had not much to lose by being mistaken for their social inferiors. The continental nobility had a very great deal to lose, and therefore made every effort to keep themselves apart as superior beings who must not be soiled by the riff-raff. The English nobility also had as a class to earn its own living, not being able to look to the State for profitable pensions or offices, or to the profits of war. Almost its only source of income was the land until the 16th century, when the profits of politics came to supply a useful supplement. As there was very little in the way of police in the provinces – and not much in London if it comes to that – the gentry had to learn to get on well with its neighbours – fellow gentry, tenants, craftsmen, farm workers – by treating them fairly and with no obvious discourtesy. Their descendants in America were never faced by the same conditions, but the habits of many generations did not quickly disappear, and their outlook on life and their own social inferiors was much the same as that of their own English forebears.

This must all be rapidly changing now. By the Second World War, the grandchildren of the great immigration were grown and active men and women. Their traditions were not those of England but of the continent, where social distinctions were always very important, and one must know one's place and stick to it.

I am not for a moment suggesting that the descendants of these immigrants still think that class distinctions are vastly important. They had come to America to escape them. But they are much more aware of the existence of class snobbery in a way that never seems to occur to those of gentry stock, and I find them often ready to take offence when clearly none is intended. These are the people who now rule the United States and why one is so much more aware of snobbery among Americans than 50 years ago.

The newer generations of immigrants, the Hispanics and Orientals, present a different form of snobbery. Whereas Italian and eastern European immigrants wanted nothing more than to become full Americans as quickly as possible, and saw the proudest day of their lives as the one on which they took their oath of allegiance to the American Constitution, the newer arrivals are determined to remain completely Hispanic or Oriental and fiercely resist any attempt to make them part of a national American culture. Which is why the United States is beginning to show signs of ceasing to be a nation. But now I really am talking about things that I know largely by hearsay.

13: Robert Smith

Addressing persons of rank

THIS is much easier than many people think. Despite political talk of "classlessness" rank is everything in every society. You rank if you have performed a courageous act. You rank if you are an old person, especially with all your faculties, to anyone much younger than you. You rank as a professor over a lecturer, as a lecturer ranks over an undergraduate. You rank as a trade union leader, just as you rank as director general of the CBI. You rank as a parent over a child, and as an older child usually ranks over a younger sibling. You rank if you live in Hampstead village over some one who lives in Tooting. You rank as a bank manager considering a loan to a would-be borrower. In this country, rank has been one of the peaceable ways to maintain order in society. Sir Peregrine Worsthorne put it well in *The Sunday Telegraph* (17 October 1993): "...once let the moral authority of those in charge be impaired, and order can only be maintained by calling on the executioner. Hence, the importance of inculcating respect for and deference to rank. If those in authority do not deserve to be looked up to personally, that is not the end of the world since it is their rank that matters most. Therein lies the central purpose of a class system: to invent respect and deference as a better way to maintain order rather than relying on fear and coercion." It has been remarked that as our society becomes less and less deferential, it has become more and more lawless, requiring more and more unenforceable laws by an increasingly large, but increasingly impotent, police force. We are encouraged by some quarters to throw off the velvet-lined gold manacles of deference and respect for the unlined, steel manacles of democracy.

According respect to the Royal Family, the nobility, ministers, members of the House of Commons, judiciary – our rulers – is seen by some people to be uncritical, even servile. A fiction has been created to deal with this state of affairs and it is that our rulers are really our servants, and that we the people are really the masters. A consequence of this is that cabinet ministers pointedly refer to one another in a television interview by their first names. Some interviewers ingratiatingly call their ministerial guests by their first names. The better sort of interviewer, who may well call the foreign secretary by his first name in private, addresses him as foreign secretary in public. But we all should know that the only thing likely to sway a government minister like a foreign secretary, is a rebellion in the back benches. The trappings of a ubiquitous familiarity make no difference to who is really "in charge". Rather than blurring the lines, therefore, we should mark them as a reminder of how things really are, and not be seduced into a spurious sense of equality, and the dangerous notion that our opinions can have an immediate impact.

None of this is to suggest even remotely that our rulers are charlatans. Very few are and a host all work very hard, for very little, particularly the much-maligned MP. Formal marks of honour and respect, with which I am about to deal, serve at least two useful purposes: (1) they remind us who really rules Britain; (2) respecting our rulers makes respecting our neighbours that much more natural, for if we cannot respect the rank of our rulers, how can we respect anyone below? This country is unusually stratified, but the extraordinary thing about this – which is a complete mystery to foreigners – is that it is a society completely open to talent. Every level of our society has its own rules, even, and perhaps particularly, the liberal establishment. If you obey the rules, you can do anything in Britain. Unlike America, you do not have to be rich; unlike Japan, you do not have to be servile; unlike Germany, you do not have to be mechanistic; unlike France, you do not have to be surly. All this is possible within a Constitutional Monarchy, an unelected House of Lords, and a House of Commons whose majority party can poll as little as 40% of the vote. I can think of no other country where a coal miner can rise, in a single generation, to become a peer of the Realm.

The Sovereign is the fount of all (formal) honour. In the United Kingdom, without the Sovereign, there is nothing at all – there is no law, no government, no armed forces, no "honour". If you can interfere with the Head of State, nothing is safe – not even the privacy of the house you live in. Through the law, the Sovereign recognizes your right to that privacy.

The conferring of titles is all of the same piece. By being confined by the law but at the same time above it, the Sovereign can theoretically confer any title on any person chosen; in practice she exercises this element of the Prerogative on the advice of her ministers, although certain honours – the Garter, the Order of Merit, the Royal Victorian Order – are in The Queen's personal gift.

THE QUEEN

Setting out the envelope:

H M The Queen
Buckingham Palace
London SW1

The form, The Queen's Most Excellent Majesty, is reserved for diplomatic letters, although it does seem a great shame that routine letters of credence and other such forgettable memoranda should be the preserve of bureaucrats. Perhaps Classical writers had it about right with "Rex" or "Regina" when they opened their addresses to sovereigns: "O King", "O Queen"; when they were addressing more than one king, they opened with "Reges": "O Kings", but perhaps it looks better in Classical texts than in a modern letter.

Begin the letter: **Madam**. Do *not* begin Dear Madam.

Never refer to the Queen by the personal pronoun (you), but as Your Majesty. This can be quite tricky, but the way to get it right is, first, to draft the letter as you would like to write it then rearrange it so that "you" does not occur. (In reports, such as this, it is quite all right to use the pronouns "she" and "her", but not in a letter directed to her). For example, the letter in draft:

Madam

I write to inform you that our local guides and scouts have raised more than £10,000, as part of a countywide scheme, for the Nether Wallop Aids Hospice.

The biggest and most profitable event was a country fair which we held on your official birthday. We held a point-to-point, gymkhana, bring-and-buy, and all the sorts of things you would expect at such an event. We concluded by singing "God save the Queen", accompanied by the Swadlincote silver band, after which everyone cheered and wished you many more years to reign.

Yours faithfully

Now we shall rewrite the letter above:

Madam

I write humbly to inform Your Majesty that our local guides and scouts have raised more than £10,000, as part of a countywide scheme, for the Nether Wallop Aids Hospice.

The biggest and most profitable event was a country fair which we held on Your Majesty's Official Birthday.   We held a point-to-point, gymkhana, bring-and-buy, and all the sorts of things one would expect at such an event. We concluded by singing The National Anthem, accompanied by the Swadlincote silver band, after which everyone cheered and wished Your Majesty many more years to reign.

I have the honour, Your Majesty, to be

Yours faithfully

If you were writing to the Queen to invite her to next year's event, the first thing to do is to telephone Buckingham Palace to find out the name of the Private Secretary, together with any decorations or title he or she might have.

Take our letter above:

Sir Robert Fellowes KCB KCVO
Buckingham Palace
London SW1

(Salutation in hand) *Dear Sir Robert*

I write to inform you that our local guides and scouts have raised more than £10,000, as part of a countywide scheme, for the Nether Wallop Hospice.

The biggest and most profitable event was a country fair which we held on The Queen's Official Birthday. We held a point-to-point, gymkhana, bring-and-buy, and all the sorts of things you would expect at such an event. We concluded by singing The National Anthem, accompanied by the Swadlincote silver band, after which everyone cheered and wished Her Majesty many more years to reign.

We are holding a similar event next year. We normally hold it in July and it would give us all the utmost pleasure if Her Majesty would condescend to be present at a date which we would be most happy to agree with you, should this humble request find favour.

Many things, linked with this charitable effort, take place in Nether Wallopshire on the same day and it may be that Her Majesty would wish to know more about these, should The Queen wish to review our efforts. Next year also marks the 98th anniversary of the incorporation of the county town of Nether Wallop by Royal Charter, a landmark in our county's history.

I would be more than pleased to send you further information and we would bend our best endeavours to working with you to make this a great success. I would be indebted to you if you would be so kind as to lay this humble request before The Queen.

(Sign-off in hand) *Yours sincerely*

You can refer to the Private Secretary by his personal pronoun "you", but the Queen's personal pronoun is switched, as seems less repetitive, between "The Queen" and "Her Majesty". Such letters should be as brief as possible: private secretaries get many of them, so to make your request keep it concise. Note also in such a letter that "The Queen" is a capital "T".

We have also added something to the letter. The Queen likes to see as much as possible, especially when she travels out of London, and if you can link your event with something else going on locally, so much the better.

Suppose the Queen comes to your event and you have to meet her.

If you are to be presented (you are introduced to everyone else in the world, including the Pope and the President of the United States) and then take over as the local leader during the Queen's stay with you, this is how it works:

i: The Lord Lieutenant, or the Chairman of the County Council (that sort of person) will have received the Queen already;

ii: When the Queen gets to you, you will have been placed at the head of a line of people, whom you will have agreed with the Palace, or perhaps through the Lieutenancy, and whom you will present;

iii: It all happens in a couple of seconds. Women curtsy, men make a neck-bow;

iv: The Queen will, simultaneously, have offered her gloved hand in greeting. *Lightly* touch her fingers because she will be shaking hands with a lot of people. A prominent politician once glad-handed so many people that he had to have medical treatment;

v: You are then in charge. Do not waste time, present your people, and get the Queen to where it is she has to be. Be sure you know everyone who should be in the lineup to be presented, but if not, make sure that you have a small list of the order. It is quite all right to refer to a list.

When presenting some one, say simply: "Your Majesty, may I present so and so, who has arranged the gymkhana?" The Queen will have a few words to say before moving on. And so it goes: You keep calling the Queen "Your Majesty" or "Ma'am" (pronounced "mam");

vi: In the mêlée of a walkabout, you may find some one who wants "to have a word". That is fine if the Queen is going in that direction, but if she is not, do not be intimidated by such supplicants who think nothing of jabbing you in the ribs from behind to get your attention. Your attention should be concentrated on the Queen and placing your body unnoticed between such a person and her. Also, beware of people who have already "had a word" filtering themselves forward to have another.

PRINCES OF THE BLOOD

Essentially, it is all the same as if you were addressing the Sovereign. Here are the addresses and salutations:

Address: **HRH The Prince Philip KG, Duke of Edinburgh**: Salutation at start of letter: **Sir**; on presentation and so forth, interpose in speech "Sir", "Your Royal Highness"

Address: **HRH The Prince of Wales KG**: then as for the Duke of Edinburgh

You will notice that we have put KG after the Queen's Consort and the Heir to the Throne. The KG (Knight of the Garter) is the only honour you use for these princes, although they hold many more. The KG is the highest formal honour the Queen bestows and the Garter is the oldest, continuous Order of Chivalry in Europe. The Queen, of course, never has letters after her title as she is the head (the fount, to use the legal term) of all honour and the sovereign of all orders. You use decorations after the names of everyone else. Most of the people you are likely to write to in this note will be in *Debrett's Peerage and Baronetage,* or *Who's Who* and you should refer to one of these publications for for their awards.

Address: **HRH The Duke of York**: then as the Duke of Edinburgh

Address: **HRH The Prince Edward**: then as the Duke of Edinburgh

For all other senior male members of the Royal Family (ie Royal Dukes of Gloucester and Kent) as for The Duke of York (Prince Andrew); for all other Princes of the Blood, as for the Prince Edward.

Just as for the Queen, you do not use the personal pronoun "you" and "he" when writing to any of them, their private secretaries, or during a meeting. Under no circumstances refer to the Queen, when addressing the Prince of Wales, as "your mother"; or, if addressing the Queen about the Prince of Wales, "your son", or "Charles", or even "Prince Charles" - he is "the Prince of Wales", or "the Duke of York", and so on.

THE QUEEN MOTHER AND PRINCESSES OF THE BLOOD

This is very like the Queen and the male members of the Royal Family:

Address: **HM Queen Elizabeth, The Queen Mother**: Salutation at start of letter: **Madam**; in speech, exactly as for the Queen. Remember the Queen Mother is "Her Majesty" too, like the Queen because she is the widow of a king. She happens also to be one of the last empresses, for she was Empress of India. There is only one other serious empress living: the Empress of Japan and her mother-in-law Dowager Empress Nagako, the widow of Emperor Hirohito. There are.the ex-wives of ex-Emperor Bokassa of Central Africa and Farah Dibah, widow of the Shah of Iran. Most interesting of all the recent empresses was Empress Zita of Austria-Hungary, who only died in 1982, and was the widow of the last Austro-Hungarian Emperor Karl who abdicated in 1918.

Address: **HRH The Princess Royal** (formally, she is no longer referred to as Princess Anne): Salute at the start of letter: **Madam**, and the rest is the same as the Queen, except in place of "Your Majesty", "Your Royal Highness".

The Royal Duchesses and Royal Princesses are treated exactly as for the Royal Dukes and Princes, though remember to change the gender where appropriate. The only slight difference is for Princess Margaret, whose address is: **HRH The Princess Margaret, Countess of Snowdon**, then as usual. "His or Her Royal Highness" is a title accorded by the Queen, usually to the wives of royal children and certain royal relations not directly of the Blood. For instance, Princess Katarina of Yugoslavia, who is married to Mr Desmond de Silva QC, a member of the Governing Council of the Manorial Society of Great Britain, has been accorded "HRH" by the Queen, so you would style her: HRH The Princess Katarina of Yugoslavia. HRH The Prince Michael of Kent's wife, on the other hand, Princess Michael, has not been accorded an "HRH", and she is simply: The Princess Michael of Kent. When Sarah Ferguson married Prince Andrew, she was accorded "HRH", and her style is: **HRH The Duchess of York**.

EVERYONE ELSE

Everyone else you may have to write to or meet starts off common. So not only are we all born naked and slough off this mortal coil with nothing, we all start common too: almost everyone. One person who starts noble is the eldest son of the Sovereign: he enters the world as a Duke, but as he is royal he does not fit into this section, though I mention him for the record. The only other person who might be born noble is the eldest son of a peer who is born posthumously.

What is this idea of nobility? Can we recognize it? The nobility of Great Britain is a very small, identifiable group of people, numbering, with Life Peers, about 1,200. Such people are noble by law so there is nothing more to be said about that here.

But as Lord Mackay says at the beginning of this book, duty and responsibility, while necessary to any aristocracy, are not exclusive. It seems to me that duty and responsibility are the two key requirements for any kind of nobility. All of us recognize these attributes in people we have met, who do not sit in the House of Lords. What does that make of members of the House of Lords? The answer is nothing because the House of Lords is simply there. Its members are noble and are accorded by courtesy, certainly, and law, sometimes, special kinds of treatment, at least when you write a letter to one of them. They used to enjoy wider privileges, such as the very useful privilege of not being arrested by their creditors while Parliament was sitting; or the less obvious privilege of beheading than hanging when sentenced to death. But the British nobility is unique among nobilities in enjoying no privileges that are not also accorded to the common man, save membership of one of the world's most exclusive clubs, the House of Lords. Otherwise a title might get you a better table in a restaurant, but it will not get you exempted from tax.

Within the peerage, there are ranks of dignity which are important on formal occasions, such as the State Opening by the Queen. There are five ranks of nobility, starting with the highest downwards: Duke, Marquess, Earl, Viscount, and Baron.

DUKES

A duke is not only the highest rank of nobility, it is a rank respected by all the others. Of course, in respecting the title, we do not necessarily have to respect the current encumbent. Apart from a handful, dukes are still well off and in the case of Westminster or Devonshire seriously well off. One duke has been prosecuted for fraud in recent years, but was cleared; another duke's eldest son was a gardener. In this context, it may be worth remarking that in earlier times if you ceased to be able to support a dignity, you lost it. George Nevil, for example, was created Duke of Bedford by Edward IV in 1469. The family lost most of their lands two years later and, in 1477, Parliament petitioned the King to degrade George Nevil from the Dukedom of Bedford which was done.

The Roman title, *dux*, meant a military leader and the rank was common in Europe from the reign of Charlemagne, Emperor of the West, from about 800 when it was an appointment at pleasure, quickly changed, under Charlemagne's weaker successors, into an hereditary fiefdom by the descendants of the holders of this imperial office: the first Capetian King of France, Hugues Capet, was Duke of Francia, a comparatively small area centred on the Ile de France. Greater dukedoms, such as Aquitaine, or the German dukedoms, were very different from the dukedoms that were to emerge in England. The former were virtually sovereign princes, while the latter derived their title of honour from the Crown and were always subservient to it. Indeed, such German duchies as Bavaria and Saxony were to become kingdoms in the 18th century. The first duke, in the specialized English sense, was Edward the Black Prince, eldest son of Edward III, who was created Duke of Cornwall in 1337: you may come across earls of earlier generations in England being referred to as *dux*, but this was not an honorific title as duke became after 1337. In much the same way, you may find an earl referred to in the documents as *marchio*, or marquess, but again this is a military rank held at pleasure by families such as the FitzOsberns who were Marcher (*marchio*) Lords in south Wales. Edward III created two younger sons Dukes of Lancaster (1351) and Clarence (1362). Edward's grandson, Richard II, created his uncles Dukes of York and Gloucester (both in 1385). These were all royal dukedoms and the first non-royal to be elevated to this rank was Richard II's favourite, Robert de Vere, ninth Earl of Oxford, whom he created Duke of Ireland in 1386. Thereafter, non-royal dukes came in comparatively rapid succession in the 15th century, none of whose titles survive today, save Norfolk.

One penultimate note: within the peerage there is a ranking based on antiquity of the title. Consequently, there is a Premier Baron (Lord de Ros), a Premier Viscount (Lord Hereford), a Premier Earl (Lord Arundel which title is subsumed under the Dukedom of Norfolk), a Premier Marquess (Lord Winchester), and a Premier Duke (Norfolk). Finally, there is a ranking by seniority of kingdom in this order: England, Scotland, Ireland, Great Britain, United Kingdom. When writing to a peer, they are all treated the same within the five ranks of nobility. *Debrett's Peerage and Baronetage* is very helpful in giving not only the holders of extant titles, their addresses, wives, and children, but brief family histories and other details. *Who's Who* also includes all peers, though much more briefly.

Today, the first nobleman of the kingdom is Miles Francis Stapleton Fitzalan Howard, Duke of Norfolk, Premier Duke and Earl and Hereditary Earl Marshal of England. Fitzalan Howard is the family surname and all peers have surnames like the rest of us which, unless they form part of the title, they do not use. If you receive a letter from the Duke of Norfolk, for example, he will sign himself "Norfolk", or from Viscount Gormanston, "Gormanston", and so on. The present Duke of Norfolk is the 17th Duke. If you consult *Debrett's*, you will see that he has many other, inferior titles. We have already mentioned the Earldom of Arundel, but he is also Earl of Surrey, Earl of Norfolk, and Earl of Norwich, and he holds numerous baronies. The ducal title was raised by Richard III in 1483 with precedence in the Dukedom and the Earldom of Arundel (which is also a feudal honour title, based on ownership of Arundel Castle) to 1433. As Earl Marshal of England, the Duke is responsible for all state occasions, such as state openings and coronations, and oversees the College of Arms. The Duke has no jurisdiction in Scotland. Titles of dignity and coats of arms in Edinburgh come under the Lyon Court, headed by the Lord Lyon, Sir Malcolm Innes of Edingight.

Envelope and top left corner of letter:

Maj-Gen The Most Noble The Duke of Norfolk KG GCB GCVO CBE MC

Salutation: **Dear Duke**

Sign-off: **Yours sincerely**

Salutation and sign-off ("top and tail") (unless Dear Sir/Madam; Yours faithfully, which are invariably typed) should as a courtesy always be written in manuscript. The assumption is that most people have letters typed by secretaries (much less the case these days as more and more people become computer/processor-literate) and it is polite to been seen to have gone to the trouble of topping and tailing personally. Unlike royalty, you can use personal pronouns even to the Duke of Norfolk, so "you" and "your" are in order. What you must not do, unless you are a supplier (such as Fortnum and

Mason) or a person seeking employment from the Duke, is to refer to him in the letter as "Your Grace". While you are not equal to the Duke, you are not subservient to him as would be a tradesman or servant, so you can write a perfectly normal letter.

If you meet a duke, you call him simply "Duke". If you are referring to him to third parties, including household servants, it is "the Duke", not "His Grace". So, if you have an appointment with a duke and his secretary asks your business, you say who you are and that you have come to see "the Duke". The secretary will almost certainly call him "Your Grace", as would, for example, a policeman or any civil servant for obvious reasons..

On the envelope style for the Duke of Norfolk, we have only used his highest title. His other titles are not used in this context. But we have added decorations which he has earned independently of the accident of birth. He is a major-general in the army and he has been decorated with various orders of knighthood and other awards. These letters always follow his name (or other letters behind other people's names as appropriate). You can check such matters in *Debrett's* or *Who's Who*. If a correspondence is struck up, the style "The Most Noble" is dropped and you would put: **Maj-Gen The Duke of Norfolk KG GCB GCVO CBE MC.**

The style you use to a duke is exactly the same as to his wife, the duchess, so in the present example: **The Most Noble The Duchess of Norfolk.** If a duke has a mother, or other female relative, who was married to a ducal predecessor, the style varies slightly as follows: **Lavinia, Duchess of Norfolk KG CBE.** Duchess Lavinia is the first non-royal female to be admitted to the Order of the Garter. She was also Lord Lieutenant of West Sussex.

Eldest son of a duke

He will take the next title down after the dukedom, so in the case of Norfolk, the next title is the Earldoms of Arundel and Surrey. This is a courtesy title and its holder is not noble until he succeeds to the Dukedom of Norfolk, so he gets no prefixes or definite articles on the envelope: **Earl of Arundel and Surrey**, then his private address (do not send letters to sons and daughters of peers and peeresses at the House of Lords as they have no entitlement to representation there).

Top: **Dear Lord Arundel** (you do not put "and Surrey" which holds good for all "multiple" titles, and do not put "Dear Earl", or "Dear Earl of Arundel"; and do not, in speech, call him "Earl" or "Earl of Arundel", but simply "Lord Arundel"). I hate receiving letters that begin "Dear Robert Smith".

The only rank of nobility, after first reference, that is different from all the rest is duke: the Marquess of X is called "Lord X"; the Earl of Y is called "Lord

Y" and so on. You do not call the Duke of Z "Lord Z", but simply Duke. The same is true for their wives who, in speech, from Marchioness down are called "Lady A".

Younger sons of dukes

All younger sons of dukes enjoy for their life the courtesy title of "Lord their first name and surname", so the Duke of Norfolk's younger son would be styled on the envelope: **Lord Gerald Fitzalan Howard**. Top: **Dear Lord Gerald**. If Lord Gerald is married, his wife would be known formally as **Lady Gerald**. Their children would have no distinctions, other than any they might have attained for themselves, or married (women). This raises another point: women who marry a titled person use the title. Men who marry titled women do not. There have been moves in the House of Lords recently to allow eldest daughters to inherit a title in preference to a younger son. Ironically, this has come from a Labour peer and would have the effect of perpetuating titles indefinitely, as opposed to ending most of them in about 200 years as calculated by Professor Carradine. I imagine that in the interests of sexual equality, it is only a matter of time.

Daughters of dukes

Style: "Lady her first name and surname", so taking the Duke of Norfolk again: **Lady Tessa Balfour**. She married Roderick Balfour. Were she still single, she would be Lady Tessa Fitzalan Howard. Top: **Dear Lady Tessa**. The sons and daughters of a duke's daughter have no automatic distinctions.

MARQUESSES

These are the second highest rank of nobility and were introduced by Richard II for his friend, Robert de Vere, Earl of Oxford, whom he made Marquess of Dublin in 1385. As titles, they took a while to gain credence among the old nobility of the late Middle Ages. The Beaufort Earls of Somerset, in the person of John Beaufort, resigned the Marquessate of Dorset and only very reluctantly resumed it, at the request of Parliament, in 1410. It was considered too much of a novelty. We shall deal with life peerages later, but the Marquessate of Dublin was granted for life. Before he married her, Henry VIII created Anne Boleyn Marquess (not Marchioness) of Pembroke. The last marquess to be created was that of Reading in 1926. Rufus Isaacs is a fine example of how, despite, or because of, our class structure, people of real talent can rise. He was a younger son of an East End Jewish tailor who rose to become Lord Chief Justice of England and, finally, Vice-Roy of India. He retired as Warden of the Cinque Ports, a position now held by Queen Elizabeth The Queen Mother, full of years and honour from his country. In writing to a marquess, we shall use the Premier Marquess of England, Lord Winchester:

Envelope and top left of letter:

The Most Hon The Marquess of Winchester
Address as normal

Top: **Dear Lord Winchester**

Tail: **Yours sincerely**

You use the personal pronouns as normal and do not refer to him as "Your Lordship". Like "Your Grace", this is for tradesmen, employees, policemen, and civil servants. In speech, simply refer to as Lord Winchester.

The style you use for a marquess is exactly the same as to his wife, the marchioness, so in the present example: **The Most Hon The Marchioness of Winchester**. Top: **Dear Lady Winchester**. If you have to write to the widow of a marquess, it would be first name, The Marchioness of X. Some marquesses are not "of anywhere", such as the Marquess Conyngham. Do not worry about this, just address the envelope **The Most Hon The Marquess Conyngham**; top: **Dear Lord Conyngham**. "Most Hon" stands for "Most Honourable", but it is always abbreviated in a letter.

Eldest son of a marquess

Like the eldest son of a duke, the eldest son of a marquess takes his father's next most senior title, in the present case Earl of Wiltshire, for whom the style is exactly the same as for the Earl of Arundel and Surrey. When you are unsure of a peer's senior courtesy title (ie the title used by his son and heir), consult *Debrett's*. They are all given.

Daughters and younger sons of a marquess

Exactly the same as for daughters and younger sons of a duke. Wives enjoy all the distinctions of their husbands, in the female gender; husbands enjoy no automatic distinctions.

EARLS

For most of the Middle Ages, after king, being an earl was the most important rank. There are different historical fashions for the introduction of "earl" into England. There was the Anglo-Saxon word "ealdoman" (roughly proximate with Alfred the Great), appointed by the king to raise the militia (*fyrd*) of a county. The Danish kings of England (1016-42) had *jarls* (pronounced "yarls"). Sir Henry Spelman thought that earls originated in the Western Empire founded by Charlemagne who appointed *comes* at pleasure to head a region (*comitatus*). Like *dux*, the *comes* quickly became hereditary, being rendered in French as *comte* and in English "count". What is sure is that there are earls in Domesday Book, compiled for William the Conqueror in 1086 as an inventory of the landholders of his kingdom of England and their lands, and "comital" quickly enters English as an adjective for counties which were traditionally headed by an earl.

As the Duke of Norfolk is also Premier Earl of England, I have chosen the Earldom of Shrewsbury, created by Henry VI in 1442 which is the oldest English earldom on the Roll of Parliament. The present 22nd Earl of Shrewsbury, Charles Henry John Benedict Crofton Chetwyn Chetwyn-Talbot, is also Earl of Waterford in Ireland and Earl Talbot of Hensol. He has other titles too, of which his senior courtesy title is Viscount Ingestre, of which Lord Shrewsbury is also Lord of the Manor. The first Earl was John Talbot, a great warrior in the French wars and after whom the claret, Chateau Talbot, is named.

Envelope and top left of letter:

The Rt Hon The Earl of Shrewsbury & Waterford
House of Lords &c

Top: **Dear Lord Shrewsbury**

Tail: **Yours sincerely**. Never refer to as "Your Lordship". Rt Hon stands for "Right Honourable" and is always abbreviated.

When writing to Lord Shrewsbury's wife:

Envelope and top left of letter:

The Rt Hon The Countess of Shrewsbury & Waterford

Top: **Dear Lady Shrewsbury**.

The widow of an earl is styled: **first name, the Countess of X**; top: **Dear Lady X**

Eldest son of an earl

Takes his father's senior courtesy title, in the present case the Viscountcy of Ingestre. Envelope: **Viscount Ingestre**; top: **Dear Lord Ingestre**.

Younger sons of an earl

Take "The Hon", standing for "Honourable", their first name and surname, so for Lord Shrewsbury's second son: Envelope: **The Hon Edward Chetwynd-Talbot**; Top: **Dear Mr Chetwynd-Talbot.**

Daughters of an earl

Take Lady first name, surname, so for Lord Shrewsbury's daughter: Envelope: **Lady Victoria Chetwynd-Talbot**; top: **Dear Lady Victoria**. Even when she marries, Lady Victoria remains Lady Victoria and takes her husband's surname. Wives of sons of earls enjoy all the distinctions of their husbands; husbands of daughters do not.

Like occasional marquesses, a few earls are not "of anywhere", such as Earl Spencer, but the style is the same as for Marquess Conyngham already given.

VISCOUNTS

This is the most recent of the peerage ranks and was first raised by Henry VI in 1440 for John de Beaumont, sixth Baron Beaumont, as Viscount Beaumont with precedence over all barons. Some sources suggest that the title was Viscount Beaumont of Swords, or simply Viscount Swords, appropriate enough considering the number of battles in which he took part, his last being Northampton where he lost his life in 1459. A descendant, Sir George Beaumont, Baronet, is still living.

Taking the Premier Viscount of England, Lord Hereford. Robert Milo Leicester Devereux (pronounced "Deverooks") is the 18th holder of the Viscountcy which was created in 1550 by Edward VI.

Envelope: **The Rt Hon The Viscount Hereford**; top: **Dear Lord Hereford**

Lord Hereford's wife: Envelope: **The Rt Hon The Viscountess Hereford**; top: **Dear Lady Hereford**. Widow of a viscount: Envelope: **first name, The Viscountess X**; top: **Dear Lady X.**

All children of a viscount

Envelope: **The Hon first name and family surname**; top: **Dear Mr, Mrs, Miss X.** So taking Lord Hereford's son: Envelope: **The Hon Charles Devereux**; top: **Dear Mr Devereux.** Wives enjoy their husbands' distinctions.

BARONS

Like earl, this is a very old title whose origin has been pored over by many historians and genealogists. For the most recent treatise on the subject, apply to the Manorial Society of Great Britain. But, essentially, a baron was the king's vassal, or *baro*, man. A barony was entirely based on a landholding which very soon became a *terrarum dignitatis*, whose holder in the early Norman period derived dignity from the property and eventually the title baron which, by the 13th century, English kings regularized by recognition.

As time passed, a landholding of great size in support of the territorial designation became less and less important, so that today, Baroness Thatcher of Kesteven holds absolutely no land at all in Kesteven. There are three types of baron: a baron by letters patent or writ of summons to Parliament (a parliamentary baron); a feudal baron or baron by tenure in England, Wales, and Ireland (not a parliamentary baron); and a Scottish baron (again not a parliamentary one).

Parliamentary barons

The Premier Baron of England is Peter Trevor Maxwell, 28th Baron de Ros (pronounced "Roos"). English and UK parliamentary barons are never called barons except in their patents of barony, or arms, or on the Roll of the House of Lords. In letters or in speech they are called just "Lords". However, a women who holds a parliamentary barony in her own right is often called baroness so-and-so, as Lady Thatcher above. I do not know why this is, but suspect that "baroness" distinguishes the holder as a peeress in her own right from "lady" which is a title largely for wives and daughters of peers. One of the loveliest titles of recent creation is Baroness Trumpington, whose name could have come out of the pages of Trollope.

Envelope and top left corner: **The Rt Hon The Lord de Ros**; top: **Dear Lord de Ros**; tail: **Yours sincerely**.

His wife: Envelope: **The Rt Hon The Lady de Ros**; top: **Dear Lady de Ros**. The widow of a baron: Envelope: **first name, Lady X**; top: **Dear Lady X**.

All sons and daughters of a parliamentary baron

The same as for viscount

All peers of the realm are entitled to bear Arms with their coronet of rank over the chief (top) of the shield, together with supporters (eg lion and unicorn as in the Royal Arms).

Feudal barons

These baronies are mostly held by the Crown and are often known as honors (sic) from the dignity emanating from such titles in the ancient duchy of Normandy; for example, Belli Fortis. They were transposed to England after the Conquest. Some are still in the hands of parliamentary peers, but some are occasionally sold which is possible as they are "estates in land", though the real estate may have been severed many years ago. Indeed, until about 1840, some holders of such baronies, who were not ennobled already, had successfully petitioned for a seat in the House of Lords, one ground being that a previous holder had been summoned to Parliament as a baron by writ. There is a manuscript in the College of Arms, London, which states that barons by tenure (feudal barons), "who, in regard thereof, ought to be summoned to Parliament." All titles are property, in law "incorporial property". One of the principal differences between parliamentary titles, and baronies and manorial lordships, is that parliamentary titles are not *in commercio*, although, as noted elsewhere in this book, some peerages effectively were. The word "lord" is Saxon: *hlaford* or *laford*:: *hlaf* a loaf of bread; and *ford* to give, because great men kept large houses, and retinues whom they fed. The specialization of peerages into purely honorific titles, as opposed to lordships and baronies that were land-based, did not begin to occur until the 13th century – so specialized by the 17th century that the Spencers were not earls of anywhere, but simply Earls Spencer, their family name. Nevertheless, the vast majority of peerages include some territorial designation (we have noted Lady Thatcher) so that the original conception of peerage as based in the land is preserved, though, as Earl Jowitt said in *The Dictionary of English Law* (1959), "the only lords of any importance at the present day are lords of manors". He did not mean by this that they could vote in Parliament, or that they were noble, like lords of Parliament. He was making the purest distinction between peers of the realm, who hold only titles of dignity (though they may also hold land), as opposed to lords of the land (manor) who, through the rights appendant to their title, have absolute rights in and over land without necessarily owning any real estate at all.

Taking a member of the Manorial Society, Paul Sleigh;

Envelope: **Baron Sleigh of Carbury**; top: **Dear Baron Sleigh**

Wives of feudal barons and feudal baronesses in their own right in England and Ireland: Envelope: **Baroness Sleigh of Carbury**; Top: **Dear Baroness Sleigh**. Children of feudal barons and baronesses have no distinctions and on the transfer of such a barony, the previous holder and his wife lose the style and revert to their former appellation.

These rules hold good for English, Welsh, and Irish feudal baronies. Additionally, the Chief Herald of Ireland will accord a feudal baron a baronial coronet and supporters for his shield (women receive a lozenge).

Scottish barons

Scottish barons, like their English and Irish feudal counterparts, do not have a seat in the House of Lords. The equivalent rank in Scotland of a parliamentary baron in England is "Lord of Parliament", and the style is exactly the same as for an English or UK parliamentary baron. Here is the use of a Scottish (feudal) baron:

Envelope: **Maurice Taylor Baron of Portlethen**; top: **Dear Baron of Portlethen**

Scottish baronesses take the female form and the style is otherwise the same as for baron. The eldest son a Scottish baron: Envelope: **Paul Sleigh of Portlethen ygr** ("younger": note the lower case "y" to distinguish the bearer, as the Lord Lyon points out, from the eminent brewers); top: **Dear Sleigh ygr**; The daughters of a baron are styled: **Miss Sleigh of Portlethen**; top: **Dear Miss Sleigh of Portlethen.**

Under the Act of Union (1707), Scotland nominated only 16 representative peers to Westminster, but in 1963, under the Peerage Act, all Scottish peers were permitted to take their seats. Irish peers sat at Westminster until 1923 when the Irish Free State was established. After that, only Irish peers who had Great Britain, UK, English, or Scottish peerages, besides their Irish title, were permitted to take their seats. For example, the Earl of Rosse, who has the inferior title of Baron Oxmantown, cannot sit in the House of Lords because his titles are all in the peerage of Ireland. The Earl of Shannon, who is also Viscount Boyle, and Baron Boyle of Bandon (titles in the Irish peerage) can sit in the Lords because he is Baron Carleton in the peerage of Great Britain. He is summoned as Lord Carleton, but is known as the Earl of Shannon, so if you were writing to him, you would address him by his Earldom and not by his GB Barony. An interesting case is that of Lord Macdonald, who lives in Skye, but because the Barony of Macdonald of Sleate (pronounced: "Slate") is in the peerage of Ireland, Lord Macdonald cannot sit in the House of Lords. Irish peers who have lost the right to sit in the House of Lords are accorded all the ceremonial styles as if they were still peers of the realm.

MANORIAL LORDSHIPS

These are, arguably, the oldest titles still in continuous use. They are not, like baronies, titles of "noblesse", but they are titles dignified by their antiquity and the historic rights still associated with them, known as "holding in Grand Serjeanty". The 1922-25 Property Acts did not affect honorific rights merged with Lordships of the Manor in England and Wales (there are no Manors *per nomen* in Scotland). At the highest level, ownership of the Manor of Bargavenny, and particularly not an earlier writ of summons, led to the recognition of Edward Nevile to be summoned to Parliament as Lord Bargavenny in the reign of James I. For an interesting account, see *First Report of the Lords' Committees on the Peerage,* p 440 (House of Lords Library). There are comparable examples for the Manor of Kingston Lisle and the Feudal Barony of Gilsland (or Gillesland). At another level, Colonel J M Dymoke is Queen's Champion in right of his Manor of Scrivelsby, Lincs, and the late Duke of Newcastle claimed the privilege of carrying the Sovereign's right hand glove at the Coronation in 1953 in right of his Manor of Worksop, Notts. The Manor of Worksop was sold at auction in July 1994 to a local man, John Hunt, together with the Right to support the Sovereign's right arm. Lesser Grand Serjeanties include the honorific right to hold by the service of keeping the king's hawks, or rendering a red rose, a golden needle, embroidered gloves - all honourable services - which minor dignities are conferred upon the holder of a Manorial Lordship by inheritance or conveyance.

Envelope: **Victor Podd Esq, Lord of Wightfield,** or **Lord of the Manor of Wightfield;** Top: **Dear Mr Podd.** Wives take the female form: **Lady of Wightfield** or **Lady of the Manor of Wightfield.** Women in their own right are, properly, Lord of X, but courtesy would permit the female form. Children enjoy no other distinctions than those they might otherwise have achieved for themselves.

BARONETS

The easiest way to think of a baronet is as an hereditary "knight". The Order was instituted in England by James I and VI in 1611, in Ireland in 1619, and in Scotland (Nova Scotia) in 1625. Essentially, it was a money-raising exercise at first and persons selected for the dignity were required to pay £3,000, ostensibly to finance the colonization of eastern Canada. Oliver Cromwell created several baronets, but payment for the title ceased with the Restoration in 1660. A significant minority of the baronetage today comprises descendants whose first recipients of the honour were lord mayors of London. The practice of creating a retiring lord mayor a baronet ceased with the election of Harold Wilson's Labour administration in 1964, although the Queen revived the honour briefly in 1990 for Lady Thatcher's husband, Dennis. A general revival, however, looks unlikely. Just as there are premier barons and viscounts, so there is a premier baronet of England who is Sir Nicholas Bacon, whom we shall take as our example:

Envelope: **Sir Nicholas Bacon Bart;** Top: **Dear Sir Nicholas**

Sir Nicholas's wife: Envelope: **Lady Bacon;** Top: **Dear Lady Bacon.** You would not address Lady Bacon as "The" Lady Bacon, as the definite article is reserved for the wives of parliamentary barons and Scottish lords of Parliament.

Sons and daughters of baronets, unless they have separate titles, are Mr, Mrs, and so forth.

KNIGHTS

This is one of the oldest titles, about which probably more could be written than any other. It is dealt with extensively in *Feudal Society* by Marc Bloch and by me, "A concept of nobility", in a *Bulletin of the Manorial Society of Great Britain.* I shall confine myself to present usage. The two main kingdoms that make up this United Kingdom have their chief knighthoods. In England it is the Garter, which we have already discussed; in Scotland, it is the Thistle. I cannot think of any Thistles that have been granted to an Englishman, although some Garters have been awarded to Scots. Therefore, a former prime minister, Sir Edward Heath, an Englishman, is a KG, but Lord Home of the Hirsel, another former prime minister and a Scot, is a KT. Ireland, when that country formed part of the UK, had the Order of St Patrick (KP), which is no longer granted. The Sovereign also used to grant honours in the Order of the Star of India when that country was an empire. The other orders of chivalry (knighthood) regularly in use (ie every six months at the Birthday and New Year Honours) are the Bath, St Michael and St George, Royal Victorian Order, and British Empire. Unlike the Garter and the Thistle, all the remaining orders have various grades of membership, the highest being "knight grand cross", followed by "knight commander", then "commander", or "companion", "officer", "member", lieutenant", variously depending on the order. If you need to check these things for the letters people like to have after their names (eg OBE, LVO), *Debrett's* and *Who's Who* cover commander/companion upwards, and some of the lesser ranks. If either publication fails on the latter, then the local phone book usually has it. As already noted, the British love their CBEs, their CMGs, so add them after people's names, but they are otherwise addressed as Mrs, or Mr, or Dr, unless knights (women, dames), and it is knights who concern us here. The rules are simple:

Except for "Bart" (being short for baronet), knights, their wives, and their children are addressed as if they were of the baronetage. The only difference is that you add the letters of the knighthood after their names: eg: "Sir John Smith KBE" (knight commander of the Order of the British Empire), or "Sir John Smith GCMG" (knight grand cross of the Order of St Michael and St George): *Who's Who* includes all knights.

Divorcées

Divorcées who keep their married title are styled: **Euphemia, Duchess (or whatever) of Coffinswell (or wherever);** Top: **Dear Duchess (or whatever).** They lose such prefixes as "The Most Noble", or "The Rt Hon". Their children, if they have any courtesy titles, are unaffected by divorce from a titled gentleman.

CLERGY

Archbishops: Envelope: **The Most Rev The Archbishop of X;** Top: **Dear Archbishop**

Bishops: Envelope: **The Rt Rev The Bishop of X;** Top: **Dear Bishop**

Deans: Envelope: **The Very Rev The Dean of X;** Top: **Dear Dean**

Cardinals: Envelope: **His Eminence The Cardinal (surname), Archbishop of X** (cardinals are usually archbishops of somewhere); Top: **Dear Cardinal**

Monsignor: Envelope: **Dear Mgr A B Wildbore;** Top: **Dear Mgr Wildbore**

Refer to in speech, as appropriate, "Archbishop", Bishop", &c

The wives of married clergy take their normal name: eg **Mrs W S Halfhide;** Top: **Dear Mrs Halfhide**

DIPLOMATS

Except for ambassadors (Envelope: **His Excellency The Ambassador of the Despotate of Epirus;** Top: **Dear Ambassador**), all other ranks and their spouses take their usual form of address.

GOVERNMENT MINISTERS

The style is essentially the same, whether you are the Prime Minister, or a Secretary of State, so I have taken the PM: Envelope: **The Rt Hon John Major, Prime Minister and First Lord of the Treasury;** Top: **Dear Prime Minister;** ditto Chancellor of the Exchequer; top: **Dear Chancellor;** ditto Secretary of State for Employment; top: **Dear Secretary of State.** They are all automatically made privy councillors (PC) when becoming a secretary of state, so they are "Rt Hon" (ie Right Honourable). Even when you have given up or been unelected from the Commons, a privy councillor is for life. Had Margaret Thatcher not taken a peerage, she would still be addressed on an envelope as: The Rt Hon Margaret Thatcher OM FRS.

Ministers and other posts below Cabinet rank, including MPs, simply use the holder's normal style, followed by his or her office: Top: **Dear usual name.** Check in *Who's Who* to see if the person you are writing to is a PC, or has another title, such as a courtesy title as the son or daughter of a peer, a knighthood, that kind of thing.

Remember, very few of the sorts of people who hold the ranks mentioned above stand on their dignity. But there is no reason to get it wrong, and to get a person's name and style right is a mark of the writer's respect, and respect goes a long way.

Notes

and further reading to all chapters.

A full reference to each work appears at its first mention in each chapter; later references in the same chapter appear under the author(s)'s surname(s) and a short title.

Abbreviations: Add, additional; BL, British Library; ed(s), editor(s); c, *circa* (about); edn, edition; fol, folio number; *ibid*, the same book or article as in the preceeding note; MS(S), manuscript(s); NS, new series; OS, old series; p(p), page(s); pt, part; repr, reprinted; rev, revised; ser, series; vol(s), volume(s).

Introduction (pages 1-20)

1   G Orwell, *Nineteen Eighty-Four* (London, 1949), pp 189, 206-7.
2   B Russell, broadcast talk, BBC Home Service, 18 May 1962.
3   W J Corbett, "The development of the Duchy of Normandy and the Norman Conquest of England" (J R Tanner, C W Previte-Orton, Z N Brooke, eds, *Cambridge Medieval History* (Cambridge, 8 vols, 1911-36), vol V, pp 508-12; D C Douglas, "Companions of the Conqueror" (*History*, vol 28 (1943), pp 129-47); J F A Mason, "The Companions of the Conqueror: an additional name" (*English Historical Review*, vol 71 (1956), pp 61-9); H C Darby, *Domesday England* (Cambridge, 1977), pp 88-9; W C Hollister, "The Greater Domesday Tenants-in-Chief", in J C Holt, ed, *Domesday Studies* (Woodbridge, 1987), pp 219-48.

4   T K Keeffe, *Feudal Assessments and the Political Community under Henry II and his sons* (Berkeley (USA), 1983), pp 42, 57-8, 86. Besides the 273 lay baronies who returned *cartae* in 1166 there were those who made no returns, usually because they were in the king's hands. The figure of 5,300 strictly refers to knights' fees.

5   See above, p 40, and references cited, p 193, n 58; I J Sanders, *English Baronies: their origin and descent, 1086-1327* (Oxford, 1960); C Moor, "The Knights of Edward I" (*Harleian Society*, vols 80-84, 1929-32); N C Denholm-Young, "Feudal Society in the 13th Century: the knights", in his *Collected Papers on Medieval Subjects* (Oxford, 1946, repr Cardiff, 1969), pp 57-61.

6   See above, pp 45-6; C Given-Wilson, *The English Nobility in the late Middle Ages* (London, 1987), pp 70-3; Denholm-Young, "Feudal Society in the 13th Century: the knights", pp 85-8.

7   H L Gray, "Incomes from land in England in 1436" (*English Historical Review*, vol 49 (1934), pp 609-39); Given-Wilson, *The English Nobility in the late Middle Ages*, pp 69-72; F M L Thompson, "The Social Distribution of Landed Property in England since the 16th Century" (*Economic History Review*, 2nd ser, vol 19 (1966), pp 505-17; J P Cooper, "The Social Distribution of Land and Men in England, 1436-1700" (*Economic History Review*, 2nd ser, vol 20 (1967), pp 419-40); J C K Cornwall, *Wealth and Society in Early 16th Century England* (London, 1988), pp 147, 187-90; see above, p 53.

8   See above, pp 70-1, and references cited in p 199, n 17.
9   Thompson, "The Social Distribution of Landed Property in England since the 16th Century"; Cooper, "The Social Distribution of Land and Men in England, 1436-

1700; B A Holderness, *Pre-Industrial England: Economy and Society from 1500 to 1750* (London, 1976), pp 32-3; P Laslett, *The World We have Lost* (London, 3rd edn, 1976), pp 35-7; G S Holmes, "Gregory King and the social structure of pre-industrial England" (*Transactions of the Royal Historical Society*, 5th ser, vol 27 (1977), pp 41-68); C G A Clay, *Economic expansion and social change: England, 1500-1700* (Cambridge, 2 vols, 1984), vol I, pp 142-3, 155-64.

10 P Mathias, "The social structure in the 18th century: a calculation by Joseph Massie", in his *The transformation of England. Essays in the economic and social history of England in the 18th century* (London, 1979), pp 171-89; J Bateman, *The Great Landowners of Great Britain and Ireland* (London, 4th edn, 1883, repr Leicester, 1971), p 515.

11 F M L Thompson, *English Landed Society in the 19th Century* (London, 1963), pp 269-345; G E Mingay, *The Gentry: the rise and fall of a ruling class* (London, 1976), pp 165-87; F M L Thompson, "English Landed Society in the 20th Century" (*Transactions of the Royal historical Society*, 5th ser, vol 40 (1990), pp 1-24; 6th ser, vol 1 (1991), p 1-20; vol 2 (1992), pp 1-23; in progress); H Clemenson, *English Country Houses and Lande Estates* (London, 1982); M Beard, *English Landed Society in the 20th Century* (London, 1989); D Cannadine, *The decline and fall of the British aristocracy* (New Haven, (USA), 1990).

12 See chapter 1 by Henry Loyn; see also F Liebermann, *The National Assembly in the Anglo-Saxon Period* (Hallé (Germany), 1913, repr New York (USA), 1961); T J Oleson, *The Witenagemot in the reign of Edward the Confessor* (London and Toronto (Canada), 1955); G B Adams, *The King's Council in the Middle Ages* (Cambridge, 1913); J E Powell, K Wallis, *The House of Lords in the Middle Ages* (London, 1968).

13 P Langford, *A polite and commercial people: England, 1727-1783* (Oxford, 1989), p 362.

14 M M Chibnall, ed, *The Ecclesiastical History of Orderic Vitalis* (Oxford, 6 vols, 1969-80), vol VI, pp 16-7; J A Guy, *Tudor England* (Oxford, 1988), pp 83, 154.

15 C V Wedgwood, T*he King's War, 1641-47* (London, 1958), p 383.

16 C Carlton, *Going to the Wars: the experience of the British Civil War, 1638-51* (London, 1992), pp 38-65, 115, 122, 192, 290-5, 304-5; C Durston, *The Family in the English Revolution* (Oxford, 1989), pp 33-56. A good recent regional study of the background to the Civil War is J Wroughton, *A Community at war: the Civil War in Bath and North Somerset, 1642-50* (Bath, 1992), pp 43, 49-50, 81-3, 130.

17 J Bossy, *The English Catholic Community*, 1570-1850 (London, 1975), pp 49-59, 78-106, 149-81. For the one Protestant among the Dukes of Norfolk, Charles, the 15th Duke, see G E Cokayne, V Gibbs, *The Complete Peerage* (London, rev edn, 14 vols 1910-59) [hereafter *CP*], vol IX, pp 633-4.

18 M Lee, *Government by pen: Scotland under James VI and I* (Urbana (USA), 1980), p vii.

19 The extent of English secular landed estates is most easily ascertained in the medieval period from the *Calendar of Inquisitions Post Mortem*, 1234-1413, 1485-1509 (London, 22 vols, 1904-92), though these inquisitions are not always complete and the stated property-values are generally considered to be under-stated in the 13th century and increasingly unrealistic thereafter. No later nation-wide survey is possible before the "New Domesday" of 1873 (Bateman, *The Great Landowners of Great Britain and Ireland,* pp 1-494, is an alphabetical list

of great landowners with their estates in each county), since the records of the 1522 muster and the lay subsidies of 1524-5 and 1543-5 are incomplete (J Sheail, "The Distribution of Taxable Population and Wealth in England during the Early 16th Century" (*Transactions of the Institute of British Geographers*, vol 55 (1972), pp 111-20); Cornwall, *Wealth and Society in Early 16th Century England,* pp 287-88), whilst surviving land-tax records after 1780 present considerable problems of comparability (L Soltow, "Wealth Distribution in England and Wales in 1798" (*Economic History Review*, 2nd ser, vol 34 (1981), pp 60-70; see critical discussion in *Economic History Review*, 2nd ser, vol 35 (1982), pp 416-33); M Turner, D R Mills, eds, *Land and Property: the English Land Tax, 1692-1832* (Gloucester, 1986).

20 Households of the greater medieval nobility normally numbered between 100 and 200, and gentry households averaged 65 (K Mertes, *The English Noble Household, 1250-1600* (Oxford, 1988); M Girouard, *Life in the English Country House* (New Haven (USA) 1978), pp 12-15; F Heal, *Hospitality in Early Modern England* (Oxford, 1990), pp 44-8). The average noble household size was still over 100 in the 16th century (Girouard, *Life in the English Country House*, pp 82-5), but fell, after 1600, to between 25 and 50 in the late 18th century and to between 10 and 50 in the early 19th century (Girouard, *Life in the English Country House*, pp 85, 208, 276; Heal, *Hospitality in Early Modern England*, p 97). In 1688 Gregory King estimated average household sizes as 40 for peers, 13-16 for baronets and knights, 8-10 for esquires and gentlemen (Laslett, *The World we have lost*, p 36). The Victorian period saw an enormous expansion in servants, partly because the expanding middle classes were employing 1-5 servants per family, and because the size of noble households was increasing: gentry families normally had at least 20 servants and the richer peers had up to 300 each (P Horn, *The Rise and Fall of the Victorian Servant* (Dublin, (Eire), 1975), pp 3-9). Most peers and richer gentry from at least the 15th century had a London house as well as one, or often more than one, country "seat".

21 F M Stenton, *The First Century of English Feudalism, 1066-1166* (Oxford, 1932, 2nd edn, 1961) pp 42-83, esp pp 74-5; N Denholm-Young, *Seignorial administration in England* (Oxford, 1937), pp 25-36, 66-85; S Painter, *Studies in the History of the English Feudal Barony* (Baltimore (USA), 1943), pp 136-41, 155; K B McFarlane, *The Nobility of Later Medieval England* (Oxford, 1972), pp 3-4, 16-8, 82-101, 136-41, 187-227; D R Hainsworth, *Stewards, Lords and People: the estate steward and his world in later Stuart England* (Cambridge, 1992); G E Mingay, "The 18th century estate steward", in E L Jones, G E Mingay, eds, *Land, Labour and Population in the Industrial Revolution: Essays presented to J D Chambers* (London, 1967), pp 3-27; E G R Taylor, "The surveyor" (*Economic History Review*, 1st ser, vol 17 (1947), pp 121-33); J R Wordie, *Estate Management in 18th Century England* (London, 1982), pp 24-74; D Spring, *The English Landed estate in the 19th Century: its administration* (Baltimore (USA), 1963); E Richards, "The Land agent", in G E Mingay, ed, *The Victorian Countryside* (London, 1981), pp 439-56; J V Beckett, *The Aristocracy in England, 1660-1914* (Oxford, 1986), pp 142-56.

22 J P Cooper, "Patterns of inheritance and settlement by great landowners from the 15th to the 18th centuries", in J Goody, J Thirsk and E P Thompson, eds, *Family and Inheritance* (Cambridge, 1976), pp 192-307; L Bonfield, *Marriage Settlements, 1601-1740: the adoption of the strict settlement* (Cambridge, 1983).

23 McFarlane, *The Nobility of Later Medieval England*, pp 47-9. As he points out, there is little evidence for noble mismanagement of their estates.

24 For the period before 1550, see McFarlane, *The Nobility of Later Medieval England*, pp 142-67, 172-6, and H Miller, *Henry VIII and the English Nobility* (Oxford, 1986), pp 2, 35-40; for the period 1550-1949, see T H Hollingsworth, "Demography of the British Peerage" (*Population Studies*, vol XVIII (1964), Supplement, pp 45-7.

25 For the "crisis of the knightly class", see P R Coss, "Sir Geoffrey de Langley and the crisis of the knightly class in 13th century England" (*Past & Present*, vol 68 (1975), pp 3-37); D A Carpenter, "Was there a crisis of the knightly class in the 13th century? The Oxfordshire evidence" (*English Historical Review*, vol 95 (1989) pp 721-52); P R Coss, *Lordship, knighthood and locality: a study in English society, c 1180-c 1220* (Cambridge, 1991), pp 218-41. For the "mere gentry", see Mingay, *The Gentry: the rise and fall of a ruling class*, pp 50-57.

26 L Stone, *The Crisis of the Aristocracy, 1558-1641* (Oxford, 1965), pp 637-49; Cooper, "Patterns of inheritance and settlement by great landowners", pp 221-4, 306-12; Clay, *Economic expansion and social change: England, 1500-1700*, vol I, pp 147-8.

27 The exception to the rule of primogeniture, generally established by 1200 (S E Thorne, "English Feudalism and Estates in Land", in his *Essays in English Legal History* (London, 1985) pp 13-30; R De Aragon, "The growth of secure inheritance in Anglo-Norman England" (*Journal of Medieval History*, vol 8 (1982), pp 381-91).), fall into three categories. The first comprises anomalies such as twin sons (eg D Crouch, *The Beaumont Twins: the roots and branches of power in the 12th century* (Cambridge, 1986).). The second results from royal preference for a younger son over his presumably less competent elder brother - Ralph de Mandeville was considered a "better knight" than his elder brother Robert by Henry I - or a female descent (Sanders, *English Baronies: their origin and descent, 1066-1327*, pp 10 (Beauchamp of Bedford), 29 (Caus), 30 (Caxton), 61 (Leicester), 64 (Marshwood), 76 (Shelford), 78 (Skirpenbeck), 80 (Southoe), 116 (Eton), 106, 134 (Papcastle), 139 (Rayne).). The third results from the peculiar situation that existed between 1066 and 1204, when the same dynasty ruled both England and Normandy. It was common for the eldest son to succeed to the "patrimony" in Normandy whilst the younger son was given the "acquired land" in England, as was exemplified by the division of the Anglo-Norman realm on the death of William the Conqueror: Robert, the eldest son, became Duke of Normandy whilst William Rufus became King of England.

28 D Crouch, *William Marshal: court, career and chivalry in the Angevin Empire, 1147-1219* (London, 1990). See also McFarlane, *The Nobility of Later Medieval England*, pp 18-40.

29 McFarlane, *The Nobility of Later Medieval England*, pp 10-15. For the medieval episcopate, see A Hamilton-Thompson, *The English Clergy and their organization in the Middle Ages* (Oxford, 1947), pp 1-43; J T Rosenthal, "The training of an élite: English bishops in the 15th century" (*American Philosophical Society Transactions*, vol 60, pt 5, 1970). For the Tudor episcopate see F M Heal, *Of Prelates and Princes: a study of the economic and social position of the Tudor episcopate* (Cambridge, 1980); for the post-Reformation parish clergy, see R O'Day, *The English Clergy: the emergence and consolidation of a profession, 1558-1642*

(Cambridge, 1979) and J Pruett, *The Parish Clergy under the Later Stuarts* (Urbana (USA), 1978), pp 32-9.

30 E Chamberlayne, *Angliae Notitia* (London, 1969), p 487; W Cobbett, *Cobbett's Parliamentary History* (London, 36 vols, 1806-20), vol XV, p 734. See also J Thirsk, "Younger Sons in the 17th century" in her *The Rural Economy of England* (London, 1984), pp 335-57; W R Prest, *The Professions in Early Modern England* (London, 1987); G Holmes, *Augustan England: Professions, State and Society, 1680-1730* (London, 1982), and the references cited in n 20 above.

31 R De Aragon, "In search of Aristocratic Women: a key to success in Norman England" (*Albion*, vol 14 (1982), pp 258-66); J C Holt, "Feudal Society and the Family: IV. The heiress and the alien" (*Transactions of the Royal Historical Society*, 5th ser, vol 35 (1985), pp 1-28); S F C Milsom, "Inheritance by Women in the 12th and 13th Centuries", in his *Studies in the History of the Common Law* (London, 1985), pp 231-60; for later times, see McFarlane, *The Nobility of Later Medieval England*, pp 142-67, 172-6; Given-Wilson, *The English Nobility in the late Middle Ages,* pp 59-65; C G A Clay, "Marriage, inheritance, and the rise of large estates in England, 1660-1815" (*Economic History Review*, 2nd ser, vol 21 (1968), pp 503-18); L Bonfield, "Marriage settlements and the 'Rise of Great Estates'" (*Economic History Review*, 2nd ser, vol 32 (1979), pp 483-93.

32 McFarlane, *The Nobility of Later Medieval England*, pp 41-60; he succinctly comments that "the rich got richer as they got fewer" (p 16). This was also notably true of the post-Restoration period (Thompson, "The Social Distribution of Landed Property in England since the 16th Century"; Cooper, "The Social Distribution of Land and Men in England, 1436-1700"; J V Beckett, "English Landownership in the later 17th and 18th centuries: the debate and the problems" (*Economic History Review*, 2nd ser, vol 30 (1977), pp 567-81); Clay, *Economic expansion and social change: England, 1500-1700*, vol I, p 143; H J Habakkuk, "The Rise and Fall of English Landed Families" (*Transactions of the Royal Historical Society*, 5th ser, vol 29 (1979), pp 87-207; vol 30 (1980), pp 199-221; vol 31 (1981), pp 195-217; Beckett, *The Aristocracy in England, 1660-1914*, pp 43-90; J Cannon, *Aristocratic Century: the Peerage of 18th Century England* (Cambridge, 1984), pp 126-47.

33 Out of a total of 207 baronies, 72 (36 per cent) passed in the female line more than once between 1086 and 1327 (Sanders, *English Baronies: the origin and descent, 1066-1327*, pp 4-15, 17-20, 23-4, 26-9, 33-5, 43, 45-7, 50-9, 61-4, 67-8, 71-8, 81-2, 86-9, 92-101, 104-5, 107-9, 111-9, 123, 125, 127, 133-5, 138, 142-4). See also McFarlane, *The Nobility of Later Medieval England*, p 144, and p 188, n 60 below for an early modern example.

34 F Pollock, F W Maitland, *The History of English Law before the time of Edward I* (Cambridge, 2 vols, 1895; 2nd edn, 1898; 3rd edn, ed S F C Milsom, 1968), vol I, pp 318-29; W S Holdsworth, *A History of English Law* (London, 16 vols, 1903-65; 4th edn, 1966), vol II, p 212; vol III, pp 61-66, 272-3; vol IV, pp 442-3, 446-7, 465-6; S F C Milsom, *The Legal Framework of English Feudalism* (Cambridge, 1976), pp 26-52, 104-5, 111-3, 118, 154-64.

35 Pollock and Maitland, *The History of English Law before the time of Edward I*, vol I, p 319.

36 Bonfield, *Marriage Settlements, 1601-1740*.

37 For the final abolition of military tenure and its "incidents' by 12 Charles II, c 24 in 1660, following Interregnum Acts of 1645-6 and 1656-7, see Holdsworth, *A History of English Law*, vol VI, pp 166-7, 426.

38 L Stone, *Uncertain Unions: marriage in England, 1660-1753* (Oxford, 1992).
39 R B Outhwaite, *Marriage and Society* (London, 1981), pp 15-80; J R Gillis, *For Better, For Worse: British Marriages, 1600 to the present* (Oxford, 1985), pts I-II; A MacFarlane, *Marriage and Love in England: Modes of Reproduction, 1300-1840* (Oxford, 1986), esp pp 174-208; Durston, *The Family in the English Revolution*, pp 10-32, 57-109. The attack on romantic love by E Shorter, *The Making of the Modern Family* (London, 1976), pp 54-78, 120-48, and L Stone, *The Family, Sex and Marriage in England, 1500-1800* (London, 1977) should be read in the light of J W Scott, "The History of the Family as an affective unit" (*Social History*, vol 4 (1979), pp 509-16).

40 D Whitelock, *Anglo-Saxon Wills* (Cambridge, 1930); M M Sheehan "The Will in Medieval England" (*Pontifical Institute of Medieval Studies, Toronto, Studies and Texts*, vol 6 (1963), pp 83-99, 151, 266-81).
41 Holdsworth, *History of English Law*, vol IV, pp 455-80.
42 P Crone, *Pre-Industrial Societies* (Oxford, 1989).
43 Corbett, "The development of the Duchy of Normandy and the Norman Conquest of England", p 508.
44 Cooper, "The Social Distribution of Land and Men in England, 1436-1700"; Cornwall, *Wealth and Society in Early 16th Century England*, pp 120-53, 253-76; Clay, *Economic expansion and social change*, vol I, p 143.
45 See references cited in n 32 above.
46 G Donaldson, *The Scottish Reformation* (Cambridge, 1960), pp 39-40, 64, 74-5; G Donaldson, *Scotland, James V to James VII* (Edinburgh, 1965), pp 105-6, 135-7; J Wormald, *Court, Kirk and Community. Scotland, 1470-1625* (London, 1981), pp 84-6, 117-20, 125-7; M Dilworth, "The Commendator system in Scotland" (*Innes Review*, vol 37 (1986), pp 51-72).

47 J V Beckett, "The pattern of landownership in England and Wales, 1660-1880" (*Economic History Review*, 2nd ser, vol 37 (1984), pp 1-22); D Spring, "Introduction", in Bateman, *The Great Landowners of Great Britain and Ireland*, p 12.

48 Darby, *Domesday England*, pp 270-5; E J Kealey, *Harvesting the Air* (Woodbridge, 1987); R Holt, *The Mills of Medieval England* (Oxford, 1988); E M Carus-Wilson, "An industrial revolution of the 13th century" (*Economic History Review*, 1st ser, vol XI, (1941), pp 39-60).

49 T A M Bishop, "Assarting and the growth of the open fields" (*Economic History Review*, 1st ser, vol 6 (1935), pp 13-29); J S Moore, *Laughton: a study in the evolution of the Wealden landscape* (Leicester, 1966); J A Raftis, *Assart Data and Land Values ... in the East Midlands, 1200-1350* (Toronto (Canada), 1974); H P R Finberg, J Thirsk, eds, *Agrarian History of England and Wales* (Cambridge, 8 vols, 1967-91, in progress), vol II, pp 134-5, 139-259.

50 J Maclean, ed, *The Lives of the Berkeleys by John Smith* (Gloucester, 3 vols, 1883-5), vol I, pp 113, 141, 169, 325-31; vol II, pp 13-16.
51 J R Wordie, "The Chronology of English Enclosure, 1500-1914" (*Economic History Review*, 2nd ser, vol 36 (1983), pp 483-505). Enclosure is now seen by most economic historians as beneficial to the economy as a whole: E E Kerridge, *The Agricultural Revolution* (London, 1967); Finberg and Thirsk, eds *Agrarian History of England and Wales*, vols IV, pp 200-55; vol V, pt 2, pp 68-9, 317-21, 378-82, 388; vol VI, pp 36, 44-9, 138-40, 160-3, 598, 605-7, 620-1, 646, 941, 968-9; Clay, *Economic expansion and social change*, vol I, pp 70-81, 104-12, 114-6.

52 For river improvements and canals see T S Willan, *River Navigation in England, 1600-1750* (Oxford, 1936, repr London, 1964); C Hadfield, British Canals (London, 1950; 2nd edn, 1959); J R Ward, *The Finance of Canal Building in 18th Century England* (Oxford, 1974); for turnpike roads, see W A Albert, *The Turnpike Road System in England, 1663-1840* (Cambridge, 1971); E Pawson, *Transport and Economy. The Turnpike Roads of 18th Century Britain* (London, 1977); for both roads and canals, Beckett, *The Aristocracy in England, 1660-1914*, pp 238-61; for the economic background to transport-improvements, see T S Willan, *The Inland Trade. Studies in English Internal Trade in the 16th and 17th centuries* (Manchester, 1976); J A Chartres, *Internal Trade in England, 1500-1700* (London, 1977); H J Dyos, D H Aldcroft, *British Transport: an Economic Survey from the 17th century to the 20th* (Leicester, 1969). Modern research has emphasised the economic importance of roads, eg D Gerhold, *Road Transport before the Railways* (Cambridge, 1993).

53 Kerridge, *The Agricultural Revolution*; Finberg and Thirsk, eds, *Agrarian History of England and Wales*, vols IV, pp 161-99; vol V, pt 2, pp 503-89; vol VI, pp 15-64, 275-383; Clay, *Economic expansion and social change*, vol I, pp 102-7, 112-6, 126-41.

54 See references cited in n 21 above.

55 S Homer, *A History of Interest Rates* (New Brunswick (Canada), 1963), pp 104-65.

56 E A Wrigley, R S Schofield, *The Population History of England, 1541-1871: a reconstruction* (London, 1981; rev edn, Cambridge, 1989), pp 208-9.

57 Beckett, *The Aristocracy in England, 1660-1914*, pp 209-25. The figures for coal-output given in J U Nef, *The Rise of the British Coal Industry*, 1550-1700 (London, 2 vols, 1932, repr 1966) are now generally agreed to be unreliable. Much better figures are given in R A Church, M W Flinn, J Hatcher, *History of the British Coal Industry*, vols I-III (Oxford, 1984, 1986, 1993).

58 Beckett, *The Aristocracy in England, 1660-1914*, pp 225-7; J T Ward, R G Wilson, eds, *Land and Industry: the Landed Estate and the Industrial Revolution* (Newton Abbot, 1971); T J Raybould, *The economic emergence of the Black Country: a study of the Dudley estate* (Newton Abbot, 1973); J Davies, *Cardiff and the Marquesses of Bute* (Cardiff, 1981); Wordie, *Estate Management in 18th Century England*, pp 75-154.

59 A L Beier, R Finlay, *London, 1500-1700: the making of the metropolis* (London, 1986); L D Schwarz, *London in the age of industrialization ... 1700-1850* (Cambridge, 1992), pp 125-55.

60 D Cannadine, *Lords and Landlords: the Aristocracy and the Towns, 1774-1967* (Leicester, 1980); Beckett, *The Aristocracy in England, 1660-1914*, pp 262-86.

61 *CP*, vol XII, pt 1, pp 434-54 (De la Poles); vol VII, p 628 (Lexinton). Here is another example of hereditary inability to produce viable male heirs: Bridget Hungerford was the daughter and heir of her father, Sir Giles Hungerford; her daughter, also Bridget, the heir of Robert Lord Lexinton, married John Manners, Marquess of Granby, heir to the duke of Rutland, in 1717 (*CP*, vol XI, p 267).

62 C G A Clay, "The price of freehold land in the later 17th and 18th centuries" (*Economic History Review*, 2nd ser, 27 (1974), pp 173-89); B A Holderness, "The English land market in the 18th century: the case of Lincolnshire" (*Economic History Review*, 2nd ser, 27 (1974), pp 557-76); Clay, *Economic Expansion and Social Change,* vol I, pp 151-2. But the role of "new money" in raising land-prices

is disputed: R C Allen, "The price of freehold land and the interest rate in the 17th and 18th centuries" (*Economic History Review*, 2nd ser, vol 41 (1988), pp 33-50).

63 Thompson, *English Landed Society in the 19th Century*, pp 9, 21, 29, 36-40, 59-61, 63, 74, 87-9, 102, 119-20, 124, 293-8, 307, 320, 337; W D Rubenstein, *Men of Property: the very wealthy in Britain since the Industrial Revolution* (London, 1981); W D Rubenstein, *Elites and the Wealthy in Modern British History* (Brighton, 1987), pp 51-82, 145-71.

64 N J Higham, "The Domesday Survey: Context and Purpose" (*History*, vol 78 (1993), pp 7-21).

65 Cornwall, *Wealth and Society in Early 16th Century England*, pp 1-4, 277-9, 281-8; L Boynton, *The Elizabethan Militia, 1558-1638* (London, 1967); J R Western, *The English Militia in the 18th Century* (London, 1965).

66 J E Neale, *The Elizabethan House of Commons* (London, 1949), pp 21-98, 140-260; D Hirst, *The Representative of the People? Voters and Voting in England Under the Early Stuarts* (Cambridge, 1975), pp 29-64, 90-105, 112-22, 213-5.

67 C O'Leary, *The Elimination of Corrupt Practices in British Elections, 1868-1911* (Oxford, 1962).

68 Walter Map, quoted in A L Poole, *From Domesday Book to Magna Carta, 1087-1216* (Oxford, 2nd ed, 1955), p 2.

69 C Johnson *et al*, eds, *The Course of the Exchequer* (Oxford, 2nd ed, 1983), p 53.

70 A Goodwin, ed, *The European Nobility in the 18th Century* (London, 1953, 2nd ed, 1967); W Doyle, *The Old European Order, 1660-1800* (Oxford, 1978, 2nd ed, 1992), pp 73-95; M L Bush, *Noble Privilege* (Manchester, 1983); M L Bush, *Rich Noble, Poor Noble* (Manchester, 1988), pp 7-102; M L Bush, *Social Orders and Social Classes in Europe since 1500* (London, 1992), pp 26-46.

71 M Dewar, ed, *De Republica Anglorum by Sir Thomas Smith* (Cambridge, 1982), pp 71-2.

72 H J Perkin, *The Origins of Modern English Society, 1780-1880* (London, 1969) pp 17-62; L Stone, J C F Stone, *An Open Elite? England, 1540-1880* (Oxford, 1984).

73 J H Plumb, *The Growth of Political Stability in England, 1675-1725* (London, 1967); P G M Dickson, *The Financial Revolution in England: a Study in the Development of Public Credit, 1688-1756* (London 1967); A Babington, *The Rule of Law in Britain from the Roman Occupation to the Present Day* (Chichester, 1978), pp 152-214; M Collison, *Public Order and the Rule of Law in England, 1688-1720* (Keele, 1987); I R Christie, *Stress and Stability in late 18th-Century England* (Oxford, 1985); B I Anderson, "Law, finance and economic growth in England; some long-term influences", in B M Ratcliffe, ed, *Great Britain and Her World, 1570-1914* (Manchester, 1975), pp 99-124; P Earle, *The World of Defoe* (London, 1976), pp 45-242.

74 E F Heckscher, *Mercantilism* (London and New York (USA), 2 vols, 1935, 2nd ed, 1956); C Wilson, *Mercantilism* (London, 1958); D C Coleman, ed, *Revisions in Mercantilism* (London, 1969).

75 R Davis, "The rise of protection in England, 1669-1786" (*Economic History Reveiw*, 2 ser, vol 19, (1966), pp 306-17); L Beer, *The Old Colonial System* (New York (USA), 2 vols, 1912).

76 This perception by foreigners of the prosperity of the English middle-class and the rising living standards of the lower orders, "a degree of wealth and extent of population of which one has no notion in France" (B Faujas de St Fond, quoted in

Langford, *A Polite and Commercial People,* p 406), is confirmed by historical analysis of archival sources such as probate inventories: N McKendrick, J Brewer, J H Plumb, eds, *The Birth of a Consumer Society: the Commercialisation of 18th Century England* (London, 1982), pts I, III; L Weatherill, *The Pottery Trade and North Staffordshire, 1660-1760* (Manchester, 1971); L Weatherill, *Consumer Behaviour and Material Culture in Britain, 1660-1760* (London, 1988); J Thirsk, *Economic Policy and Projects: the Development of a Consumer Society in Early Modern England* (Oxford, 1978; C Shammas, *The Pre-Industrial Consumer in England and America* (Oxford, 1990), pp 17-51, 76-193, 225-65; J Brewer, R Porter, eds, *Consumption and the World of Goods* (Cambridge, 1993).

77 J C Holt, *Magna Carta* (Cambridge, 1965, 2nd ed, 1992), pp 448-73; A MacFarlane, *The Origins of English Individualism* (Oxford, 1978); C B Macpherson, *The Political Theory of Possessive Individualism* (Oxford, 1962); see also references in n 73 above.

78 W Blackstone, *Commentaries on the Laws of England* (London, 4 vols, 1765, 10th ed, 1787), vol I, pp 126-7.

79 This remark is generally attributed to William Pitt, though it is not included in the earliest collections of his speeches: J Almon, *Anecdotes of the Life of William Pitt, Earl of Chatham* (London, 3 vols, 1797), or F S Thackeray, *A History of William Pitt, Earl of Chatham* (London, 2 vols, 1827).

80 Cobbett, *Cobbett's Parliamentary History*, vol XV, pp 725-8, 735-40.

81 See references in n 11 above.

82 P Beresford, S Boyd, "Britain's Rich: the Top 400" (*Sunday Times*, 4 April 1993).

83 I am very grateful to Robert Smith, Chairman of the Manorial Society of Great Britain, for offering me the opportunity to edit this book with him; I must also thank my collaborators for their courtesy and efficiency in producing their contributions on time and for their prompt response to my editorial enquiries. I am grateful, once again, to my friends and colleagues Professor Christopher Clay and Dr Ronald Hutton for their kindness in answering further queries. I also wish to thank Professor Bernard Alford for allowing me a term's study leave to complete this and other work. My wife Brenda and my children have, as always, cheerfully put up with my attempts at historical scholarship. Finally, I offer to the reader my reflection at the end of the Conference at which the papers were first delivered: I think the academics did the audience proud.

Chapter 1 (pages 21-27)

1 F M Stenton, *Anglo Saxon England* (Oxford, 1943; 3rd ed 1971): index under *Witan.*

2 F Liebermann, *The National Assembly in the Anglo-Saxon Period* (Hallé (Germany), 1913; repr, New York USA, 1961).

3 T J Oleson, *The Witenagemot in the reign of Edward the Confessor* (London and Toronto (Canada), 1955).

4 S D Keynes, *The Diplomas of King Aethelred "the Unready"*,Cambridge, 1980.

5 Keynes, *The Diplomas of King Aethelred* pp 48-69, especially pp 61-2.

6 Keynes, *The Diplomas of King Aethelred*, pp 213-4 and Table 6. Eadric appears consistently at the head of witness-lists from 1012 to the end of the reign (1016).

7 F Liebermann, *Die Gesetzel der Angelsachsen*, vol i, Hallé, 1903 (reprint 1960), pp 26-47: the negative Golden Rule, ch 49.6, p 44.

8 Liebermann, *Die Gesetze der Angel-Sachsen*, vol i, p. 46.

9   D Whitelock, "Wulfstan and the Laws of Cnut" (*English Historical Review*, 63, 1948, pp 433-52): also *English Historical Documents*, vol i (2nd edn), 1980, p 358.

10 *Anglo-Saxon Chronicle* 978, trs and ed D Whitelock, London, 1961, p 79.

11 *ibid*, 1051 for the clearest evidence for the actions of a Council, ed Whitelock, pp 119-20.

12 F M Stenton, *The First Century of English Feudalism, 1066-1166* (Oxford, 1932; 2nd edn, 1961)

13 S B Chrimes, *An Introduction to the Administrative History of Medieval England* (Oxford, 2nd edn, 1959), pp 18-85: B D Lyon, *A Constitutional and Legal History of Medieval England* (New York 1960), pp 152-66 and 279-99.

14 *Anglo-Saxon Chronicle*, 1137, ed Whitelock, p 198.

15 H R Loyn, *The Governance of Anglo-Saxon England* (London 1984) p 102.

16 *Anglo-Saxon Chronicle* 1087, ed Whitelock, p 162, and regularly during the reigns of William II and Henry I.

17 Lyon, *A Constitutional and Legal History*, pp 245-50.

18 *Magna Carta*, clauses 12 and 14 (J C Dickinson, *The Great Charter* (London, 1968), pp 17-29; H Rothwell, ed, *English Historical Documents*, vol III (London, 1975), pp 316-26; J C Holt, *Magna Carta* (Cambridge, 1965, repr 1976), pp 316-37.

19 Whitelock, ed, *Anglo-Saxon Chronicle,* p 162 (entry for 1085, E text).

20 *English Historical Documents*, vol II, ed D C Douglas, G W Greenaway (London, 1953 2nd edn 1981), no 84.

21 Whitelock, ed, *Anglo-Saxon Chronicle,* p 191 (entry for 1125, E text).

22 Warren, *Henry II* (London, 1973), pp 473-475.

23 Butt, *A History of Parliament: The Middle Ages* (London, 1989), p 47.

24 Poole, *Domesday Book to Magna Carta* (London, 2nd edn 1955), p 292.

25 Warren, *Henry II*, p 485.

26 Poole, *Domesday Book to Magna Carta*, p 368.

Chapter 2 (pages 28-43)

1   J Todd, *Waterperry Church* (Oxford, 1955, repr Eynsham, 1969), pp 9-11.

2   For these "cadaver" tombs, see L Stone, *Sculpture in Britain. The Middle Ages* (Harmondsworth, 2nd edn, 1972), pp 213-6

3   Stone, *Sculpture in Britain*, pp 162, 258 n 23, and L Southwick, "The armoured effigy of Prnce John of Eltham in Westminster Abbey and some closely related military monuments" (*Church Monuments*, 2 (1987), pp 9-21), although the Boughton tomb is not mentioned here. *Victoria County History of Oxfordshire*, IX, p 100, is wrong in stating that the effigy is of Thomas of Broughton (died c 1375), rather than John, who died c 1350.

4   They are best represented in glass in Waterperry church: E A Greening-Lambourn, *The Armorial Glass of the Oxford Diocese 1250-1850* (Oxford, 1949). p 162 and plate 53.

5   H E Salter, *Cartulary of Oseney Abbey* (6 vols, Oxford Historical Society, lxxxix, 1928-36), IV, pp 372-88; *Victoria County History of Oxfordshire*, V, p 296-8.

6   E M Thompson, ed, *Chronicon Galfridi le Baker de Swynebroke* (Oxford, 1889), p 8. I owe this reference to the kindness of Henry Summerson.

7   *Cal. Fine Rolls 1337-47*, 247, 250, 300; *Cal. Patent Rolls 1321-4*, 123-4, 186; *Cal. Patent Rolls 1324-7*, 8.

8   P Meyer, ed, *L'Histoire de Guillaume le Maréchal* (Société de l'histoire de France, 3 vols, 1891-1901), II, lines 16, 753-68.

9   For these battles, see D A Carpenter, *The Battles of Lewes and Evesham 1264-5* (Keele, 1987).

10 N Denholm-Young, ed, *Vita Edwardi Secundi The Life of Edward II* (London, 1957) p 28.

11 *Ibid*, p 126

12 J Stevenson, ed, *Chronicon de Lanercost* (Bannatyne Club, 1839) p 245.

13 W R Childs, J Taylor, eds, *The Anonimalle Chronicle 1307-34* (Yorkshire Archaeological Soc Record Ser, CXLVII, 1987), p 142-3.

14 "For two centuries after the Conquest, the frank open rebellions of the great folk were treated with a clemency which, when we look back to it through intervening ages of blood, seems wonderful": Sir F Pollock and F W Maitland, *The History of English Law* (2nd edn, S F C Milsom ed, 2 vols, Cambridge, 1968), ii, p 506.

15 *L'Histoire de Guillaume le Maréchal*, ii, lines 16, 732-52.

16 *Chronicon Galfridi le Baker*, 14.

17 W A Wright, ed, *The Metrical Chronicle of Robert of Gloucester* (Rolls Ser, 2 vols, 1887), II, line 11,736.

18 H Rothwell, ed, *The Chronicle of Walter de Guisborough* (Camden Soc, LXXXIX, 1957), p 201.

19 T Wright, ed, *The Chonicle of Pierre de Langtoft* (Rolls Ser, 2 vols, 1866, 1868), II, 145; W Stubbs, ed, *The Historical Works of Gervase of Canturbury* (Rolls Ser, 2 vols, 1879, 1880), II, p 111.

20 See particularly, J Gillingham, "War and Chivalry in the *History of William Marshal*" in P R Coss, S D Lloyd, eds, *Thirteenth Century England II, Proceedings of the Newcastle-upon-Tyne Conference,1987* (Woodbridge, 1988), pp 1-13.

21 Carpenter, *Battles of Lewes and Evesham,* pp 22-3.

22 *L'Histoire de Guillaume le Maréchal*, ii, lines 16, 977-96.

23 *The Metrical Chronicle of Robert of Gloucester*, ii, lines 11,103-5.

24 For the new tactics, see J Bradbury, *The Medieval Archer* (Woodbridge, 1985), pp 87-90.

25 J Dunbabin, "Government", in J Burns, ed, *The Cambridge History of Medieval Political Thought c350-c1450* (Cambridge, 1988), p 492; Dunbabin is here influenced by J G Bellamy, *The Law of Treason in England in the Later Middle Ages* (Cambridge, 1970), pp 23-58. See also, Pollock and Maitland, *History of English Law*, II, pp 505-6.

26 Bellamy, *The Law of Treason*, pp 1-14.

27 M Chibnall, ed, *The Eccesiastical History of Orderic Vitalis*, (Oxford, 6 vols, 1969-80), VI, p 353; see C W Hollister, "Royal Acts of Mutilation: The Case against Henry I" in *Monarchy, Magnates and Institutions in the Anglo-Norman World* (London, 1986), pp 291-301.

28 H R Luard, ed, *Flores Historiarum* (Rolls Ser, 3 vols, 1890), II, p 493.

29 C L Kingsford, ed, *The Song of Lewes* (Oxford, 1890), lines 250-2, 186-8.

30 G D G Hall, ed, *Glanvill* (London, 1965), 3,171; G E Woodbine, ed, *Bracton on the Laws and Customs of England* (translated with revisions and notes by S E Thorne, Cambridge, Mass, USA, 1968-77), II, p 334. It is difficult, therefore to accept

Maitland's view that Edward III was the first monarch since the Conquest who could regard making war against the king as treasonable, he being the first such king who was in no danger (having assumed the crown of France) of being accused of such a treason himself: Pollock and Maitland, *History of English Law*, II, 505-6. Equally the king of England's fear of setting a precedent for his own royal overlord cannot explain the period of clemency which ended while that overlordship was still accepted.

31 *Foedera*, I, pt i, pp 207-8.

32 H R Luard, ed, *Annales Monastici* (Rolls Ser, 5 vols, 1864-9), IV, pp 170.

33 For ducal Normandy see D Bates, *Normandy before 1066* (London, 1982) and E Searle, *Predatory Kinship and the creation of Norman power, 890-1066* (Berkeley (USA), 1988).

34 For the political problems posed by the division of England and Normandy, see J C Holt, "Politics and Property in Early Medieval England", *Past and Present*, 57 (1972), pp 3-52, esp pp 19-21 and C Lewis, "The King and Eye: a study in Anglo-Norman politics", (*English Historical Review*, CIV (1989), 569-87), esp pp 585-7. For wider discussions of the relationship between England and Normandy, see D Bates, "Normandy and England after 1066", (*English Historical Review*, CV (1990)).

35 *Orderic Vitalis*, IV, pp 284-5.

36 William the Conqueror's clemency will be discussed by John Gillingham in a forthcoming article. See also his "Conquering the Barbarians: War and Chivalry in 12th Century Britain", (*Haskins Society Journal*, 4 (1993), pp 69-86), esp pp 83-4.

37 W Stubbs, ed, *Willelmi Malmesbiriensis Monachi De Gestis Regum Anglorum* (Rolls Ser, 2 vols, 1887, 1889), II, pp 372-3.

38 Hollister, "Royal Acts of Mutilation: the Case against Henry I", pp 291-301.

39 For these feuds, see R C H Davis, "What Happened in Stephen's Reign, 1135-54" (*History*, XLIX (1964), pp 1-12); H A Cronne, *The Reign of Stephen. Anarchy in England 1135-54* (London, 1970), ch 5.

40 W Stubbs, ed, *Chronica Magistri Rogeri de Houedene* (Rolls Ser, 4 vols, 1868-71), II, pp 64-5, 68, 118.

41 H R Luard, ed, *Matthaei Parisiensis Chronica Majora* (Rolls Ser, 7 vols, 1884-9), II, pp 626; F Michel, ed, *Histoire des Ducs de Normandie et des Rois Angleterre* (Société de l'histoire de France, 1840), p 163. For noble pressure brought on Stephen to spare the garrison of Exeter Castle, see K R Potter, ed, *Gesta Stephani* (London, 1955), p 28.

42 For examples at the battles of Lewes and Evesham, see *Annales Monastici*, IV, pp 175, 452.

43 *Vita Edwardi*, pp 19-20; *Flores Historiarum*, ii, pp 493-4.

44 *Vita Edwardi*, pp 14-16.

45 *Annales Monastici*, IV, p 294.

46 *Chronica Majora*, III, p 498; IV, p 196; Bellamy, *The Law of Treason*, pp 22-3.

47 *Lanercost*, p 205.

48 *Lanercost*, p 244.

49 For this aspect of the Charter, see J C Holt, *Magna Carta* (Cambridge, 2nd edn, 1992), ch 8.

50 R F Treharne and I J Sanders, eds, *Documents of the Baronial Movement of Reform and Rebellion* (Oxford, 1973), pp 97-113 (caps 1, 17), 118-21.

51 *Statutes of the Realm,* I (Record Commission, 1830), pp 157-67 (caps 10, 11, 19). The Ordinances are translated in Rothwell, ed, *English Historical Documents III* (London, 1975), pp 527-39.

52 For a recent article on Simon, see D A Carpenter, "Simon de Montfort: The First Leader of a Political Movement in English History" (*History,* LXXVI (1991), pp 3-23). A new biography by J R Maddicott is forthcoming.

53 *Documents of the Baronial movement,* pp 110-111, 105 (caps 21, 22, 10).

54 *Ibid,* pp 292-3, 302-3.

55 C Bémont, *Simon de Montfort, Earl of Leicester* (new edn, translated by E F Jacob, Oxford, 1930), p 277.

56 T Stapleton, ed, *De Antiquis Legibus Liber Cronica Maiorum et Vicecomitum Londoniarum* (Camden Soc, 1846), pp 75-6.

57 *Annales Monastici,* I, p 164; D A Carpenter, "What Happened after 1258?", in J Gillingham and J C Holt, eds, *War and Government in the Middle Ages. Essays in Honour of J O Prestwich* (Woodbridge, 1984), pp 110-2.

58 W B Stevenson, "England and Normandy, 1204-1259" (unpublished University of Leeds PhD thesis, 1974), p 202 and appendix IV; see also F M Powicke, *The Loss of Normandy* (2nd edn, Manchester, 1961), 328-58.

59 W W Shirley, ed, *Royal and Other Historical Letters Illustrative of the Reign of Henry III* (Rolls Ser, 1862, 2 vols, 1866), i, pp 220-2; See D A Carpenter, *The Minority of Henry III* (London, 1990), pp 261-2, 272-3. For a discussion of Englishmen and foreigners, see chapter 5 of M Prestwich, *English Politics in the 13th Century* (London, 1990).

60 S Painter, *Studies in the History of the English Feudal Barony* (Baltimore, 1943), ch vii, esp pp 170-4.

61 C Given-Wilson, *The English Nobility in the Later middle Ages* (London, 1987), 12. Given-Wilson's book is a valuable introduction to recent work on the medieval nobility, the foundations of which were laid by K B McFarlane, *The Nobility of Later Medieval England* (Oxford, 1973).

62 J E Powell and K Wallis, *The House of Lords in the Middle Ages* (London, 1968), p 226.

63 *Ibid,* p 230.

64 *Ibid,* ch 18 onwards; but see the reservations in Given-Wilson, *The English Nobility,* pp 58-66.

65 *Documents of the Baronial Movement,* pp 111, 105 (caps 21, 22, 10).

66 *Feudal Aids,* IV, p 168; I, p 114; *Cal Charter Rolls,* IV, p 486; *Victoria County History of Oxfordshire,* V, pp 296-8; *of Buckinghamshire,* IV, pp 81, 127.

67 *Parliamentary Writs,* II, pt ii, p 593; *Feudal Aids,* IV, p 167; *Cal Fine Rolls 1347-56,* pp 269, 334, 376; W F Carter, *The Quatremains of Oxfordshire* (Oxford, 1936), pp 10-12, 35, 61-2 and plate facing p 16; *Victoria County History of Oxfordshire,* VII, pp 173, 208. The Quatremains increased their property in the course of the 14th century.

68 This was true of Gloucestershire, for example, where 30 of the 50 were knights: N Saul, *Knights and Esquires: The Gloucestershire gentry in the 14th Century* (Oxford, 1981), pp 34-5; for other figures, see Given-Wilson, *The English Nobility,* pp 70-3.

69 *Parliamentary Writs*, II, pt ii, p 593; Saul, *The Gloucestershire Gentry*, p 6; pp 6-9 of this work has an important discussion of the rise of the squires.

70 D A Carpenter, "Was there a crisis of the knightly class in the 13th century? The Oxfordshire evidence", (*English Historical Review*, XCV (1980)), pp 727, 729; P R Coss, *Lordship, Knighthood and Locality, a Study in English Society c 1180-c1220* (Cambridge, 1991), pp 218-41. The question of ow many knights there were in the early 13th century is being studied by Kathryn Faulkner.

71 Carpenter, "Was there a crisis of the knightly class?", pp 722, 737; Coss, *Lordship, Knighthood and Locality*, pp 241-57; S L Waugh, "Reluctant Knights and Jurors: Respites, Exemptions and Public Obligations in the Reign of Henry III", (*Speculum*, 58 (1983), pp 937-86); J Quick, "The Number and Distribution of Knights in 13th Century England: The Evidence of the Grand Assize Lists" in P R Coss and S D Lloyd, eds, *Thirteenth Century England I: Proceedings of the Newcastle upon Tyne Conference, 1985* (Woodbridge, 1986), pp 114-24.

72 N Denholm-Young, "Feudal Society in the 13th Century: The Knights", *Collected Papers of N Denholm-Young* (Cardiff, 1969), pp 85-8.

73 Saul, *The Gloucestershire Gentry*, p 6.

74 H E Salter, ed, *The Boarstall Cartulary* (Oxford Hist Soc, LXXXVIII, 1930), pp 9-10.

75 For the growth of representation in the period immediately after 1265, see J R Maddicott, "The Crusade Taxation of 1268-70 and the Development of Parliament" in PR Coss and S D Lloyd, eds, *Thirteenth Century England II: Proceedings of the Newcastle upon Tyne Conference, 1987* (Woodbridge, 1988), pp 93-118.

76 For the political views of local society in the years after 1215, see particularly J R Maddicott, "Magna Carta and the Local Community", (*Past and Present* 102 (1984), pp 25-65).

77 See the example given in D A Carpenter, "Debate: Bastard Feudalism Revised", (*Past and Present* 131 (1991), p 183).

78 For the fullest statement of these views, see P R Coss, "Sir Geoffrey de Langly and the Crisis of the Knightly Class in 13th Century Englan", (*Past and Present* 68 (1975), pp 3-37). P R Coss, *Lordship, Knighthood and Locality*, chs 6-9 takes the same basic line but with important qualifications; see next note.

79 Carpenter, "Was there a crisis of the knightly class?", pp 721-52, makes this case for Oxfordshire. Coss has now found a comparable pattern in Warwickshire; Coss, *Lordship, Knighthood and Locality*, pp 294-304.

80 *Feudal Aids*, V, p 279; *Cal Charter Rolls*, IV, p 286; *Victoria County History of Wiltshire*, IX, p 121; Carpenter, "Was there a crisis of the knightly class?", pp 735-7.

81 *Oseney Cartulary*, IV, pp 20, 258.

82 See the references in note 66 above.

83 I J Sanders, *English Baronies 1086-1327* (Oxford, 1960), p 54.

84 *Cal Patent Rolls 1313-17*, p 277; *ibid 1321-4*, p 186.

85 K B McFarlane, introduction by G L Harriss, *England in the 15th Century: Collected Essays* (London, 1981), p xviii.

86 These sentences merely touch on current debates about structures of local power in late medieval England; for introduction to some of the problems see Prestwich, *English Politics in the 13th Century*, ch 3; Given-Wilson, *The English Nobility*, pp 73-83.

87 See above, n 3.

88 Lord Macaulay, *The History of England* (Penguin English Library, 1979), pp 58-9.

89 I am most grateful to John Gillingham who commented on a draft of this chapter, discussed the whole subject with me on numerous occasions, and provided many references. I read D Crouch, *The Image of the Aristocracy of Britain, 1100-1300* (London, 1992) only after I had completed this chapter. It touches on many of the issues raised and is indispensable for future work on the aristocracy.

Chapter 3 (pages 44-51)

1   J E Powell, K Wallis, *The House of Lords in the Middle Ages* (London, 1968).

2   Bruce McFarlane calculated that in 1300 there were 136 families whose head had received at least one personal writ of summons to Parliament, and 221 more over the next two centuries. Of these only 61 survived in unbroken male descent until 1500 (K B McFarlane, *The Nobility of Later Medieval England* (Oxford 1972), p 144). On the other hand despite the growth of baronies by patent, in 1483, two thirds of those summoned were considered as holding baronies "time out of mind").

3   Ransoms could be huge: the Archbishop of Sens, taken at Poitiers by Warwick, fetched £8,000 (McFarlane, *The Nobility of Later Medieval England*, p 30)

4   Henry VI was to institute the new order of Viscounts in 1440 with Lord Beaumont.

5   He was so rich that he could afford to give away a jewelled collar valued at £2,667, partly as a repayment for debt, but partly as a pure gift (McFarlane, *The Nobility of Later Medieval England*, p 95).

6   McFarlane, *The Nobility of Later Medieval England*, p 91.

7   Carole Rawcliffe, *The Staffords, Earls of Stafford and Dukes of Buckingham, 1341-1521* (Cambridge 1979), pp 24-5. A comparison might be made with the Percies who had an income from land of about £3,000 in the mid-15th century, about half of which went on administration, annuities and fees to retainers. The 4th Earl of Northumberland had 33 knights in his retinue and could afford a funeral costing £11,000 in 1489 (J M W Bean, *The Estates of the Percy Family 1416-1537*, (Oxford, 1959), pp 81-2, 134).

8   McFarlane, *The Nobility of Later Medieval England*, p 111.

9   The map of the Stafford estates in Rawcliffe, *The Staffords, Earls of Stafford and Dukes of Buckingham*, p xiii is instructive. Land, like money lending, brought in about 5 per cent per annum (McFarlane, *The Nobility of Later Medieval England*, p 57). Although, on the Percy estates, income from land may have declined by as much as one quarter in the first half of the century (Bean, *The Estates of the Percy Family*, pp 29-30, 41-2, 88-9.).

10 McFarlane, *The Nobility of Later Medieval England*, p 49. McFarlane gives a good example of peculation in action: Thomas of Woodstock, Duke of Gloucester, was made the king's lieutenant in Ireland in 1392 and drew £6,332 from the exchequer. He spent £1,340 on soldiers, £300 on artillery and travel arrangements, and £200 on silver plate for his own use. The remaining £4,500 was spent on the Duke's affairs (McFarlane, *The Nobility of Later Medieval England*, p 26).

11 Rawcliffe, *The Staffords, Earls of Stafford and Dukes of Buckingham*, p 93. In the mid 15th century, a Percy heiress spent £30 on cloth of gold for a dress; at the Field

of the Cloth of Gold, the Percies spent £80 10s on 111/2 yards of the same material (Bean, *The Estates of the Percy Family*, pp 100, 141).

12 Kate Mertes in her study of *The English Noble Household 1250-1600* (Oxford 1988) notes that her most significant finding is that "they settled down... In every household document I have found, instead of a regular movement once or twice a month, a long, steady habitation of from four to six, sometimes eight months in a single dwelling..." (p 185).

13 McFarlane, *The Nobility of Later Medieval England,* p 96.

14 F J Furnivall, *Early English Meals and Manners*, EETS, 1868.

Chapter 4 (pages 52-65)

1   D M Palliser, *The Age of Elizabeth* (2nd ed, London, 1992), p 419. I am very grateful to Cliff Davies and John Watts for their helpful comments on this chapter.

2   C A Sneyd, ed, *A Relation, or rather a True Account of the Island of England,* (Camden Society, OS, 37, 1847), p 39.

3   H Miller, *Henry VIII and the English Nobility*_(Oxford, 1986), pp 10, 99, 126.

4   *Ibid*, p 255; G L Harriss, "The King and his Magnates" in G L Harriss, ed, *Henry V: The Practice of Kingship* (Oxford, 1985), pp 43, 47.

5   K B McFarlane, *The Nobility of Later Medieval England* (Oxford, 1973), pp 143, 146; L Stone, *The Crisis of the Aristocracy 1558-1641* (Oxford, 1965), pp 758-9; Miller, *Henry VIII and the English Nobility*, p 35.

6   P J Holmes, "The Great Council in the Reign of Henry VII", *English Historical Review,* 101 (1986), 840-62; J A Guy, "The Privy Council: Revolution or Evolution?", C Coleman, D R Starkey, eds, *Revolution Reassessed: Revisions in the History of Tudor Government and Administration* (Oxford, 1986), pp 59-85; D R Starkey, "Court, Council and Nobility in Tudor England", in R G Asch, A M Birke, eds, *Princes, Patronage and the Nobility: The Court at the Beginning of the Modern Age c. 1450-1650,* (Oxford, 1991), pp 175-203; A L Brown, "The King's Councillors in Fifteenth Century England" (*Transactions of the Royal Historical Society*, 5th ser 19 (1969), 95-118); J L Watts, "The Councils of King Henry VI, c1435-1445" (*English Historical Review*, 106 (1991), pp 279-298). As these articles demonstrate, the history of the king's council in the 15th and 16th centuries is a subject of formidable complexity.

7   P Williams, *The Tudor Regime,* (Oxford, 1979), pp 453-6; J J Goring 'Social Change and Military Decline in Mid-Tudor England', (*History,* 60 (1975), 188-97); L. Boynton, *The Elizabethan Militia 1558-1638* (London, 1967), pp 145, 196.

8   G A Bergenroth *et al.*, eds, *Calendar of State Papers, Spanish*, (15 vols, London, 1862-1954), XIII, no 164.

9   A. L. Brown, *The Governance of Late Medieval England 1272-1461* (London, 1989), pp 40, 234.

10 F M Heal, *Of Prelates and Princes: A Study of the Economic and Social Position of the Tudor Episcopate* (Cambridge, 1980), pp 328-9.

11 J Cornwall, *Wealth and Society in Early Sixteenth Century England* (London, 1988), p 141; S J Payling, *Political Society in Lancastrian England: The Greater Gentry of Nottinghamshire* (Oxford, 1991), p 3.

12 Stone, *Crisis of the Aristocracy*, pp 129-64; J H Hexter, "The English aristocracy, its crises, and the English revolution, 1558-1660", (*Journal of British Studies,* 8

(1968), pp 38-49); B Coward, *The Stanleys, Lords Stanley and Earls of Derby, 1385-1672* (Chetham Society, 3rd ser 30 (1983), pp 22-64).

13 L Stone, *Family and Fortune: Studies in Aristocratic Finance in the Sixteenth and Seventeenth Centuries* (Oxford 1973), pp 180-4, 214-19; G W Bernard, "The fortunes of the Grey, Earls of Kent, in the early sixteenth century", (*Historical Journal*, 25 (1982), pp 672-5); B J Harris, *Edward Stafford, Third Duke of Buckingham, 1478-1521* (Stanford (USA), 1986), pp 100-34; Stone, *Crisis of the Aristocracy*, pp 324-34, 482-6.

14 Stone, *Family and Fortune*, pp 188-92; *Crisis of the Aristocracy*, pp 294-380, 555-83.

15 M Howard, *The Early Tudor Country House: Architecture and Politics, 1490-1550* (London, 1987); M Girouard, *Robert Smythson and the Elizabethan Country House* (New Haven (USA), 1983); Stone, *Crisis of the Aristocracy*, pp 549-55.

16 J M W Bean, *From Lord to Patron: Lordship in Late Medieval England* (Manchester, 1989), pp 164-74, 211-25: K Mertes, *The English Noble Household, 1250-1600* (Oxford, 1985), p 187: S J Gunn, "The act of resumption of 1515", in D T Williams, ed, *Early Tudor England: Proceedings of the 1987 Harlaston Symposium* (Woodbridge, 1989), p 102; J P Cooper, *Land, Men and Beliefs: Studies in Early Modern History* (London, 1983), pp 78-96.

17 F M Heal, *Hospitality in Early Modern England* (Oxford, 1990), pp 56-9, 88-117; Coward, *The Stanleys*, pp 84-93; Stone, *Crisis of the Aristocracy*, pp 207-14.

18 Coward, *The Stanleys*, pp 94-5.

19 J G Bellamy, *Criminal Law and Society in Late Medieval and Tudor England* (Gloucester, 1984), pp 15-19; J A Guy, *The Cardinal's Court: The Impact of Thomas Wolsey in Star Chamber* (Hassocks, 1977), Stone, *Crisis of the Aristocracy,* p 237; S E Kershaw, "Power and duty in the Elizabethan aristocracy: George, Earl of Shrewsbury, the Glossopdale dispute and the Council", in G W Bernard, ed, *The Tudor Nobility* (Manchester, 1992), pp 266-95; W T MacCaffrey, "Talbot and Stanhope: an episode in Elizabethan politics" (*Bulletin of the Institute of Historical Research*, 33 (1960), pp 73-85).

20 McFarlane, *Nobility of later Medieval England*, pp 216-17; M M Condon, "Ruling elites in the reign of Henry VII" in C D Ross, ed, *Patronage, Pedigree and Power in Later Medieval England*, (Gloucester, 1979), p 123; S J Gunn, P G Lindley, "Introduction", in S J Gunn, P G Lindley, eds, *Cardinal Wolsey: Church, State and Art* (Cambridge, 1991), pp 19-21.

21 D Willen, *John Russell, First Earl of Bedford* (London, 1981); S J Gunn, *Charles Brandon, Duke of Suffolk c1484-1545* (Oxford, 1988); S L Adams, "Eliza enthroned?: The court and its politics", in C A Haigh, ed, *The Reign of Elizabeth I* (London, 1984); pp 55-77.

22 S Doran, "The finances of an Elizabethan nobleman and royal servant: a case study of Thomas Radcliffe, 3rd Earl of Sussex", (*Historical Research*, 61 (1988), pp 286-300); Stone, *Crisis of the Aristocracy*, p 469.

23 Miller, *Nobility of later Medieval England*, p 204; Stone, *Crisis of the Aristocracy*, p 741; C A Haigh, *Reformation and Resistance in Tudor Lancashire* (Cambridge, 1975), pp 140-1, 219, 252-4.

24 G S Thomson, *Lords Lieutenants in the Sixteenth Century* (London, 1923); R R Reid, *The King's Council in the North* (London, 1921); pp 59-239; P Williams, *The Council in the Marches of Wales under Elizabeth I* (Cardiff 1958), pp 36-7,

234-6, 267-96; G W Bernard, *The Power of the Early Tudor Nobility: A Study of the Fourth and Fifth Earls of Shrewsbury* (Brighton, 1985), pp 139-44, 204-5.

25 A Wall, "Patterns of politics in England, 1558-1628" (*Historical Journal*, 31 (1988), pp 955-8); Coward, *The Stanleys,* pp 115-22; C Cross, *The Puritan Earl: The Life of Henry Hastings, Third Earl of Huntingdon 1536-1595* (London, 1966); W Hunt, *The Puritan Moment: The Coming of Revolution in an English County* (Cambridge (USA), 1983), pp 160-72.

26 M E James, *Society, Politics and Culture: Studies in Early Modern England* (Cambridge, 1986), pp 416-65; R C McCoy, *The Rites of Knighthood: The Literature and Politics of Elizabethan Chivalry* (Berkeley (USA), 1989), pp 79-102.

27 Bernard, *The Tudor Nobility,* p 4; J Scott, *Algernon Sydney and the English Republic, 1623-1677* (Cambridge, 1988), pp 39-41, 45-8.

28 Condon, "Ruling elites", p 121; Miller, *Henry VIII and the English Nobility*, pp 124-6.

Chapter 5 (pages 66-86)

1   J H Hexter, *Reappraisals* in History (London, 1961; Chicago (USA), 2nd edn, 1979), p 20.

2   S R Gardiner, *History of the Great Civil War* (London, 4 vols, 1893), IV, 284-5; B Worden, *The Rump Parliament* (Cambridge, 1974), p 73.

3   Worden, *The Rump Parliament*, p 172; A Woolrych, *Commonwealth into Protectorate* (Oxford, 1982), pp 122-3, 167.

4   J Scott, *Algernon Sidney and the English Republic 1623-1677* (Cambridge, 1988); J Scott, *Algernon Sidney and the Restoration Crisis, 1677-1683* (Cambridge, 1991).

5   K B Macfarlane, *The Nobility of Later Medieval England* (Oxford, 1973), pp 146-7; J F Naylor, *The English Aristocracy and the Peerage Bill of 1719* (New York, 1968), p 159.

6   L Stone, *The Crisis of the Aristocracy, 1558-1641* (Oxford, 1965), p 53; E Chamberlaine, *Angliae Notitiae or the Present State of England* (London, 1669), p 459; G Miege, *The New State of England* (London, 1691), pt II, p 223.

7   H R Trevor Roper, *The Gentry 1540-1640* (*Economic History Review Supplement*, no 1, 1953), p 6.

8   Stone, *Crisis of the Aristocracy,* p 59.

9   Stone, *Crisis of the Aristocracy,* p 123; A à Wood, *Life and Times*, ed A Clark (Oxford Historical Society, 5 vols, 1891-1900) II 16.

10   G E Cokayne, V Gibbs, eds,*Complete Peerage* (London, rev edn, 14 vols, 1910-59) [hereafter *CP*], V, pp 329-32 (Ferrers), III, p 402 (Lansdowne), X, pp 560-2 (Windsor); see also D J Backhouse, "The Crown, the Peerage and High Politics 1689-1760", unpublished PhD thesis, University of London, 1990, p 69.

11   Chamberlayne, *Angliae Notitiae* (1669 edition), p 451.

12   *CP* XII(i) 29; II 177; Backhouse, "The Crown, the Peerage and High Politics, p 49; W D Cooper, ed, *Savile Correspondence* (Camden Society, 1858) p 57.

13   British Library, Egerton MS 3330, fol 05, 71, 101.

14   Backhouse, "The Crown, the Peerage and High Politics, pp 60-2; above pp 75, 77.

15 *47th Report of the Deputy Keeper of the Public Records* (London, 1886), pp 118-9;
    G Holmes, *British Politics in the Age of Anne* (London,rev edn, 1987), pp 395-6.

16 *CP* V 364, IX 25-6.

17 J P Cooper, *Land Men and Beliefs* (London, 1982) pp 15-16; Stone, *Crisis of the
    Aristocracy,* p 99; Naylor, *The English Aristocracy,* p 159; J V Beckett, *The
    Aristocracy of England 1660-1914* (Oxford, 1986), p 486; Backhouse, "The Crown,
    the Peerage and High Politics", p 376. These figures are necessarily a little vague:
    the picture was a fluid one, with creations and extinctions occurring irregularly;
    there were also a few peerages whose legality was challenged.

18 The figures in *CP* VIII 740 are clearly wrong, especially for Anne's reign; those in
    Beckett, *The Aristocracy of England*, p 486, are totals, not creations.

19 Stone, *Crisis of the Aristocracy,* p 99; Beckett, *The Aristocracy of England,* p 486.

20 Stone, *Crisis of the Aristocracy,* pp 97-9; W T Maccaffrey, "England: The Crown
    and the New Aristocracy, 1540-1600" (*Past and Present*, no 30 (1965), pp 54-6).

21 Based on *47th Report*, pp 96-124 and *CP*.

22 Trevor Roper, *The Gentry, 1540-1640*, pp 12, 54.

23 *CP* XII(i) p 159; Trevor Roper, *The Gentry, 1540-1640,* pp 12, 16.

24 *CP* VI 321; *DNB*; Trevor Roper, *The Gentry, 1540-1640,* p 23.

25 *CP* VII 531.

26 Richmond, Carr and Hay; the indirect case was Clifton.

27 Stone, *Crisis of the Aristocracy,* pp 101-2

28 Stone, *Crisis of the Aristocracy,* pp 98-9, 468-9.

29 Stone, *Crisis of the Aristocracy,* pp 105-6; *CP* ii 229, iii 193-4, vi 586

30 C R Mayes, "The Sale of Peerages in Early Stuart England" (*Journal of Modern
    History* xxix (1957), pp 27-8); *CP* XI 486; C Russell, *Parliaments and English
    Politics, 1621-9* (Oxford, 1979), p 152.

31 R Lockyer, *Buckingham* (London, 1981), p 448.

32 Mayes, "The sale of peerages", p 28 and *passim*; Stone, *Crisis of the Aristocracy,*
    pp 105-17

33 L L Peck, "Corruption at the Court of James I", in B C Malament, ed, *After The
    Reformation: Essays in Honour of J H Hexter* (Manchester, 1980), pp 75-94 (esp
    pp 82-3).

34 *CP* III 247-8; Mayes, "The sale of peerages", pp 23-4, 36; Trevor Roper, *The Gentry,
    1540-1640,* pp 10-12.

35 *CP* II 37, 515, III 300-1; Stone, *Crisis of the Aristocracy,* pp 106, 114n; Mayes, "The
    sale of peerages", pp 31-3.

36 Mayes, "The sale of peerages", pp 29-30; Stone, *Crisis of the Aristocracy,* p 114.

37 Trevor Roper, *The Gentry, 1540-1640,* pp 10-11; Mayes, "The sale of peerages",
    pp 24, 27.

38 *CP* XII 283, VIII 488, III 476.

39 Stone, *Crisis of the Aristocracy,* p 119.

40 *CP* XII(II) 342-3.

41 *Calendar of State Papers, Domestic, 1660-1*, pp 564-5.

42 E Hyde, Earl of Clarendon, *Life* (3 vols, Oxford, 1827), II 314, 362.

43 *CP* IX 791.

44 Bodleian Library, Carte MS 219, fol 416. See *CP* VI 43-4 (Grafton), IX 740-1
    (Northumberland), X 836-8 (Richmond), XI 286-8 (St Albans).

45 J Miller, "The Crown and the Borough Charters in the Reign of Charles II" (*English Historical Review*, 100 (1985), pp 69, 72, 76); P Jenkins, *The Making of a Ruling Class: The Glamorganishire Gentry, 1640-1790* (Cambridge, 1983), pp 25-32.

46 Backhouse, "The Crown, the Peerage and High Politics", p 74.

47 *CP* II 323.

48 Holmes, *British Politics in the Age of Anne,* pp 227, 516, n 49.

49 Stone, *Crisis of the Aristocracy,* ch 5; much of Stone's argument was prefigured in Hexter, *Reappraisals*, pp 142-8.

50 This paragraph is based on Professor Conrad Russell's inaugural lecture at King's College, London.

51 C Dalton, *The Life and Times of General Sir Edward Cecil, Viscount Wimbledon* (London, 2 vols, 1885) ii 402.

52 H C Foxcroft, *Life and Letters of Halifax* (London, 2 vols, 1898) II 206.

53 J Cannon, *Aristocratic Century: The Peerage of Eighteenth Century England* (Cambridge, 1984), pp 118-20.

54 Chamberlayne *Angliae Notitiae,* (London, 1669), pp 456-7.

55 Chamberlayne *Angliae Notitiae,* (London, 18th edn, 1694), pp 413-4.

56 Miege, *The New State of England* (London, 1691), pt II, p 219; Miege, *The Present State of Great Britain* (London, 1707), pt I, p 254.

57 H C Foxcroft, ed, *Supplement to Burnet's History of his Own Time* (Oxford, 1902), p 127.

58 R North, *Lives of the Norths,* ed A Jessopp (London, 3 vols, 1890) I 170.

59 Stone, *Crisis of the Aristocracy,* ch 5; M E James, *Family Lineage and Civil Society: Durham 1500-1640* (Oxford, 1974); James "The Concept of Order and the Northern Rising of 1569" (*Past and Present*, 60 (1973), pp 49-83); Hexter, *Reappraisals in History,* p 144; A Fletcher, "The Coming of War" in J S Morrill, ed, *Reactions to the English Civil War, 1642-9* (London, 1984), p 36.

60 Stone, *The Crisis of the Aristocracy,* ch 5; Cooper, *Land Men and Beliefs,* pp 78-96; North, *Lives of the Norths,* i 171.

61 James, *Family, Lineage and Civil Society.*

62 Stone, *Crisis of the Aristocracy,* pp 201-8; Cooper, *Land Men and Beliefs,* pp 87-90.

63 S A Strong, ed, *A Catalogue of Letters and Other Historical Documents Exhibited in the Library at Welbeck* (London, 1907), p 212.

64 Stone, *Crisis of the Aristocracy,* pp 475-6, 775; Trevor Roper, *The Gentry, 1540-1640,* pp 54-5; N Cuddy, "The Revival of the Entourage: James I", in D Starkey *et al,* eds, *The English Court* (London, 1987), ch 6.

65 B Manning, ed, *Politics, Religion and the English Civil War* (London, 1973), ch 2; J Adamson, "The Baronial Context of the English Civil War" (*Transactions of the Royal Historical Society,* 5th Series xl (1990), pp 93-120); C Russell, *The Fall of the British Monarchies, 1637-42* (Oxford,1991).

66 P R Newman, "The Royalist Party in Arms: The Peerage and Army Command, 1642-6", in C Jones, M Newitt, S Roberts, eds, *Politics and People in Revolutionary England* (Oxford, 1986), pp 81-93; D Hirst, *Authority and Conflict* (London, 1985), p 227.

67 Adamson, "The Baronial Context of the English Civil War"; D Pennington, "The Rebels of 1642", in R H Parry, ed, *The English Civil War and After* (London 1970), ch 2.

68 C Clay, "Landlords and Estate Management", in J Thirsk, ed, *The Agrarian History of England and Wales*, v (Cambridge, 1985) pp 119-54.

69 R Scrope, T Monkhouse, eds, *Clarendon State Papers* (Oxford, 3 vols, 1767-86), III pp 361-2.

70 D H Hosford, *Nottingham, Nobles and the North* (Hamden, 1976).

71 R Beddard, *England without a King* (Oxford, 1988); J Miller, *Popery and Politics in England, 1660-88* (Cambridge, 1973), pp 257-61; *London Moderate or Protestant Intelligencer,* no 1 (15 Dec 1688); T Bruce, Earl of Ailesbury, *Memoirs,* ed W E Buckley (Roxburghe Club, 2 vols, 1890), I 204-7.

72 A Simpson, "Notes of a Noble Lord" (*English Historical Review,* lii (1937), p 95).

73 Stone, *Crisis of the Aristocracy,* pp 465-6; Holmes, *British Politics in the Age of Anne,* pp 387-90, 436-9.

74 J Brewer, *The Sinews of Power: War, Money and the English State, 1689-1763* (London, 1989); J H Plumb, *The Growth of Political Stability in England 1675-1725* (London, 1967).

75 Cannon, *Aristocratic Century*; Beckett; *The Aristocracy of England;* J Cannon, "The Isthmus Repaired: The Resurgence of the English Aristocracy, 1660-1760" (*Proceedings of the British Academy,* lxviii (1982), pp 431-53).

76 Adamson, "The Baronial Context of the English Civil War", p 119, sees an embryonic version of such noble power in the 1640s; if so, the embryo was soon aborted.

Chapter 6 (pages 87-97)

1 T B Smith, "The Union of 1707 as fundamental law" (*Public Law* (1957), pp 99-121; M Upton "Marriage vows of the Elephant: the constitution of 1707" (*Law Quarterly Review*, 105 (1989), pp 79-103).

2 Sir T Innes in Viscount Dunedin, ed, *Encyclopaedia of the Laws of Scotland*, (Edinburgh, 18 vols, 1926-51), XI, p 202 ("Peerage").

3 Scots Law Commission, "The Abolition of the Feudal System" (*Discussion Paper,* 93 (1991), para 5.12).

4 For a discussion of this form of descent see D O'Corrain, "Irish regnal succession a reappraisal", (*Studia Hibernica*, 11 (1971), pp 7-39.

5 Sir T Innes in Lord Macmillan, ed, "Sources of Scots Law" (*Stair Society*, 1 (1936), p 434).

6 Lord Keith of Kinkel in *House of Lords Debates*, 27 June 1977, paraphrasing Sir T Craig, *Jus Feudale*. (Edinburgh, 3rd edn, 1732, repr and trans Lord Clyde, Edinburgh, 2 vols, 1934).

7 Macmillan, ed, "Sources and Literature of Scots Law", p 435.

8 ""Lady Ruthven of Freeland, Petitioner", Scots Law Times (Lyon Court), 1977, p 9.

9 *Ibid.*

10 Lord Chancellor Talbot, "Viscountcy of Oxenfoord" (Journal of the House of Lords (1733), p 379).

11 "Lady Ruthven of Freeland, Petitioner", p 2.

12 J Riddell, *Inquiry into the Law and Practice in Scots Peerages*, (Edinburgh, 2 vols, 1842), II, p 1052.

13 "Viscountcy of Oxfuird", 1986, (*Scots Law Times (Lyon Court)*, 1986) pp 9, 17A (per Lord Fraser of Tullybelton).

14 The ability to exclude the apparent heir is discussed by A F Steuart, "The exclusion of apparent heirs in Scottish peerages" (Juridical Review, OS 16 (1904), pp 285-96).

15 The importance of Crown recognition was emphasised by James VI (D Masson, ed, *Register of the Privy Council of Scotland* (London, 14 vols, 1877-98), X, pp 310-11 (15 March 1615).). Cp the *Kincardine* case J Lauder, Lord Fountainhall, The Descisions of the Lords of Council and Sessions from .. 1678 to .. 1712 (Edinburgh, 2 vols, 1759-61), II, pp 367-8); the Earl of Kincardine attempted to resign his Earldom into the hands of his eldest daughter, to the exclusion of the apparent heir.

16 R Rait, *The Parliaments of Scotland* (Glasgow, 1924), 533.

17 C Thomson, C Innes, eds, *Acts of the Parliament of Scotland 1124-1707* (London, 13 vols, 1814-75), VI, p 43.

18 Rait, *The Parliaments of Scotland*, p 520.

19 *Ibid*, p 521

20 G Mackenzie, *Memoirs of the Affairs of Scotland* (Edinburgh, 1821), p 60.

21 Rait, *The Parliaments of Scotland*, p 301.

22 See "The Riding of Parliament", in N de Guerdeville, *Atlas Historique* (Paris (France), 2 vols, 1720), II, plate 56.

23 Thompson and Innes, eds, *Acts of Parliament in Scotland*, III, pp 443-4.

24 W F Skene, *Celtic Scotland*, (Edinburgh, 3 vols, 1876-80), III, p 566.

25 Anon, "Historical Notes on Titles of Nobility in Scotland" (*Journal of Jurisprudence*, XXV (1881), p 566).

26 A Seton, "De jure prelationis" (*Maitland Club Miscellany*, I, pt 2 (1834), p 355.

27 F W Pixley, *A History of the Baronetage*, (London, 1900), p 210.

28 A Seton, Lord Saltoun, *The Frasers of Philorth*, (Edinburgh, 2 vols, 1879) II, p 41.

29 He should be addressed as "Lord Clashfern" (Scottish Law Times (News), 1984, p 196).

30 Chalmers of Ormonde, *La Rescherche des Singularitez Plus Remarquables Concernant l'Etat d'Ecosse* (Paris (France), 1579).

31 "Lord Daer v Freeholders of Wigton" (1702) (W M Morison, *The Decisions of the Court of Session, from its institution until .. 1808* (Edinburgh, 42 vols, 1811), XXI, pp 8692-726).

32 Riddell, *Inquiry into the Law and Practice in Scots Peerages*, p 114.

33 This system is now under review (Scots Law Commission "The Abolition of the Feudal System").

34 A Bruce "Barony Title: a response" (*Journal of the Law Society of Scotland*, 1993, pp 156-7).

35 W Scott, *Waverley*, (Edinburgh, 1814), ch 10.

36 J Wormald, *Lords and Men in Scotland: bonds of manrent*, 1442-1603 (Edinburgh, 1985), p 34.

37 *Ibid*, p 44.

38 *Ibid*, pp 165 *et seq*.

39 K Brown "Playing second fiddle? The Nobility and Regal Union" in *The Landed Élite in Scotland, 1440-1914* (Association of Scottish Historical Societies (1989), pp 15-33).

40 Brown "Playing second fiddle?"

41 K Brown, "Noble Indebtedness", (*Transactions of the Royal Historical Society*, 5th ser, 39 (1989), p 260).

42 M Lynch, *Scotland: New History* .(London, 1991, repr 1992), p 250.

43 D Stevenson, "The Government of Scotland under the Covenanters, 1637-1651" (*Scottish Historical Society*, 4th ser, 18 (1982), p 14.

44 C Larner, *The Enemies of God.: the Witch-Hunt in Scotland* (Baltimore (USA), 1981).

45 Lynch, *Scotland: a New History*, p 314.

46 See chs 7-8 above.

Chapter 7 (pages 98-108)

1 T B Macaulay, *The History of England* (London, 6 vols, C H Firth, ed, 1913-15), III, pp 1310-12.

2 Kathleen Wilson summarized the orthodox view, writing, as recently as 1992, that "most scholars have reached a consensus that the Revolution was largely an episode in patrician politics, unrelentingly "conservationist" in ideological, political and social effect" (K Wilson, "A Dissident Legacy: 18th century popular politics and the Glorious Revolution", in J R Jones, ed, *Liberty Secured? Britain Before and After 1688* (Stanford (USA) 1992), pp 299-334.

3 *Hansard*, 136 (7 July 1988), p 1245.

4 See, particularly, the introductory chapter "The Revolution in Context" in *Liberty Secured?* Professor Jones stresses widespread resistance to James II and popular participation, especially in Scotland.

5 The best scholarly example is J C D Clark, *English Society, 1688-1832.* (Cambridge, 1985)

6 J R Western, *Monarchy and Revolution: the English State in the 1680s.* (London, 1972), p 3.

7 J R Jones, *The Revolution of 1688 in England* (London, 1972), p 331.

8 W A Speck, *Reluctant Revolutionaries: Englishmen and the Revolution of 1688.* (Oxford, 1988).

9 J E C Hill, *A Century of Revolution* (London, 1961), p 277.

10 J R Kenyon, *The Stuart Constitution* (Cambridge, 2nd edn, 1986), p 3.

11 J A Cannon, *Aristocratic Century: the Peerage of 18th century England* (Cambridge, 1984), pp 115-23.

12 *The Nation and Athenaeun*, 14 July 1928, reprinted in L B Namier, *Skyscrapers and Other Essays* (London, 1931), pp 44-53.

13 *Hansard's Parliamentary Debates*, (London, 3rd series, 356 vols, 1830-91), II, p 1194.

14 J Hawkins, *Life of Johnson* (London and Dublin (Ireland), 1787; repr, New York (USA), 1974), p 227.

15 G B Hill, ed, *Boswell's Life of Johnson* (Oxford, 6 vols, 1934-50), III, p 326; IV p 177.

16 eg N McKendrick,*The Birth of a Consumer Society: the Commercialisation of 18th Century England*. (London, 1982). The concept of an industrial revolution has been questioned by, among others, J C D Clark, *Revolution and Rebellion: State and Society in England in the 17th and 18th Centuries* (Cambridge, 1986), pp 37-9.

17 P Langford, *A Polite and Commercial People: England, 1727-1783* (Oxford, 1989) and P Langford, *Public Life and the Propertied Englishman, 1689-1798* (Oxford, 1990).

18 Langford, *A Polite and Commercial People*, ch 12.

19 Langford, *Public Life and the Propertied Englishman*, p 510.

20 See particularly J V Beckett, *The Aristocracy in England 1660-1914* (Oxford, 1986), pt ii.

21 C Jones, ed, *A Pillar of the Constitution: The House of Lords in British Politics, 1640-1784* (London, 1988), p 18.

22 J Black, "The House of Lords and British Foreign Policy 1720-1748", in Jones, ed, *A pillar of the constitution* p 135.

23 J W Croker, ed, *Memoirs of John Lord Hervey* (London, 3 vols, 1884), I, p 249.

386   Quoted by P G D Thomas, "'Thoughts on the British Constitution' by George III in 1760", (*Bulletin of the Institute of Historical Research*, LX (1987), p 362).

24 Quoted J Brooke and L B Namier, eds, *The House of Commons, 1754-1790* (London, 3 vols, 1964), II, p 93.

25 Cannon, *Aristocratic Century*, p 112-3.

26 *Ibid*, p 114.

27 Property qualification for MPs was brought in in 1711 and for JPs in 1732.

28 The act to exclude copyholders was carried after the hotly disputed Oxfordshire election of 1754 and passed in 1758. It confirmed an act of Anne's reign.

29 A bill to reform and reconstitute the militia passed the Commons in 1756 but was rejected by the Lords. Sandys doubted whether the officers could stop their men becoming "riotous and seditious" and warned that "no free state ever trusted the arms of the commonwealth in the hands of the poor and indigent". Hardwicke thought the bill "too democratical". A modified version, aiming at only half the total number of recruits, passed in 1757 with substantial safeguards. Colonels were to be landowners worth at least £400 pa or heirs apparent worth double that amount. This qualification was considerably higher than that for a member of parliament sitting for a borough. (Stat 30 George II, cap 25; W Cobbett, *Parliamentary History of England* (London, 36 vols, 1806-20), XV, pp 704-69, esp pp 731, 757-8).

Chapter 8 (pages 109-122)

The literature on the modern British aristocracy is as vast and as varied as the subject itself. There are memoirs a-plenty, of uneven quality, and almost every major novelist, from Jane Austin and Anthony Trollope to Evelyn Waugh and P G Wodehouse, has much of value to say. The number of biographies, of family histories and of case studies increases exponentially, year by year. The following list is a selection from the most important books which address large subjects:

A Adonis, *Making Aristocracy Work. The Peerage and the Political System in Britain, 1884-1914* (Oxford, 1993).

J V Beckett, *The Aristocracy in England, 1660-1914* (Oxford, 1986).

M Bence-Jones, *Twilight of the Ascendancy* (London, 1987).

J Camplin, *The Rise of the Plutocrats: wealth and power in Edwardian England* (London, 1978).

D Cannadine, *Aspects of Aristocracy: Grandeur and Decline in Modern Britain* (to be published, 1994).

D Cannadine, *The Decline and Fall of the British Aristocracy* (New Haven (USA), 1990).

D Cannadine, *Lords and Landlords: The Aristocracy and the Towns, 1774-1967* (Leicester, 1980).

J Cannon, *Aristocratic Century: The Peerage of Eighteenth-Century England* (Cambridge, 1984).

R Carr, *English Fox-Hunting: A History* (London, 1976).

H Clemenson, *English Country Houses and Landed Estates* (1 London, 982).

L Colley, *Britons: Forging the Nation, 1707-1837* (New Haven (USA), 1992)

M Girouard, *Life in the English Country House: A Social and Architectural History* (London, 1978).

M Girouard, *The Return to Camelot: Chivalry and the English Gentleman* (New Haven, 1981)

D W Howell, *Land and People in Nineteenth-Century Wales* (London, 1978).

G Jackson-Stops (ed), *The Treasure Houses of Britain: Four Hundred Years of Private Patronage and Art Collecting* (New Haven (USA), 1985).

C Jones, D L Jones, eds, *Peers, Politics and Power: The House of Lords, 1603-1911* (London, 1986).

D Itzkowitz, *Peculiar Privilege: A Social History of Fox-Hunting, 1753-1885* (Hassocks, 1977).

A Lambert, *Unquiet Souls: The Indian Summer of the British Aristocracy, 1880-1914* (London, 1984).

J M Lee, *Social Leaders and Public Persons: A Study of County government in Cheshire since 1888* (Oxford, 1963).

G E Mingay, *The Gentry: The Rise and Fall of a Ruling Class* (London, 1976).

G E Mingay (ed), *The Victorian Countryside* (London, 2 vols, 1981).

G D Phillips, *The Diehards: Aristocratic Society and Politics in Edwardian England* (Cambridge, 1979).

W D Rubinstein, *Men of Property: The Very Wealthy in Britain since the Industrial Revolution* (London, 1981).

G R Searle, *Corruption in British Politics, 1895-1930* (Oxford, 1987).

D Spring, ed, *European Landed Elites in the Nineteenth Century* (Baltimore (USA), 1977).

L Stone and J C Fawtier Stone, *An Open Elite? England, 1540-1880* (Oxford, 1984).

F M L Thompson, *English Landed Society in the Nineteenth Century* (London, 1963).

There are no footnotes or further reading for chapters 9 and 10.

Chapter 11 (pages 134-143)

N Baldwin, "The House of Lords: its constitution and functions" (*University of Exeter Research Group Discussion Paper* 8, 1982).

D R Beamish, "The house of Lords Select Committee on Practice and Procedure, 1976-79" (*The Table*, vol 47 (1979), pp 37-47).

L Blom-Cooper, G Drewry, *Final Appeal: a study of the House of Lords in its judicial capacity* (Oxford, 1972).

R L Borthwick, "Public Bills Committees of the House of Lords" (*Parliamentary Affairs*, vol 26 (1973), pp 440-53).

P A Bromhead, *The House of Lords and contemporary politics, 1911-57* (London, 1958).

P A Bromhead, "The Bishops and the House of Lords" (*Church Quarterly Review*, 158 (1957), pp 491-502)

H Burrows, "Powers of the House of Lords" (*Journal of Clerks at the Table in Empire Parliaments*, vol 20 (1951), pp 115-25).

Church of England, Archbishops' Commission on Church and State, "The House of Lords", *Church and State: report of the Archbishop's Commission* (London, 1970), pp 45-7).

G Drewry, "One appeal too many: an analysis of the House of Lords as a final court of appeal" (*British Journal of Sociology*, vol 19 (1968), pp 445-52).

G Drewry, "Judges in Parliament" (*New Law Journal*, vol 119 (1969), pp 431-2).

G Drewry, "Lord Chancellor as Judge" (*New Law Journal*, vol 122 (1972), pp 855-6).

G Drewry, J Brock, "Prelates in Parliament" (*Parliamentary Affairs*, vol 24 (1971), pp 222-50).

G Drewry, J Morgan, "Law Lords as Legislators' (*Parliamentary Affairs*, vol 22 (1969), pp 226-39).

Lord Du Parcq, "The Final Court of Appeal" (*Current Legal Problems*, vol 2 (1949), pp 1-12).

Lord Eccles, Lord Drumalbyn, Lord Boyd-Carpenter, Earl of Lauderdale, "The need to retain a second chamber" (*Association of Independent Unionist Peers*, 1980).

Lord Gardiner, "The Trials of a Lord Chancellor" (*Holdsworth Club of the University of Birmingham*, 1968).

V Goodman, "The judicial business of the House of Lords" (*Journal of Clerks at the Table in Empire Parliaments*, vol 18 (1949), pp 122-27).

Lord Hailsham, "The problems of a Lord Chancellor" (*Holdsworth Club of the University of Birmingham*, 1972).

P Henderson, "Legislation in the House of Lords" (*Parliamentary Affairs*, vol 21 (1968) pp 176-77).

"The House of Lords Committee for Privileges" (*The Table*, vol 26 (1957), p 146).

"The House of Lords and the European Communities" (*House of Lords Information Office Factsheets*, 2, 1978).

"The Judicial work of the House of Lords" (*House of Lords Information Office Factsheets*, 8, 1982).

Earl of Kilmuir, "The Office of Lord Chancellor"(*Parliamentary Affairs*, vol 9 (1956), pp 132-39).

Earl of Longford, *A History of the House of Lords* (London, 1988).

Viscount Massereene and Ferrard, *The Lords* (London, 1973).

J Morgan, *The House of Lords and the Labour Government, 1964-70* (Oxford, 1975).

J Morgan, "The House of Lords in the 1980s" (*Parliamentarian*, vol 62 (1981), pp 18-26).

P Norton, "The forgotten Whips: Whips in the House of Lords" (*Parliamentarian*, vol 57 (1976), pp 86-92).

P Norton, *The Constitution in Flux* (Oxford, 1982).

A Patterson, *The Law Lords* (London, 1982).

R W Perceval, G C A S Snowden, "Delegated Legislation: debates in the House of Lords" (*Journal of Clerks at the Table in Empire Parliaments*, vol 21 (1952), pp 39-43).

J Plaskitt, "The House of Lords and harminization in the European Communities" (*Public Administration*, vol 59 (1981), pp 203-14).

Viscount Samuel, "The administration of the House of Lords", in his *See how they run: the administration of venerable institutions* (London, 1976).

Scottish Young Conservatives, *House of Lords Reform* (Edinburgh, 1981).

Lord Shackleton, "The role of second chambers: the report of a study group of the Commonwealth Parliamentary Association" (*Parliamentarian*, vol 64 (1982), pp 199-252).

D R Shell, *The House of Lords* (London, 1988; 2nd edn, New York (USA), 1992).

D R Shell, D Beamish, eds, *The House of Lords at Work* (Oxford, 1993).

C Sopwith, "The European Communities Committee of the House of Lords: the work of the legal advisor" (*The Table*, vol 50 (1982), pp 62-9).

Lord Windlesham, "The House of Lords: a study of influence replacing power", in his *Politics in Practice* (London, 1975).

There are no footnotes or further reading for chapters 12 and 13.

Index

(I) or (S) denotes creation in the Irish or Scottish peerages. Illustrations are not included in the index.

Charles I, *King* (b 1600, r 1625-49) 5, 70, 72, 73-5, 90; Civil War 82-4, 96

Charles II, *King* (b 1630, r 1660-85) 9, 96, 102; children 68, 69, 70, 76; peerage creation 76-7, 84

Charteris, Hugh and Ivo 114

Chatham, William Pitt "the Elder" (1708-78), *1st Earl of*, quoted 18, 106, 111

Chester Cathedral 114

Chivalry, Orders of: 121-2, 160, 177; Order of the British Empire 117; Order of the Garter 44-5, 129-33, 164; Order of Merit 117; Order of the Thistle 177

Church of England 6, 62, 116; and House of Lords 138, 141; forms of address 177-8

Churchill family 118; John Churchill (1650-1722), *1st Duke of* Marlborough 77, 79; Sarah Churchill, *1st Duchess of* Marlborough (1660-1744) 5, 77; *Viscount* Churchill 118; *Sir* Winston Leonard Spencer Churchill (1874-1965) *Prime Minister* 1940-5, 1951-5 120

Cinque Ports: wardens 49, 169

City, the 118, 153

civil service 111, 116

Civil War (1642-9) 82-4, 96

Clarence, Lionel of Antwerp (1330-80), *Duke of* 166

Clarendon, Edward Hyde (1609-74), *1st Earl of* and *1st Baron* Rochester, quoted 76, 96

Cleveland, Barbara Villiers (1641-1709), *1st Duchess of* 71

Clifford family, *Earls of* Cumberland 102-3

Cloth of Estate 130, 131

Cnut, *King* (b c995 r 1016-35) 22, 148

Colchester, *Viscounts* 70

College of Arms 48, 167, 174

Commentaries (Sir William Blackstone, 1723-78), quoted 18, 104

Committee Stage 139-40

constitution: monarch 27, 28, 36, 41-2, 85-6, 100; parliament 100, 103-4, 123-8

continental nobility 15, 56; exempt from taxes 149, 157-8; France 18-19, 149-50 151; 14, 36 (Revolution); 89 (succession law)

Conway, barony of 69

Conyers, John, MP (19th c) 107

Copt Hall 74

copyhold 2, 9-10, 107, 204n391

Corbett, *Sir* Vincent 81-2

Corn Laws 110

coronations 26, 167, 175

coronets 47, 173

Council, Kings *see* Great Council

Council in the Marches 61, 70

Council of the North 61, 63, 70, 73

courts, central 26-7, 61, 64

Court of Session (Scotland) 87, 88, 91, 95

Courtenay family 52; Edward Courtenay (late 14th c), *Earl of* Devon 48; Henry Courtenay (c1498-1539) *Marquess of* Exeter 62

courtesy titles 15, 169, 170, 171-2, 173, 174; in Scotland 93, 174-5

Coventry, Thomas Coventry (1578-1640), *1st Baron* 73, 75

Devereux family: Robert Devereux (1566-1601), *2nd Earl of* Essex 57-8, 62, 64, 79, 103, 65 (quoted); Robert Devereux (1591-1646), *3rd Earl of* Essex 72, 83 (quoted): Robert Milo Leicester Devereux, *18th Viscount* Hereford (Premier Viscount of England) 172

Devon, Edward Courtenay (late 14th c), *Earl of* 48 *see also* Courtenay family

Devonshire, *Dukes of* (Cavendish family) 13, 111, 112, 113, 121 *see also* Cavendish, William

Devonshire, Charles Blount (1563-1606), *8th Baron* Mountjoy, *1st Earl of* 71

Die Hards, Tory (1911) 119

diffidatio 31-2

diplomats 85, 113, 116; form of address 178

Disraeli, Benjamin, *1st Earl of* Beaconsfield (1804-81) 103, 112

Dissolution of the Monasteries 54, 57, 61, 71

Domesday Book 3, 13, 25, 148, 170-1

Donovan Commission 135

Dormer, Robert (c1610-43), *Earl of* Carnarvon, *Viscount* Ascot 75

Dorset, Thomas Sackville (1535/6-1608), *1st Baron* Buckhurst, *1st Earl of* 60-1, 62

Douglas (S), *Earls of* 91

Douglas-Home, Alexander Frederick, *Baron* Home of the Hirsel, KT 121, 177

Douglas-Scott-Montagu, John Walter Edward (1866-1929), *2nd Baron* Montagu of Beaulieu 118

Ducie, Basil Howard Moreton (1917-91), *6th Earl of* 20

Dudley family 53; John Dudley, *Viscount* Lisle 54

Dufferin and Ava, Frederick Temple Hamilton Temple Blackwood (1826-1902), *1st Marquess of* 118

dukes 46, 71, 102, 168-9; form of address 167-9

Dumont, Monsieur (visitor, 1787) 152

Dunfermline (S), *Earls of* 91

Dunraven, Windham Thomas Wyndham Quin (1841-1926), *4th Earl of* 119

Dunsmore, *Lord* 73

Duras, *Baron* Louis (c1640-1709) 70

Durham (castle) 25

Dymoke, J M 175

Eadric Streona 21-2, 148

Eadwig, King (b c943, r 955-9); charters 21

earls 2, 46, 71, 91-2, 96, 173-4; crowns 47; form of address 171-2

Edward the Confessor, *King* (b 1002-5, r 1042-66) 148

Edward I, *King* (b 1239, r 1272-1307) 10, 31-2, 37; personal writs of summons 39

Edward II, *King* (b 1284, r 1307-27) 5, 29-30, 35, 44

Edward III, *King* (b 1312, r 1327-77) 44-6, 48, 50-1, 150, 166

Edward IV, *King* (b1442, r 1461-83) 47, 50-1, 59, 61, 166

Edward VI, *King* (b 1537, r 1547-53) 63, 71

Edward VII, *King* (b 1841, r 1901-10) 117

Edward the Black Prince, *Prince of Wales* (1330-76) 166

electorate *see* franchise

Elizabeth I, *Queen* (b 1533, r1558-1603) 16, 53, 55, 71, 81

Her Majesty Queen Elizabeth II, (a 1952) 125, 131; form of address 160-3 *see also* constitution; Crown